A Long Way from Runnemede

MEMOIRS AND OCCASIONAL PAPERS
Association for Diplomatic Studies and Training

In 2003, the Association for Diplomatic Studies and Training (ADST) created the Memoirs and Occasional Papers Series to preserve firsthand accounts and other informed observations on foreign affairs for scholars, journalists, and the general public. Sponsoring publication of the series is one of numerous ways in which ADST, a nonprofit organization founded in 1986, seeks to promote understanding of American diplomacy and those who conduct it. Together with the Foreign Affairs Oral History program and ADST's support for the training of foreign affairs personnel at the State Department's Foreign Service Institute, these efforts constitute the Association's fundamental purposes.

- Claudia E. Anyaso, ed., *FIFTY YEARS OF U.S. AFRICA POLICY: Reflections of Assistant Secretaries for African Affairs and U.S. Embassy Officials*
- Thompson Buchanan, *MOSSY MEMOIR OF A ROLLING STONE*
- J. Chapman Chester, *FROM FOGGY BOTTOM TO CAPITOL HILL: Exploits of a G.I., Diplomat, and Congressional Aide*
- John Gunther Dean, *DANGER ZONE: A Diplomat's Fight for America's Interests*
- Robert E. Gribbin, *IN THE AFTERMATH OF GENOCIDE: The U.S. Role in Rwanda*
- Allen C. Hansen, *NINE LIVES, A FOREIGN SERVICE ODYSSEY*
- Frankling Huffman, *YOUR DIPLOMATS AT WORK: A Comedy in Seven Acts*
- James Robert Huntley, *ARCHITECT OF DEMOCRACY: Building a Mosaic of Peace*
- Joanne Grady Huskey, *UNOFFICIAL DIPLOMAT*
- John G. Kormann, *ECHOES OF A DISTANT CLARION: Recollections of a Diplomat and Soldier*
- Nicole Prévost Logan, *FOREVER ON THE ROAD: A Franco-American Family's Thirty Years in the Foreign Service*
- Helen Lyman, *NOT TO THE MANNER BORN*
- Henry Mattox, *PRESENT AT THE FOOTNOTE: Personal Commentary on American Diplomacy*
- Armin Meyer, *QUIET DIPLOMACY: From Cairo to Tokyo in the Twilight of Imperialism*
- William Morgan and Charles Stuart Kennedy, eds., *AMERICAN DIPLOMATS: The Foreign Service at Work*
- James M. Potts, *FRENCH COVERT ACTION IN THE AMERICAN REVOLUTION*
- Howard L. Steele, *BUSHELS AND BALES: A Food Soldier in the Cold War*
- Hans N. Tuch, *ARIAS, CABALETTAS, AND FOREIGN AFFAIRS: A Diplomat's Quasi-Musical Memoir*
- Daniel Whitman, *A HAITI CHRONICLE: The Undoing of a Latent Democracy*
- Susan Clough Wyatt, *ARABIAN NIGHTS AND DAZE: Living in Yemen with the Foreign Service*
- Ginny Carson Young, *PEREGRINA: Unexpected Adventures of an American Consul*

A Long Way From Runnemede

One Woman's Foreign Service Journey

Theresa Anne Tull

ASSOCIATION FOR DIPLOMATIC STUDIES AND TRAINING
MEMOIRS AND OCCASIONAL PAPERS SERIES

Washington, DC

VELLUM/New Academia Publishing 2012

The opinions and characterizations in this book are those of the author and do not necessarily represent official positions of the Government of the United States or the Association for Diplomatic Studies and Training.

Printed in the United States of America

Library of Congress Control Number: 2012934879
ISBN 978-0-9845832-9-4 paperback (alk. paper)

 An imprint of New Academia Publishing

 New Academia Publishing
PO Box 27420, Washington, DC 20038-7420
info@newacademia.com - www.newacademia.com

All photos courtesy of the author.

To the memory of my parents,
John James Tull and Anna Paull Tull,
with deep appreciation

Contents

Acknowledgments

I wish to acknowledge gratefully the computer help given to me in connection with this project by some skilled and loving relatives: Priscilla and Kristin McLane, Laurie Tull, Lynn Tull, and Michael Gatti.

Prologue

It was a beautiful day in Da Nang. The sun was flashing on the river outside the window of my office in the American Consulate General. But the news I had become privy to the day before was not happy news. I knew that bright days were going to be few and far between for the people of Da Nang and South Vietnam in the spring of 1975.

I returned my attention to the task at hand: drafting a telegram informing the embassy in Saigon that I wanted to evacuate the Americans and Vietnamese staff and their families from Da Nang immediately, in a phased manner, in anticipation of what I felt sure would be the final assault of the North Vietnamese Communists upon this northern region of South Vietnam. As I was finishing the cable recommending that a U.S. naval fleet be sent to the South China Sea to assist what I expected to be a massive flood of refugees from South Vietnam, there was a knock on my door. My secretary answered it and showed in Mary Francis, the wife of the American consul general, whose deputy I was at the time and who had himself been evacuated to the United States a few weeks before for medical reasons. She had hosted a coffee that afternoon for the wives of American staffers and wanted to bring me a treat from it. She gave my secretary and me a few Chinese fortune cookies and left us to our work.

The cable completed, I sat back and once more surveyed the lovely Han River outside my window. I knew that my cable would not be welcome in Saigon or in Washington. I knew that the ambassador in Saigon—who at that very moment was in Washington pressing his views on the administration—would not share my analysis of the intelligence that had prompted me to seek permission to begin an evacuation. As I dispatched the telegram, I had every expectation that the response from Saigon and Washington would be a demand for my own immediate recall.

My secretary brought me a cup of coffee, and we opened our fortune cookies. I relaxed on the sofa for a moment and read, "You've come a long way, baby."

1

Runnemede Beginnings

Da Nang, South Vietnam, was indeed a long way from Runnemede, New Jersey, a small blue-collar town on the Black Horse Pike. The Pike was one of two main arteries that brought Philadelphians, and Jerseyites, to the wonderful beaches of the South Jersey shore. I was born in Runnemede on October 2, 1936, the seventh child and third daughter of John James Tull and Anna Cecelia Paull. Runnemede was a town of simple pleasures, and not a bad place at all to be when growing up in the 1930s and 1940s.

A town with a population then of about 3,500, Runnemede offered next to nothing in the way of the recreational opportunities common today—there were no public tennis courts, no public swimming pool. There was a movie theater, however, which saw good business from me whenever I could obtain twelve cents for the child's admission price, and my parents' permission. Friday night frequently saw me in the middle row, with friends or occasionally a brother, enjoying the newsreel, cartoon, short subject, previews, and feature, which were standard fare at the time. Another five cents bought a candy bar or Jujubes, a hard gumdrop confection that was a favorite because one box, judiciously managed, could last the entire evening.

Despite the lack of township-provided recreational amenities, Runnemede offered ample entertainment to children with imagination. The Tull family lived at 22 East Fourth Avenue, a few houses from the Black Horse Pike. There were several houses on the street, but diagonally across the street for most of my childhood was a large vacant field with plenty of room to play and explore. The field had been part of a farm, apparently, as asparagus grew wild there, as did blackberries galore; picking these shiny black beauties just before breakfast so they could be enjoyed on cereal was a nice way to start a summer's day. Daisies, bluebells, and sweet peas were among the flowers growing wild in the field, waiting to be plucked for bouquets for a mother who always welcomed them gratefully and gave them pride of place in the dining room.

The field also provided the space for softball games, which my older brothers and their friends enjoyed. The terrain was uneven, causing occasional slips when running for a high fly ball, and the stickers were omnipresent, but it was a field, it was close by, and it was used a lot by major league wannabes.

I was five years younger than my nearest-in-age brother, and frequently felt wistful that while Charles and the next brother, fourteen months older than he, had each other as boon companions, I, as the youngest child, had no built-in family playmates. Charles and Jay were very nice to me, but they had each other and their friends, and their interests were commensurate with their ages. Although they were good-natured when I wanted to play with them, as I frequently did, my mother would not let me be a pest too often. I remember with a smile one summer day when the boys were playing softball in the field and—because they weren't hard up for teammates on this occasion—had no place for me in the lineup. It was a particularly hot day, and my brothers decided I could be their "official water girl." My job was to keep them supplied with water from our garden hose. I made several happy trips across the street to our driveway to fill the milk bottle with water from the garden hose for the players. After a few such trips, my mother called out the kitchen window to ask what I was doing. I told her I was getting water for the boys. She said that they were perfectly capable of getting their own water. I explained proudly that I was the official water girl for the game. She made it clear that whenever I wished to stop being the water girl, I was free to do so, but I skipped happily back to the game and continued my work. At that point, I apparently had not yet read *Tom Sawyer* and learned how he had gotten Aunt Polly's fence painted.

War Years

Clouding these simple pleasures of childhood, however, was World War II. One of my earliest memories is driving home with my parents and younger brothers from a Sunday visit to Holy Cross Cemetery in Philadelphia, where we had visited the graves of my mother's parents, and hearing on the car radio that the Japanese had bombed Pearl Harbor. Our lives immediately changed. My two oldest brothers, Jack and Bob, were soon to leave for the armed forces, Jack to join the army air force, Bob to be a carrier pilot with the navy. My father became the head of civilian defense for our town. My sister Hazel became a nurse's aide at the West Jersey Hospital, caring for wounded servicemen, and an air raid warden.

We children made our small contributions. We collected aluminum foil from cigarette packs, gathered milkweed pods, which apparently had some use, we were told, in the making of parachutes, and saved our pennies to buy savings stamps (ten cents each), which could be converted into a twenty-five-dollar war bond when seventeen dollars and fifty cents' worth of stamps filled a little book. My brothers helped my father collect newspapers throughout the town, all for the war effort.

The terms "war effort" and "duration" were key words of my early childhood years. So much had to be done for the war effort. So much would last for the duration of the war. Men were drafted for the duration. Rationing—of meat, sugar, butter, and other foodstuffs, and gasoline—was for the duration. There were rationing books with ration stamps, and little rationing tokens of different colors. When the war was over, my mother used the rationing tokens as bingo markers.

Our family loved the seashore. My mother had two sisters who lived in Wildwood, New Jersey—Elizabeth and Margaret. They had apartments or rooms to rent, and we occasionally visited them overnight. More often, though, we took day trips to Wildwood or to Atlantic City for a day on the beach, or an evening stroll on the boardwalk. We generally had a lovely time. We would pack a picnic lunch, eat on the beach, and try to avoid sunburn (though we fair-skinned Tulls generally failed in that endeavor in those days before sunscreen).

Atlantic City, in particular, changed a lot during the war. The glamorous boardwalk hotels became nursing homes or recuperation centers for wounded servicemen. The boardwalk itself was crowded with crippled and seriously injured men. Although the mainland United States was spared the horror of war, seeing these maimed men and the black oil smears on the beaches from sunken ships brought some of the reality of the war home to us.

For me, having two brothers in the service was perhaps why my memories of the war years are stronger than those of my contemporaries without older brothers involved. I missed my brothers dreadfully, particularly the oldest, Jack, who had been especially sweet to me. He was the farthest away from us, in England. Bob, two years younger than Jack, was for most of the war in training in the United States, and we saw him from time to time. But at one point, it had been more than two years since we had seen Jack. My mother told me later that she could not mention his name or express concern about him in my presence, because I would start crying. She could not even miss her son in peace.

Our front window proudly bore a small flag with two blue stars, signifying that two members of the armed forces had lived in our house. Mercifully, our stars remained blue; my brothers returned unharmed from the war. Others on our street were not as fortunate. The houses on both sides of ours had to exchange their blue stars for gold ones—their sons had been killed in action. Another family at the upper corner of our street also gave a son to the country. Three young men on one small street died during the three and a half years of bitter warfare that saw the defeat of Hitler's Germany and Hirohito's Japan. People on many blocks throughout the country must have experienced such poignancy.

"Hello There, Young Fellow"

This was my father's usual greeting when called to the telephone innumerable times during my childhood by people seeking help or information. Daddy had been a councilman in our town, and later the mayor, and was elected a freeholder of Camden County on the Democratic ticket in 1940. Throughout the war years he was intimately involved with many aspects of the war effort, and our phone was seldom quiet, particularly around dinnertime, when callers seemed to sense they could catch him at home. I remember his greeting was always cheery, no matter how tired or sick he may have been; he also always stood ready, as I remember it, to extend himself for others.

My pleasant childhood, wartime–related worries and difficulties aside, came to an end in the summer of 1947, with the onset of my father's terminal illness. Daddy, who was a lieutenant in the army during the First World War, had been gassed during experiments with new gas masks at the Frankford Arsenal in Philadelphia; his health afterward had suffered off and on for many years. He had been near death in 1940, but rallied to live a full life for seven more years. He could not manage another rally in 1947, however. He was hospitalized in June. The summer was a blur of missing him, of my mother taking two buses to visit him in the Naval Hospital in Philadelphia, of relatives coming to visit. I was taken to see him at least once—against regulations, as I was only ten years old—and I remember that I enjoyed sitting in his wheelchair. I didn't know then that I was not to see him again; my mother said that he didn't want me to see him as ill as he was. He died on September 25, 1947, one week before my eleventh birthday. I miss him to this day.

My father had a profound influence on me, despite our few years together. I remember his intense interest in public affairs and international events. I would sit on his lap during the war years as he read the newspaper, and I think I learned a lot about reading almost by osmosis. At dinner, we discussed national and international events—the coal miners' strikes, President Roosevelt's programs, the war effort. I have a brief but sharp memory of going to Camden in 1944 when President Roosevelt was campaigning for reelection. The president spoke on the steps outside Camden's City Hall, with local politicians, including my father, on the platform with him. My mother and I had seats close by; I could see the president, and I saw that my father was up there with him. I fantasized as a child about a future in which I would be a politician, too, perhaps a congresswoman. Precociously interested in current events, I once asked the young man dating my sister Hazel, in all innocence, what he was doing for the war effort. Her hapless 4-F date remembered that exchange for decades!

School Days

I was a few weeks shy of six years when I proudly went off to school for the first time. I joined my two brothers Jay and Charles at St. Rose of Lima School in Haddon Heights, New Jersey, a small town a few miles from Runnemede. We had to walk about four blocks to Clements Bridge Road to catch the school bus, which deposited us at the school well before class time. There were separate school yards for boys and girls, and I remember being the only girl waiting in the girls' yard for activity to begin, while my brothers and their friends went off to the boys' yard.

Charles and Jay liked St. Rose very much. I did not. I was perhaps excessively sensitive. The harsh first grade teacher was a stern nun whose grim manner greatly unnerved me. My frequent reaction to her outbursts, even when they were not directed at me, was to throw up. Then one of my brothers would be summoned from his class, and in due course my father would arrive to take me home.

I reported the nun's actions to my parents. They were unfailingly sympathetic toward me, but apparently felt that they had to encourage me to persevere and overcome my aversion. My mother's methods of encouragement were varied: She tried to give me a "good start" to the day by cajoling me to eat breakfast; one morning she even served me my favorite drink, grape juice, which made for a particularly colorful episode when the nun slapped the boy behind me. My mother went so far as to meet our school bus one fall afternoon with a dear little black and white puppy in her arms—a warm, wiggly incentive that did not, unfortunately, act as an antiemetic. We all loved Teddy, but I continued to be sick almost daily in school.

My salvation came unexpectedly. My parents decided to surprise me one afternoon and pick me up after school. My father arranged to leave work early, and they drove over to the school. They remained in their parked car, waiting for school to let out.

Fortunately for me, the nun was in her usual form. The drill was that the teachers walked their classes out of the school to the corner, where the students dispersed to school buses or began their walk home. As we walked, the nun herded us with sharp words, smacks, and snatches at jackets. My mother told me that my father, witnessing this, muttered, "Well, Theresa is right," and they arranged my transfer to the Grace Downing public school around the corner from us in Runnemede. My detestable two months at St. Rose were over. My brothers remained, happily so. Both of them graduated from St. Rose, and they retain fond memories of the experience—except for the trips they made to the first grade classroom because their little sister had been sick again.

The public school, for me, had a totally different atmosphere. There was classroom discipline—no rowdiness allowed—yet this state of order was achieved without any unpleasantness on the part of Miss Stafford, the first-grade teacher. I soon lost my dread of going to school. I remained shy and easily unsettled, but I soon adapted to the less severe environment. I could read before starting school, more or less, and had no difficulty with any of the subject matter. I excelled easily and made friends.

Religious education was accommodated by means of an excellent program of that era called "released time." The churches arranged to provide an hour a week of religious training by nuns or ministers at children's homes near the school. Parents who wanted their children to attend signed authorizations to that effect; children whose parents did not remained in class. I enjoyed the novelty of getting out of school early and going to a friend's house a few doors down from the school. Nuns from St. Theresa's Church in Runnemede were the teachers. St. Theresa's nuns were fine women, good catechism teachers, musicians, and firm but pleasant. Their behavior never evoked the anxiety I'd experienced under the tutelage of the first-grade teacher at St. Rose's. She was an aberration, and I was an exceptionally sensitive child. I have great respect for the outstanding academic results most teaching nuns extracted from the large numbers of students in their classrooms in that era.

A bonus for me in attending Grace Downing School was that I could go home for lunch. With my brothers at St. Rose's, I had my mother entirely to myself for that hour. As the youngest of seven children, it was a treat to have my busy mother's unshared company. When I was deemed old enough, I walked down Third Avenue and crossed the Black Horse Pike with the help of a policeman, picked up our mail at the post office near Third Avenue—there was no home delivery in those days—recrossed the Pike with the policeman's help, and headed home for, on most days, a nice hot lunch with my mother. My favorite lunch was corn fritters, sprinkled lightly with powered sugar. Occasionally, my mother's brother, Uncle Ray Paull, would stop by for coffee. At that time, he was a Freihofer's bread man whose route was in our town. He was a warm, friendly man, and I enjoyed having him stop in. If my mother bought a box of chocolate-covered doughnuts from him, my day was well and truly made.

Another delight of my grade school days was the treasured "one session." Our school day started at 9:00 a.m., stopped at 12:00 noon for lunch, resumed at 1:00 p.m., and concluded at 3:30 p.m. Because most of the students walked to school, if the weather was particularly bad—heavy rain, or even better, snow—we had one session. Our fire company would blow a whistle at noon to alert parents that school would continue uninterrupted until 1:00 p.m., when we would be released for the afternoon.

How we prayed for heavy rain to worsen, or for snowflakes to turn into a major storm! On such a morning, I suspect that from 11:00 a.m. on, not much was learned as we eyed the elements and yearned for one session. On those occasions when we were granted that boon, we splashed happily homeward, or trudged through freshly fallen snow as we dodged snowballs, with the rare gift of unexpected free time. My mother, who was an excellent cook and baker, welcomed me home with hot soup and concern ("Better get out of those wet clothes") and could frequently be persuaded to let me help her bake cookies or a scrumptious cake. The kitchen and house would fill with the scent of cinnamon and nutmeg as the treats baked. I settled in cozily in our warm house with a good book, a glass of milk, and a sample of baked delights as the elements raged outside. Everyone should have a few "one sessions" in his or her life.

Go, Irish!

I completed grammar school in seven years, skipping fourth grade. I later learned that the school authorities had recommended to my parents that I skip another grade (seventh) but my parents vetoed that. I already was the youngest by far in my class, and socially I would not have been in the same league with my classmates. As it was, my mother determined my social activities by my age, not by my class, and I was not allowed to do many of the things my classmates were permitted to do. I recall, for example, serving as president of our church sodality, a religious-social organization for young teens. We were organizing a dance, but technically I wasn't yet permitted to attend dances. Mother acquiesced on this occasion, however. Nonetheless, my youth often made me feel socially awkward.

In retrospect, skipping a grade level was helpful in some respects. I was bored with the class work at my regular grade level, which, through no effort of my own, I was easily able to master. Skipping a grade made me stretch a bit to cover the omitted material. And, since my father died while I was in the seventh grade, it meant that I graduated from high school and entered the working world a year earlier than usual, which helped my cash-strapped mother considerably.

My father and my mother both encouraged me to think about attending college. When I was quite young, I recall my father suggesting that I might want to consider being a lawyer when I grew up, which I regard as a quite enlightened suggestion to a daughter in that era. But there were no family funds for it, and Pell grants, government-subsidized student loans, and even community colleges had not yet arrived. College, from my point of view, was out of the question. Besides, from the time my father died, I was anxious to grow up, get a job, and ease my mother's burdens. I frankly disliked school. I found it boring at times, and deeply resented the collective punishments frequently meted out to the entire class because of the misbehavior of a few. I increasingly wanted to be free of school constraints, to be my own person. Not attending college directly after high school was not a hardship for me.

I was the seventh member of my family to attend Camden Catholic High School, as several of the teaching sisters duly noted ("What, another Tull?" or, more gently, "Oh, are you Hazel's sister?"). I commuted by public bus to Camden each day, a twenty- to twenty-five-minute trip. Initially, I was very nervous in my new environment, but I gradually adjusted and calmed down. I managed a ninety-plus average for four years; earned a citizenship award for broad participation in school activities; worked on the school newspaper, *The Spire,* for four years; appeared in the school play, "The New Moon," in my senior year; and thoroughly enjoyed attending Camden Catholic's football games. (The Fighting Irish had a good team in those days, but when I was a sophomore, our star player, Sonny Morrell, died after being tackled in our game against Bridgeton High. All of us at the school were devastated by his death.)

A couple of teachers made a strong impression on me. Working on the school paper with our journalism instructor, Sister Laura, sharpened my writing skills. Sister Coleman, who taught world history, made the subject come alive; she never tolerated less than a full effort from those she knew were capable of it. She pulled me up short once when I had sloughed off a pop quiz—that only happened once. She also strongly recommended that I participate in the Forensic Society. I joined and did well in original oratory and debates, honing my public speaking skills and boosting my confidence. I quit the club when an afterschool job opportunity arose.

2

On the Road to the Foreign Service

I was graduated from Camden Catholic in June 1953. I was delighted to be set free. I was sixteen years old. I started work full-time the next morning as a secretary at Rose & Epstein, a Camden law firm where I had been working part-time for several months. My salary was $35 per week. I enjoyed the work, and my freedom. No more homework! No more listening to rants from my senior homeroom nun who had selected me as her punching bag of the year. I did my job, met friends for lunch, and turned my salary over to my mother on payday, receiving a small allowance. This continued for two years; when I turned eighteen, I began instead to pay room and board and to manage my own money and expenses. Mother warned me that I had been better off under the previous arrangement, and she was right, but we both agreed it was time for me to take over my own finances.

I stayed with Rose & Epstein for two years. When I turned eighteen, I was eligible to try for employment with Camden's then star employers, RCA Victor and the Campbell Soup Company. I opted for Campbell's, and was hired as a secretary in their legal department and paid $10 per week more than I had been getting. I was then informed I would have to regularly make calculations using a slide rule to chart certain expenses. I was a bit intimidated by the vastness of the facility and the factory-like atmosphere. I gave it two weeks and resigned, determined never to work again in a large organization (little did I know!).

I then joined the office of another lawyer, Raymond Sirus, on Cooper Street in Camden. Sirus was a one-lawyer operation. He shared office space with friends—a father and son legal team, and a real estate broker-manager. The four secretaries shared a common office space, but each worked exclusively for one individual employer. It was a pleasant working arrangement. I was at least twenty years younger than the other secretaries, but we got along well.

After a few months in this arrangement, a lawyer friend of Raymond Sirus died suddenly. Mr. Sirus called me into his office and told me that the deceased had a wonderful, experienced secretary who was shocked by her boss's death, and was looking for a job. He insisted that he was very satisfied with my work, but this woman had twenty-plus years of legal experience. He asked if I would consider working instead for Alex Malamut, the real estate broker. Malamut's elderly secretary was leaving (perhaps nudged out—she had been increasingly unpleasant and erratic over the preceding months). I said yes and became Malamut's secretary.

This was an agreeable change. Alex Malamut was very pleasant and kind. The work was not particularly taxing, and he insisted that I should never pretend to be busy. If my work was up-to-date, I was free to read a newspaper, type letters to friends, or otherwise amuse myself. Sometimes he brought in school papers for his high-school-aged daughter for me to type. This was fine with me. It was a good arrangement for me; I had just begun taking college courses at Rutgers University's evening college, and it was very helpful to be able to study occasionally at my desk.

Mr. Sirus's legal secretary arrived, but, despite her supposed experience, she could not adjust to Mr. Sirus or to his work. She frequently asked me for advice on how to perform certain rather routine tasks, and loudly expressed her dislike for the work and for her new employer. Arguments could be heard from behind his closed office door. Then one day when the new secretary was at lunch, Mr. Sirus called me into his office and said that the new arrangement was not working out. He had been misled about his new secretary's abilities. Would I consider returning to his employ? I would not, I said. I was enjoying working with Mr. Malamut, and it would not be fair to leave him when I had just really learned the job. Mr. Sirus did not press the matter, but within a few days, his vaunted, experienced legal secretary quit in a huff. I happily stayed with Mr. Malamut.

A Profession Calls

I probably would have stayed with Alex Malamut for some time had I not become aware of an opportunity to enter the teaching profession. A high school friend had been employed as a teacher with the Diocese of Camden. By this time, I was no longer enamored with secretarial work; I yearned for work that would stretch my brain and my abilities. I had already started attending college at night, but a long span of years would pass before that route would produce a degree. But the Catholic school system was in dire need of teachers, and was able to make its own determination concerning teacher qualifications. I looked into it, and on the basis of my high school standing, I suppose, I was hired as a fourth-grade teacher at Sacred Heart Church on Ferry Avenue in Camden.

My fling as a teacher was short-lived. When I took over a sixty-five-student fourth grade class in October, I was the third teacher the class had had that year. I liked the children, and they seemed to like me; occasionally, they even seemed to be learning something from me. But I had difficulty maintaining classroom discipline. I was attending night school, and the college work, together with class preparation, was too much. I believe I stayed for three weeks, but it might have only been two. The principal and the students seemed genuinely sorry to see me go, but I think they were well rid of me. I had bitten off more than I could handle.

Vincent G. Kling, AIA—Architect Extraordinaire

I was once again looking for a job. This time I thought I might venture farther afield, to Philadelphia, where wages were higher and the opportunities more abundant. Skimming the want ads, I spotted an advertisement for a secretary at the firm of Vincent Kling, a noted Philadelphia architect. I knew about Kling's work through Ken, a man I had dated for two years. He was an interior decorator, and occasionally on Sundays we and some of his friends would drive around the city and surrounding area, where they would point out buildings they admired. Kling's Lankenau Hospital was one such building. Through Ken I had acquired a minieducation in art and architecture, and I was intrigued at the thought of working for Vincent Kling.

My mother was concerned about the neighborhood in which Kling's office was located, near Corinthian and Girard Avenues. When I called in response to the ad, Kling's executive secretary, Mary Matthews, asked me to come in for an interview. I told her about my mother's misgivings, and Mary suggested that I bring my mother with me so she could see for herself that the immediate neighborhood of the office was quite acceptable.

Mother and I decided to take her up on the suggestion. We made a day of it. We took the bus to Philadelphia to Thirteenth and Market Streets, and from there we took a trolley up to Nineteenth Street to Girard. We then walked a block to Kling's office on Corinthian Avenue. It was a large, old frame house, complete with front porch, nicely painted in cream with blue trim. Inside, the house had been converted into very attractive modern offices that retained a welcoming atmosphere. I took and passed the requisite shorthand and typing tests, and was hired. Mary Matthews was quite impressed with my mother, and mother was satisfied with the neighborhood and office arrangements. We celebrated my new job, which paid me the staggering sum of $70 per week, double the salary at which I had started my full-time work three years before, by lunching at Schrafft's on Chestnut Street and taking in a movie. The next Monday, I began what was to be a very happy seven years of employment with Vincent Kling.

The Foreign Service Beckons

I thoroughly enjoyed my seven years at Vincent Kling's. The atmosphere was vibrant, the people interesting, the work fascinating. It was exciting to be part of an endeavor that resulted in long-standing, beautiful buildings. From the moment a prospective client entered the office, through preliminary sketches, to formal renderings, to preparation of specifications, to ground breaking, through building completion, and frequently to an office tour of the completed structure, the work excited me.

I progressed in the firm, from one of four pool stenographers to an appointment as executive secretary to Mr. Kling's four senior executives. I had my own small office adjoining theirs, and eventually I was authorized to engage a secretary for myself. This worked out well—the lady I hired, Marge Ely, became a friend. One of the executives, Harry Ahrens, was responsible for preparing contracts for the architectural projects. I gradually evolved into the person who prepared the first draft for his review—not the usual secretarial duty, but I enjoyed stretching my brain, and he welcomed it.

Meanwhile, I was continuing to pursue my college degree at Rutgers University's Camden campus. Inspired by my brother Jay, who had begun night school a few years earlier, I decided when I was working in Camden that I would give it a try. There was one semester when I dropped out, in part because my mother became ill and was hospitalized, and I missed several classes. Mostly, however, it was because I was tired of the effort, the classes, the homework, and the term papers—and I wanted time for myself. I gave myself a semester off, during which I devoted spare time to writing short stories and short plays. I never got anything published. The high point of my writing career came when the *Ladies' Home Journal* sent me a personal letter of rejection (instead of the usual mimeographed form rejection note), encouraging me to continue and to send them more stories.

After this brief interlude, I decided to try college again. I signed up for one course in the fall semester, enjoyed it, and decided that I should knuckle down and work seriously toward my degree. I was never tempted to abandon this course of action again. I had gotten restlessness out of my system. And despite my enjoyment of my work at Kling's, I knew I did not want to be a secretary all of my life.

About this time, I found an article in the magazine *Good Housekeeping* about careers in the Foreign Service. It highlighted careers for women, both clerical and professional. This was the first time I had heard that women could become Foreign Service officers (FSOs), and perhaps advance through the ranks and become ambassadors. I decided that this would be the career for me, once I had gotten my college degree. My love of travel, history, current events, and government combined to make this the career at which

I thought I could succeed. Meanwhile, the slow slog toward the degree continued.

One of the professors at Rutgers with whom I had become close friends, Hal Emery, gave me some worthwhile information. When I told him of my Foreign Service goal, he informed me that a college degree was not a prerequisite for admission into the Foreign Service. You had to pass an extensive written examination and an oral exam, he explained, but there was no requirement for the degree, as such. I sent away for information from the State Department. Although the material I received said the best preparation for the exam was a college degree in history, political science, economics, etc., I saw nothing that said the degree was a prerequisite.

Hal, whose class in Western civilization I had taken, assured me that I could pass the written test. I decided to give it a try. An additional incentive to take the plunge was that, at that time, FSOs had to enter the program before their thirty-first birthday. I did not see this as a problem, because if I persevered in my night school effort, I would have the degree by then. Subsequently, however, the State Department decided that as of a certain date, anyone entering as an FSO had to be prequalified in a foreign language. I saw no way I could meet this requirement, so thought it best to try to get in before this requirement took effect. [*Note:* This proved to be a short-lived requirement. When too few young people were found to be prequalified in a foreign language, the requirement was dropped.]

I registered to take the FSO exam, and did so at the post office building in Philadelphia. The written exam took seven or eight hours. It was exhaustive, and exhausting. I did not feel overwhelmed by it, and was delighted when after several weeks I was informed that I had passed the exam and was invited to proceed to the oral exam. Prior to the oral exam, however, you had to undergo an extensive security investigation. Unfortunately, this included interviews with my current employer. My bosses at Vincent Kling were not happy to learn that I was planning to leave them.

I opted to take the oral exam at the U.S. Mission to the United Nations in New York City. Hal had assured me that I would have no difficulty passing the oral, having easily passed the written exam. He knew that I was well spoken and not easily flustered. He assured me that the oral would not be another minute fact-seeking test—he had taken these exams himself a few years earlier, although he decided to remain in academia—but one to test my maturity and ability to think on my feet.

Wrong. My oral exam was ninety minutes of specific fact-seeking questions. I couldn't believe it. What Indians were native to California? In flying from Addis Ababa to Rabat, what would the terrain look like? Describe it, name details, and so on. There were also specific economic-related questions, and I had not yet studied economics. But I kept my cool, did not pretend to know an answer when I didn't. Germaine Greer and Betty Friedan would be interested in knowing that one of the questions I was asked, not fact specific, was along these lines: Since I was a woman and probably would marry, why should the State Department hire me and spend money training me, when I would be required to resign when I got married? Indicative of these pre–women's lib times, I thought this was a reasonable question. I replied that since I would be working in embassies, the likelihood was that if I married it would be to another FSO, in which case the U.S. government would be getting two for the price of one.

Nonetheless, the panel flunked me. The chairman kindly said that they were truly impressed by the fact that I had passed the written exam when I had accumulated only about sixty-five college credits. They strongly encouraged me to try again, which would mean, I learned, that I had to take the written exam all over again.

I was crushed. I had never before failed at anything in my life. Making it worse was the fact that I had to return to Kling's, crestfallen, and inform them that I would not be leaving them just yet, thank you.

I decided that despite the lack of a specific requirement for a college degree, the State Department did not want nondegree folks in their FSO program. I resolved to continue college at night, acquire the degree, and, if possible without the language prerequisite, try again for the Foreign Service.

My mother, however, who had stood to lose a lot personally if I had succeeded in my Foreign Service quest, strongly encouraged me to take the exam again immediately. I told her that the panel had recommended that I try again, but probably just to make me feel better, I felt. But mother said they would not have urged me to test again unless they thought I could make it. I decided to sign up and take the exam at the next opportunity—the test was administered only once a year—to prove, I said, that my passing it the first time was not a fluke.

So I took the exam, passed again, and proved my point. I then decided I would wait until I had the degree to pursue the matter further. My mother, again, was the catalyst for me abandoning this cautious approach. Take the oral exam as soon as it is offered, she urged. "What do you have to lose," she pressed, "a day's vacation?" I decided, why not? By this time, the department had abandoned the practice of conducting the security investigation prior to the oral, so I knew my employer would not be approached again. I followed my mother's advice.

Again, I went to New York City, to the U.S. Mission to the United Nations. This time the oral exam was conducted along the lines that Hal Emery had prepped me on—no individual fact-seeking questions, but broader, more thoughtful, shall I say, essay-type questions. One, for example, gave me the opportunity to select a world leader I would have the opportunity to interview, and devise five questions to ask him or her. Another asked me to describe the purpose of U.S. foreign aid programs. I felt comfortable with the questions and with my responses, but was convinced that the panel was only going through the motions. I would once again be encouraged to try again at some vague future date.

After the panel met in private to discuss the exam, I was called back into the room and was greeted with "Welcome to the Foreign Service, Miss Tull." I was genuinely surprised. "Are you telling me that I passed?" I asked. "Yes, of course," I was told. "We had the recommendation in your file from the previous panel, encouraging you to try again, and we're pleased that you did." Needless to say, my trip home that day was much more pleasant than the previous year's similar journey had been.

To Washington

This time, I vowed to tell no one—not even my brothers and sisters—of my plans until I had a firm date to go to Washington and be sworn into the Foreign Service. My mother was tremendously proud and supportive. As a final "civilian" fling, we went to Miami Beach for a week in June. I found an incredibly inexpensive deal at the Carillon Hotel on the beach, because it was off-season. The package included airfare, hotel, and all breakfasts and dinners. We were delighted to find that our dinners would be offered in a beautiful ballroom-type dining space, complete with crystal chandeliers and tuxedoed pianist at a grand piano. We cherished this time together, taking sightseeing boat rides, lounging around the beach, and even seeing a couple of movies. *Lawrence of Arabia* was the current hit, and we made a special effort to see it. Mom was not a keen movie fan, but she was agreeable to going, knowing how much I enjoyed films. I had selected Florida for our trip because mom and I had never been there. I knew that mom would enjoy telling her sister, Libby, who wintered in St. Petersburg every year, about her stay on Miami Beach.

Thus it was that in August 1963, 1 found myself waiting for the Greyhound bus at the Runnemede exit of the New Jersey Turnpike. It seemed unreal that I was actually leaving home, the home in which I had been born twenty-six years before, and embarking on a professional career—from secretary to diplomat, overnight. I was thrilled, yet nervous. Would I succeed? How would I fare, competing with college graduates and people with advanced degrees?

The State Department had suggested that I begin my stay in Washington at the Meridian Hill Hotel on upper Sixteenth Street. It was a women-only establishment, the destination of choice for a range of new government employees. I recall checking into the hotel, unpacking, and sitting down at the tiny desk in my small room. I started reviewing the implications of my departure from my widowed mother's home.

While I lived at home, I paid for room and board. In addition, at least one of my siblings sent mom a small check regularly each month. This, combined with a modest pension as the widow of a World War I veteran and mom's excellent money-managing skills, kept the household running smoothly. But now that I was no longer there, that weekly cash input would cease, yet in all of my preparations for the move to Washington, mom had never raised this matter. This was typical of her attitude throughout my life.

In the wake of my father's death, I was to consider myself free to pursue any undertaking. I recall her saying in this regard that my brothers and sisters had all been able to pursue their lives as they wished, and just because I was the youngest, there was no reason that I shouldn't do the same. When I demurred about leaving her alone, she said bluntly that if I held back from pursuing my dreams because of her, I should remember that before too long she would be dead, and I would still have the bulk of my life to live. Mom was right, of course. I immediately wrote her a letter telling her that I'd arrived safely, and informing her that I would continue to send her the rough equivalent of the money I had paid for room and board. When she got the letter, she objected, but I insisted. I cite this episode as indicative of my mother's totally unselfish, supportive attitude.

The next morning, August 12, 1963, I reported to the State Department and was sworn in as an FSO. A mild disappointment awaited, however. Although I was supposed to begin the A-100 course (a sort of basic training, without the calisthenics, for FSOs), I was told that because of overbooking, I had been assigned instead to a course that began in October. Meanwhile, various busy-work assignments were found for us. I recall a couple of dreadful days in a personnel office, separating travel orders into at least eight different stacks. This did not sit well with the other fledgling FSO who shared this task with me, but I was still too awed about actually working in the State Department to fuss.

Rescue came fairly soon. Within a week I was assigned to assist on the Philippine desk in the East Asia Bureau. I was given a desk in the corner of the office director's office. Bob Ballantyne was a fine man, an excellent role model, and a good teacher. He allowed me to stay in his office during all of his meetings, and gave me genuine work to do. I was already strongly inclined toward a career in Southeast Asia when I entered the Foreign Service, and this six-week stint on the Philippine desk reinforced my interest.

The office director took me to bureau staff meetings, where I learned about the major issues the bureau faced. I recall that an important development during this period was the establishment of Malaysia, cobbled together from several former British colonies, including the Federation of Malaya, Singapore, and the former crown colonies of Sabah and Sarawak. Singapore's membership proved short-lived. This predominantly ethnic Chinese entity was expelled from the federation in 1965 because the leader of Malaysia feared that Singapore's leader, Lee Kuan Yew, was attempting to substitute a multiethnic community for ethnic Malay political dominance.

Another highlight was meeting John D. Rockefeller IV. Jay was an intern in the bureau, considering options about his own career. He was tall, handsome, single, and, of course, incredibly rich. He was also very nice. He resisted my charms, however, and those of the State Department, going on to become West Virginia's governor and, later, senator, a position he still holds.

I was privileged to be in Washington on August 28, 1963, and witnessed, on my lunch hour, the historic March on Washington on behalf of civil rights. This gathering of a quarter million people had been organized principally by the Reverend Martin Luther King, Jr. People from all over the country, largely blacks but not exclusively, convened on the Washington Mall to march for civil rights for Negroes (this was before "black" or "African American" came into favor). Washington was very nervous about this "invasion," as there were concerns that it could turn violent. Many businesses closed, but the government remained open.

I sympathized with the purpose of the march, but was uncertain, as someone who had just been sworn in as a government employee, whether I could join it. I cautiously decided that I would not march, but would go to the mall to observe and hear the speeches.

I am so glad I overcame my qualms (some people stayed away, in misplaced fear). The march was entirely peaceful. Throngs of disciplined but determined Americans marched down the mall, carrying banners calling for equal rights, voting rights, fairness in housing, and the like. And the main address, some of which I heard over the public address system set up at the Lincoln Memorial, was Martin Luther King's "I have a dream" speech—that was a truly historic event, and I was at least a peripheral witness. My Washington life was well launched.

The Housing Search

Housing, of course, had to be obtained. I scanned the *Washington Post* for likely opportunities and found an ad from a group of women in Georgetown seeking a new addition to their household. Although I doubted I could afford Georgetown, I decided to check it out. The house was lovely and large, and the three women interviewing me were pleasant enough. One of them was Vice President Lyndon Johnson's secretary. I passed their inspection, as these women, all secretaries, thought it would be acceptable to have an FSO as a roommate. The cost, however, as I had feared, was beyond my means. My share of the rent alone would have been $85 per month, and I knew there would doubtless be other shared costs. I thanked them for their time and linked up with three young secretaries I had met at the hotel—two friends from Buffalo, New York, working at the Pentagon, and a perky young girl who had just joined the CIA (Central Intelligence Agency). The four of us found an apartment in a private home in Arlington, Virginia. My share of the rent was $35 per month, which was much more manageable for me. We shared food costs, and the arrangement worked out well. At age twenty-six, I became a de facto den mother for these twenty-one- and twenty-two-year-olds. The place was conveniently situated, and our landlords, a young couple who lived above us, were quite nice. Later in the year, when President Kennedy was assassinated and Lyndon Johnson became president, I wondered how his secretary with whom I had almost shared a house had fared. I wondered whether he had taken her with him to the Oval Office. I assume he did.

Horseback Problems

I settled into my new life with my three roommates smoothly. The low cost of our shared rental made it possible for me to enjoy some outside activities. One beautiful Saturday, the four of us decided to go out to Maryland and rent horses. I made it clear to the folks at the stable that I was very inexperienced and wanted a quiet horse that would be content to walk. No problem, I was assured. Business was brisk that day, however, and a friend of the stable owner, a woman in her thirties, joined us; she offered to lead the group on a trail ride through the woods. I reiterated to her my insistence that I had to maintain a very moderate pace.

This apparently fell on deaf ears. She was so happy to be riding on that beautiful afternoon that she soon set a rapid pace, up hill and down dale—all the while through thick woods. I attempted to get her attention, without success. Suddenly, a large branch whipped me off and under the horse, which promptly stepped on my calf. Suffice it to say that we returned home, but after an hour or so I decided that I had to get medical treatment. At the hospital emergency room, x-rays revealed that I had a severe contusion on the right leg, plus a broken finger on my right hand. The leg injury was such that the doctor said it had to be treated like a broken leg. The leg was put into a cast and I was fitted out with crutches. The finger was placed firmly in a splint.

Thus encumbered, I continued my A-100 course, the FSO's basic training-cum-introduction to government and the Foreign Service. In exchange for using my car, a classmate carted me to and from the Foreign Service Institute. My mother came down from Runnemede to look after me for about two weeks—being right-handed, I was rather helpless. This proved to be a blessing for all of us. Mom became everyone's mom in our apartment. They reveled in her delicious cooking, told her their troubles, and generally enjoyed her warm, helpful presence.

Thanks to the transportation arrangements and mom's attentions, I was able to participate almost fully in the A-100 course activities, with only one potential glitch: We were given a language aptitude test, and I discovered that I could not record my answers fast enough with my left hand. I alerted the instructor, but as it developed, I still scored high enough to avoid having to take the test again. I regret, however, that my A-100 class photo reveals a pair of crutches on the floor, insufficiently concealed despite my efforts.

November 22, 1963

This fateful day began like any other for the A-100 class. The shocking news that President John F. Kennedy had been shot in Dallas was broken to us shortly after it occurred. We were all stunned. Our course coordinator took the position that we should behave as if we were at an overseas post and continue our work as usual. Shortly thereafter, however, the news came that the president had died of his wounds, and we were dismissed. I recall standing on the street corner, weeping, waiting for my ride, and watching as cars pulled over to the curb as drivers and passengers listened to the news on the radio and added their tears to those that the rest of the nation was shedding.

It was a devastating blow to the country, to the world, and to the hopes of this bright, eager, young group of diplomats in training. How could it have happened? Why? I had avidly supported Jack Kennedy's presidential bid. I volunteered in Philadelphia as a "citizen for Kennedy," and worked, time permitting, at the Democrats' Chestnut Street office, doing mailings, culling lists, and the like. On my lunch hour at Kling's, I made phone calls to prospective voters. This got me into hot water with Vincent, a rock-ribbed Republican, who was furious to discover that votes for Kennedy were being solicited from his premises. I had not seen anything wrong with doing this during my lunch hour, and as I only called Philadelphia numbers, no additional charges were incurred. In retrospect, I came to understand that campaigning while at the office was inappropriate.

During the campaign, I got to see Kennedy in person twice. When he visited the Levittown, Pennsylvania, shopping center, my sister Hazel and I went down and got a good, close look at the handsome candidate. I recall running after his car, at a point when there were for some reason few people near us. He waved at us with an expression that seemed to ask, "Are you two out of your mind?" Later in the campaign, he was due to arrive at the Philadelphia International Airport about 9:00 p.m. My brother Jay called and offered to take mom and me over to join the welcoming crowd. We asked my mother's sister, Aunt Kit, to join us. As happened frequently, Kennedy arrived late, and many of the crowd were refreshing themselves in the terminal when word came that the plane had landed. We scooted out and made it to the first ranks of the welcomers, and were rewarded with handshakes from the future president.

Now, all of that youthful enthusiasm and patriotic leadership had been silenced forever. It was devastating.

I was so glad that my mother was still with us in Virginia. She was extremely saddened, and it was helpful to both of us to have each other for support. Complicating our sorrow was the fact that Dick Waldis, son of my oldest sister, Betty, and mom's oldest grandchild, was getting married the following day. The rehearsal dinner was that evening. We did not know what to do, but it was too late for weddings to be canceled, so we swallowed hard and attended the dinner.

The wedding day dawned with torrential rains adding to the general gloom. Somehow we got through it. I felt so sorry for Dick and Sue, to have had such a tragedy overshadowing their special day.

Lying in State; the Funeral Procession

The president lay in state at the U.S. Capitol, under the rotunda, on Sunday night. My FSO friend-chauffeur drove mom and me to the city, and somehow we managed to view the coffin. I think we took folding chairs to use as we waited in line. My crutches also helped us get some preferential treatment. It was a very moving experience.

The next day, we decided to go to Arlington National Cemetery for the funeral procession itself. Again, my crutches helped us get front-row placement, with our trusty folding chairs. We arrived well before the procession. The crowd was subdued, serious, and kind. When the procession entered the cemetery, we got a good view of the entire entourage. It was so sad to think of this young, vibrant, intelligent man cut down in the prime of his life, before he had been able to achieve all that might well have been possible had he lived to complete his term. On this day, ironically, the sun was shining brightly. We probably would not have chanced attending if it had been as miserably rainy as Saturday had been.

Sunday morning, mom and I were watching television over breakfast when we saw Jack Ruby break past police officers in Dallas and murder Kennedy's accused assassin, Lee Harvey Oswald. This despicable act bothered me almost as much as the assassination itself. What kind of country were we becoming, I wondered, if this was the way "justice" was carried out?

Sold into Slavery–to Chicago

At last, the two-month A-100 course was over. I had found it a most interesting, stimulating introduction to the government at large and to the State Department in particular. I liked my fellow FSOs very much. We had some fun parties, and I dated a couple of the young men a few times. I was subject to some mild interest when brief bio sketches were distributed about each class member. It did not take some of the men long to discover that I did not have a college degree, nor did it take me long to note that all of my fellow FSOs had at least a bachelor's degree. Moreover, some had master's degrees, a couple were lawyers, and one had a PhD.

One Yale graduate with whom I became friendly was particularly interested in how I scored on the frequent exams we were given in the consular affairs section of the course. He would sidle over to me and try to read my score when the tests had been returned. I made it difficult for him to peek, so he had to ask how I'd done. I always managed to score higher than he did, which annoyed him in a humorous way. I remember him saying, exasperated, after the third such experience, when my ninety-six had edged out his ninety-three or ninety-four, that he didn't know how to explain to his father that the tens of thousands of dollars he had spent on his son's Yale education apparently had not been particularly productive, since I could best him with no degree.

The big day—when we would receive our overseas assignments—dawned. We had been offered a choice of general areas of interest for our first assignment. I had selected Asia, Africa, and the Middle East. But when assignments were announced, there was a major change in plans. Because the State Department was facing a budget crisis, we were told, our class of FSOs would not be going abroad just yet. Instead, we were being assigned to the Passport Agency—"sold into slavery," as we put it—and would be sent to various passport offices throughout the United States. A few officers were diverted into the Diplomatic Courier Service. At least they would get to live abroad, the rest of us groused, while we processed passport applications back in the states.

Thus it was that in January 1964 I drove out to Chicago, with my mother, to begin a seven-month stint adjudicating passport applications. I was pleased to get assigned to Chicago, as my brother Charles and his wife and family were living there at the time. Charles was a professor of American history at DePaul University. Mom and I stayed with them while we searched for an affordable apartment for me. Luckily, I found a charming efficiency-plus in an old brownstone just off Lake Shore Drive, at 416 North Arlington Street. Mom and I were very pleased with the place. The owners had kept the first floor of the old house for themselves, and converted the second and third floors into separate apartments. Mine had a decent-sized living and dining room combination, a tiny kitchen, a large bath, and a separate sleeping area off of the living room. The space was separated from the living room by a floor-to-ceiling drape, but it was large enough to stand on its own as a bedroom. It had a full-sized bed, nightstands, bureau, mirror, and closet. The apartment was no more than a mile from Charles and Mickey's apartment, and we saw a fair amount of each other. I frequently attended Sunday mass at their church and joined them for breakfast afterward.

Mom and I enjoyed having this quality time with Charles and Mickey and their children, and seeing Chicago. After a brief stay in Chicago, mom returned to Runnemede. When I completed my tour in August, mom came out by bus and stayed with me for about two weeks. We did some more sightseeing, including a very interesting day trip to Springfield to visit the Abraham Lincoln house and grave. Mom particularly enjoyed the Lincoln Park Zoo, which was just a few blocks from my apartment. There was a huge polar bear there, which mom enjoyed visiting. She spoke to him, and he responded. He would come over to the side of the den where she was (above him, of course, and completely safe) and look at her intently as she murmured softly to him. I called him "mom's polar bear." They had a good relationship.

The atmosphere in the Passport Office in the old Chicago Federal Building was very good. The capable director, Bruce Weaver, took pains to blend his temporary Foreign Service help smoothly into the mix with his permanent civil service staff. We cooperated fully with the experienced hands, some of whom confided to me later that they had feared that the FSOs—there were four of us—would think they were too good for the work required. They were pleasantly surprised when this proved not to be the case.

Shortly after I arrived at work, the trial of Teamster Union leader Jimmy Hoffa took place in a courtroom in the Federal Building. As the workload permitted, Bruce allowed us on a staggered basis to attend segments of the trial, which was major national news at the time. I recall a short, heavy-set, dark man sitting impassively as his crimes were detailed. Hoffa was convicted and spent time in prison. Some time after his release he disappeared after going to a restaurant for an appointment. He is widely believed to have been murdered, but his body has never been recovered.

3

First Overseas Assignment: Brussels

Orders finally came to Chicago for my first overseas assignment: a rotational training assignment as a junior officer at our embassy in Brussels, Belgium, preceded by four months of French language training. I was delighted, although I had not sought a European assignment. My first preference was for Asia, followed by Africa and the Middle East, as I had never been to those places, while I had had a wonderful vacation in Europe in 1961. As a little girl, I had been intrigued by the book *Anna and the King of Siam,* and resolved to visit Thailand. But that could wait—Europe beckoned.

In Washington, I linked up with a fellow FSO, Sarah Nathness, to share an apartment in Arlington Towers, the same complex where we would be studying languages—she, German, preparatory to an assignment in Bern, and I, French. Sarah was a very intelligent and pleasant young woman and I had hoped we could socialize together, exploring Washington and the like, but it developed that she was quite a homebody and rarely left the apartment. A chain-smoker, she did me a great favor when she volunteered that she would never smoke in the bedroom we shared. Not having lived with a smoker, I did not realize how thoughtful this was at the time, but as the rest of the apartment became permeated with her cigarette smoke, I appreciated her gesture.

Being in Washington gave me an additional opportunity to visit Runnemede on weekends, as mom and I knew that within months

I would be living across the sea. She remained my staunchest supporter, although we both dreaded the impending separation. Fortunately, mom's older sister and best friend, Aunt Kit, remained a regular companion, and my brothers and sisters who lived in the area were very supportive of her. Still, despite my excitement at going to work in a European embassy, the thought of leaving my mother to live alone was wrenching.

We enjoyed our last Christmas together in December 1964. At the last minute, I invited two friends to come to Runnemede and share the holiday. One, Louise DuMont, had been one of my original Arlington roommates. When I left for Chicago, she kept in touch with my mother, and occasionally drove to Runnemede to spend the weekend with her. The other was a lovely Hispanic communicator from California, with whom I had served in Chicago. I discovered that she was not flying home to California for Christmas, and after checking with mom, I invited her, and Louise, to come home with me.

Christmas had always been very special for me, and I was initially reluctant to ask others to join us. Although I felt I should share the holiday with these girls who otherwise would go to a restaurant in the Washington suburbs on that special day, part of me selfishly wanted to have everything at home just as it had always been. I am glad I overcame the selfish impulse, because the girls were so appreciative, and we had a wonderful Christmas weekend. I felt particularly rewarded when the communicator called her family in California on Christmas and told them what a fine time she was having with us. Both girls were very grateful to mom, who treated them like a couple of extra daughters.

To Brussels: The Embassy, Apartment Hunting

After a flurry of last-minute shopping (much of it accomplished by my sister, Hazel, as I nursed a heavy cold) and packing, I said my goodbyes and emplaned for Belgium. The embassy had me met at the airport and whisked through the formalities—a new and pleasant experience. They had made a reservation for me at the Metropole Hotel in downtown Brussels, an old Grand Hotel–type structure, attractive in a formal, dark way. It was within walking distance of the embassy, about a thirty-minute walk. It all felt very strange, initially, and the perpetual gloom of the rainy weather the region is infamous for was not designed to remove butterflies from the stomach of someone about to launch a new career. It was midwinter, of course, which meant that daylight, such as it was, began about 8:30 a.m. and lasted until approximately 4:30 p.m. This was not conducive to bright spirits. But, hey, I was living in Europe!

I was processed through the administrative section of the embassy, and learned that finding housing was totally my responsibility (this was before the time when the embassy in Belgium leased residences for its entire staff). Also, protocol required that I pay a courtesy call on the wives of everyone on the diplomatic list who outranked me—that is, everyone. So between trying to read into my new duties in the admin section, where I went first as part of my rotational training assignment, I had to absent myself frequently to make calls on some forty-two wives and present them with my personal calling card. If they were not at home, I left the card, bent at the top-left corner, in the silver tray provided in the entry hall for this purpose. Most often, however, I was received politely and offered tea or coffee and perhaps a cookie. Although distracting from what I regarded as my "real" duties, these protocol calls did provide an overview of the city as I visited various neighborhoods where our scattered personnel lived, and I was happy to meet the wives of the men I was gradually getting to know at the embassy.

The atmosphere in the embassy, per se, was not very welcoming to newcomers. You were left on your own, as typified by the general services officer who suggested that I find an apartment by taking a trolley car and getting off when I saw an *A Louer* (For Rent) sign—this while knowing nothing about the safety of the various neighborhoods. Fortunately, an A-100 classmate, Bill Barraclough, his wife Beryl, and their preschool son had also been assigned to Brussels and were staying at the Metropole. I had assumed that as a married couple they had been invited to dinner by other couples, while I had been ignored, except for tentatively offered invitations from secretaries to join them at dinner at restaurants, which I quickly accepted. Bill corrected that impression—they had been left completely on their own and were unhappy about it. He and

Beryl resolved to change that situation when they were settled, and did so, establishing an informal welcoming committee to greet the newcomers, invite them to dinner, take the wives shopping, and so on. Meanwhile, I joined them for occasional meals.

My salvation regarding the apartment search came from a young FSO, Bob Houdek, and his wife, who invited me to dinner the second week I was in Brussels—my only such invitation. They had a charming little apartment in the university district of Brussels—57 Square des Latins, second floor. They were nearing the end of their Brussels tour. In the course of the evening I asked what the rent was (doable) and whether the apartment had been rented. They did not think so, and put me in touch with their landlord. It was available. I grabbed it, and was very happy there for my two-year assignment.

In Brussels at that time, an apartment was either furnished completely (down to china, glassware, pots and pans, etc.) or unfurnished, which meant one had to provide one's own large appliances, light fixtures, drapes, and so on. Finding a fully furnished apartment saved me a lot of money and time that would have been spent buying appliances and all of the other accoutrements of apartment life.

The apartment was on the second floor of a town house, in a row of similar structures overlooking the oval-shaped "square." The skull of an African water buffalo dominated the entry hall— the landlord had been a Belgian civil servant in the Congo. I left it up; it was quite a conversation piece. To the right was a bright, cozy living room, and to its right was a pleasant dining room. There was a small kitchen down the short hall, a WC (water closet, a small room containing a toilet and wash basin), a separate bathroom, a very small bedroom across from the bath, and at the end of hall, a larger bedroom. In the living room, what appeared to be an attractive wooden cupboard was actually a Murphy-type bed, which meant I could accommodate guests, and I did so on occasion. I thoroughly enjoyed the apartment and the neighborhood. There was ample street parking for the 1965 Mustang I had treated myself to, a silver blue beauty, my first brand new car. (I recently read that a woman had donated her 1965 silver blue Mustang to the Smithsonian for display as an American artifact!) And there was a trolley at the corner, which went right to the embassy.

I enjoyed living in Brussels. It is a beautiful old city. Elaborately decorated medieval guildhalls border the Grande Place at the center of the city. On Sundays, the Grande Place glowed with the kaleidoscopic colors of the weekly flower market. Restaurants and cafés rimmed the periphery. Sitting outside with a "martini rouge," a Dubonnet cocktail, was an inexpensive way to drink in the centuries-old atmosphere. The Belgian cuisine was excellent and less expensive than in France. Near the Grande Place, La Rue des Bouchers, a charming little street, offered a wide choice of restaurants. The dollar was strong in 1965, and I was able to enjoy restaurant meals often. A favorite spot for inexpensive *boeuf Béarnaise* or *moules avec pommes frites* (French fries, which the Belgians claim to have invented) was Chez Leon.

Brussels also was a cultural center. The Palais des Beaux Arts offered plays, concerts, ballets, and art exhibits, which I attended frequently. And Belgium's location made exploring Europe on long weekends very convenient. The only negative about living there was the depressingly gray, too often rainy, weather.

Briefing by the Ambassador

The U.S. ambassador to Belgium when I arrived in January 1965 was Douglas MacArthur II, the nephew of the famous general. He was, not surprisingly, authoritarian in his manner and approach to his staff, and was not exactly beloved. I was very impressed, however, that shortly after my arrival, when I paid a call on him in his office, he spent a half hour outlining the current situation in Belgium and the state of U.S.–Belgian relations.

Rotational Duties: The Administrative Section

At that time, new FSOs were assigned to larger embassies and were rotated over the course of two years through the four major sections of the embassy: political, economic, consular, and administrative. This practice gave new recruits an excellent overview of the embassy's work, as well as an opportunity to discover which line of work they found appealing and for which they had some aptitude. I was assigned initially to the administrative section and placed under the supervision of the personnel officer.

This woman had had a most interesting career as a secretary in various government agencies, including several years working for a high official in the American occupation administration in Germany. She assumed increasingly responsible work, and eventually entered the Foreign Service under a program that did not require taking the competitive FSO exam, and became a personnel officer.

She was pleasant, but it became apparent to me that she was in a bit over her head. She was easily flustered, and grew visibly angry when questioned civilly by her boss, the administrative counselor, Ken Lindstrom, about aspects of her work. She used me as a secretary, which I found unsatisfactory. Once I determined that this was how she intended to continue to "train" me, I went to the administrative counselor and complained that I was not being given real work to do. I knew that my performance would be evaluated after each stint in the various sections, and I was concerned that there would be nothing to say about me from this rotation except that I typed well. This would not be helpful for my promotion prospects in the highly competitive Foreign Service.

Lindstrom asked me for patience, and explained that the officer was on her last Foreign Service assignment, which was why he was showing forbearance about her sometimes almost erratic (and certainly disrespectful) behavior. He assured me that meaningful work would be found for me, and asked me to hang on and help her as much as I could.

Not long thereafter, Lindstrom assigned me and Bob Lamb, a fellow junior FSO, to work with a senior Foreign Service local employee to conduct a local wage survey. Periodically, embassies survey the local employment scene to ensure that embassy wages and benefits for its local national employees are fair and competitive with other employers in the capital cities. This assignment was welcome release for me from the personnel office, and proved to be a very interesting and meaningful task. With the guidance of the FSN (Foreign Service national, our local employee), we developed a list of companies in Brussels with which the embassy competed for employees. We arranged meetings with their personnel people, obtained copies of their wage and benefits scales (and in return provided them with ours), and studied the results, comparing these data with our own wage scales. Visiting the major companies in Brussels to compare notes on wages and benefits was very educational.

Bob and I required a large work space to finalize our work—developing a revised wage and benefits plan for the embassy's large FSN staff—and found ourselves allotted the ambassador's office for this chore while he was away for a couple of weeks. We settled into his large, attractive office with the expansive view of the city for several days and did our work, which was well received. The embassy leadership accepted the wage plan, and Bob and I were commended for our work.

Bob was multitalented, and excelled in whatever section he was assigned. I recall asking him later why he had decided to specialize in administration rather than political or economic work. He explained pragmatically that he was already married, with young children, and he had determined that he could advance much more quickly in the administrative field, which he also enjoyed, than in the other fields where advancement would most likely be slower. He made the right decision. Bob rose quickly through the ranks, and ultimately served very capably as assistant secretary of state for administration.

Duty Officer: Crisis in the Congo

Three weeks into my assignment in Brussels, I found myself on the roster as embassy duty officer. Every embassy and consular post has an officer on call to deal with emergencies during nonworking hours. I was a little surprised that after such a short period at post I would be entrusted with this task, but swallowed hard when the time came and assumed my duties. The duty began at the close of business on Friday night and ran until that same time the following Friday. I picked up the bulky duty-officer book from the outgoing officer. This tome contained miscellaneous information about whom to contact for various problems that might arise, emergency phone numbers for police and hospitals, and the like. I took the book with me to my new temporary residence. I had found the Metropole Hotel a bit grim, and had moved a bit closer to the embassy, to the Westbury Hotel, a newer, modern facility.

Saturday mornings the duty officer had to work at the embassy reviewing cables, alerting more senior officers to items of interest or concern. My first morning passed uneventfully. I felt that I had not blown anything yet. So far, so good.

Saturday night—or, rather, early Sunday morning, about 2:00 a.m.—I got a phone call at my hotel from the embassy communications office. A "NIACT immediate" (night action immediate) cable had come in, requiring my review. I could not believe this. Was war breaking out? Nervously, I dressed and took a cab to the embassy.

I reviewed the cable, which was from one of our posts in Zaire, the former Belgian Congo. The country had been experiencing civil war in certain areas. I read the message several times and could not determine what, if anything, the embassy could or should do about the situation described. I could not understand what action we could possibly take. Yet, the duty-officer instructions clearly stated that after reviewing such messages, the duty officer should immediately inform either the deputy chief of mission (DCM) or the appropriate embassy counselor, who then, presumably, would have to come in and review it themselves.

I decided that there was no reason to disturb either gentleman's sleep for this particular message. Hoping I was doing the right thing and that I had not missed something in this message that I later would regret not acting on, I returned to the hotel for a few more hours of restless sleep.

At 8:00 a.m. I returned to the embassy, retrieved the message from the code room, and called the political counselor, Bob Beaudry. I had met him briefly, but it was clear he was initially puzzled about who this young woman claiming to be the duty officer could be— and then his concern about my not calling him in the middle of the night surfaced when he curtly said, "I will be right in."

Within a half hour, Bob was reading the message in the code room with me, and to my great relief, he said in disgust, "There's no reason for this to have been sent NIACT immediate. There's no action for us." He was clearly pleased with my good judgment. He wanted to know when I would be coming to the political section to work. I didn't know, but I said that was the field in which I wished to specialize.

This episode had a very favorable impact on my tour in Brussels, and ultimately on my entire Foreign Service career. Bob took an interest in me, and he included me occasionally in representational dinners at his home, where I met Belgian political figures, journalists, and the like. He nagged the administrative counselor to assign me to his section—in vain, as it was only at the end of my two-year tour that I finally entered that promised land. When this finally happened, he gave me interesting work to do and praised it liberally.

Bob's long-term impact on my career, however, came when I was about to leave. He, too, was finishing up his assignment. I told him I had received an indication that I was going to be assigned to Saigon, which pleased me, but as a consular officer, which did not. I wanted to be a political officer, period, not a consular officer, where most women officers who were not shunted into personnel work were frequently assigned in those days. Bob asked how I felt about going to Saigon. I told him I wanted to go—Southeast Asia was the area in which I was most keenly interested, and the war in Vietnam was dominating U.S. foreign policy and U.S. public attention at that time. But I said I wanted very much to be a political officer, and I was concerned that the consular assignment would start me down the wrong career path. "Would you still go to Saigon if you had to go as a consular officer?" Bob asked. I said I would. Bob then told me that a good friend of his in the department was in charge of junior officer assignments, and he would have a word with him when he got to Washington. A few weeks later, I was assigned to Saigon as a political officer, for which I remain grateful to Bob Beaudry, because that assignment launched me on the career in political work that led ultimately to three assignments as chief of mission.

A Tragic Loss

By February I was fairly well settled into my new life in Belgium. I had moved into my Square des Latins apartment; I was feeling more comfortable about my work at the embassy; and I had developed friendships with several of the embassy secretaries, a lively group of intelligent, interesting, fun-loving young women. I was pleased to accompany three of them for a long weekend in Paris over the Presidents' Day weekend. Train service in Europe was fast and cheap, and we found an inexpensive pair of rooms in the city that were well situated for sightseeing. It was cold and damp that weekend, but we had a fine time, enjoying the museums, the fascinating street scenes of Paris, and the delicious food.

I returned to Brussels late in the evening on Monday. Shortly after I entered my apartment, the phone rang. It was the embassy duty officer, calling to read a telegram informing me that Hazel's husband, Bob McLane, had been killed in an automobile accident. It was shattering news. They had five great children, aged six to sixteen. How could this have happened? Bob and Hazel had bought my car, a 1955 Chevrolet, when I left for Belgium, and I prayed that the accident had not been caused by a mechanical failure of the car.

The next day I undertook to find a flight to Philadelphia. The World Cup was playing somewhere in Europe, and most flights were booked. I ended up having to fly to Frankfurt. From there, I took a plane to London, and thence to Philadelphia. It was a sad journey. I arrived home in time for the wake and funeral, and stayed with Hazel for about ten days in all, doing what I could to help her deal with the tragedy. The accident was not the fault of my car, for which I was extremely grateful. A drunken teenager had lost control of his car, crossed the median strip, and crashed head-on into Bob's car, killing him instantly. The teenager reportedly was also gravely injured.

Hazel faced her loss bravely. A strong, courageous woman, she raised the children alone, and they all grew into successful, kind, loving adults. I returned to my hitherto exciting life in Brussels with a heavy heart. In only six weeks abroad, I had experienced one of the most negative aspects of Foreign Service life—being separated by thousands of miles from loved ones in times of need, when you would like to be closer and more helpful. This would not be the only time I endured this situation.

Consular Trials

Next on my rotation through the embassy was the consular section, to which I was assigned well in time for the busy summer season. The consul was Sara Andren, a competent, somewhat theatrical woman who had risen through the ranks of staff positions to head a consular section in a busy European capital. Sara saw it as her duty to shape up junior officers, and she did so with a sharp tongue. She could be downright nasty, and in the next breath invite her victim to join her at a *vernissage* (an art exhibition opening, usually with wine and cheese) and be as pleasant as can be. I learned a lot from her, but her manner rankled. At one point, her behavior toward me and another woman junior officer was so egregious that we complained to the administrative counselor. He urged us to be forbearing, but said he would monitor the situation. I don't know whether he spoke with Sara or not, but somehow the months passed and I survived. I learned quickly that I detested consular work, and resolved that if I ended up consigned to this specialty, I would resign. I would rather have been a secretary in the political section than the head of a consular section. I have great admiration for these officers with the patience and skills to handle this important but trying work, but I quickly realized that I was not one of them.

Sara took occasional days off, and I was in charge of the section on those occasions. I recall one particularly difficult citizen assistance case. A fortyish-looking man came into my office and asked to see the consular officer. I assured him that I was that person. No, he wanted to discuss his problem with a man. Sorry, said I; I was all he could get. The consul, who was on vacation, was also a woman, so I hoped I would be able to help him. Chagrined, the man began his tale.

While living in Florida, he said, he had learned the location of a sunken Spanish galleon. After some preliminary dives, he had, to his delight, located the vessel. He had mortgaged his house, sold furniture, and taken other drastic steps to raise the money for a proper attempt at salvaging the sunken treasure on the ship. He had managed to glean some gold coins from the wreck, and had decided to go to Spain and see if he could engage the Spanish government in financing a full-scale excavation of the vessel. He had brought his wife and seven children with him to Spain, where, after spending most of his remaining money, he had been rebuffed by the Spanish authorities. He had managed to make it as far as Brussels with his family, all of whom, down to a two-year-old child, were sitting in the consular waiting room. The man wanted assistance in being repatriated to the United States. (When citizens find themselves in desperate circumstances, the State Department can arrange repatriation loans to return destitute citizens to the United States.)

My mind boggled at the thought of processing what might well have been the largest repatriation case in this embassy's history. Still, he was entitled, so I gathered the necessary information and told him I would seek funding from the department to return him and his family to the United States. He wondered if perhaps I could arrange for him to sail as a crew member on a ship bound for the United States, taking his family along with him. Brussels was not a port, and I said that this would not be possible. Besides, I said, I doubted that any ship in need of a crewman could accommodate that crewman's wife and seven young children.

Meanwhile, we had to find food and lodging for this family. Our embassy had no funds available to assist in this regard. Some larger embassies, I learned, had some funds established by gifts from private citizens to aid in this type of case, but Brussels did not. On several occasions while working in the section, I gave destitute Americans small amounts of cash from my own pocket to tide them over for a meal or two. In a few cases, the loans were eventually repaid.

In this case, the American said that his wife was a Mormon, and he was confident that if there were any Mormons in Brussels, they would aid his family while he was waiting for the repatriation loan to be processed. I was skeptical, but I called the Mormon office and relayed the story. The gentleman who took my call was unreceptive to providing assistance, but I pressed him, saying how convinced these folks were that their fellow Mormons would not turn them away, and he reluctantly agreed that they could come by the Mormon facility. I had arranged for the family to spend the night at a temporary hospice; what I was seeking was money for food and a generally helping hand.

I sent off the cables requesting the repatriation loan. The next day, however, my destitute American came by the consular section to tell me that he would not be leaving for the United States from Belgium, after all. He had been encouraged by the Mormon group to take his family to Rotterdam, a large port where they thought he might be able to get a job on a ship and return to the United States with his family via that route. The Mormons had given them transportation money for the trip to Rotterdam. I tried to talk the man out of it—I saw little chance that he would be successful in that effort. In my view, the Mormons were simply trying to push him out of their territory. His best bet was to remain in Brussels, take the repatriation loan, and return in that manner. But he would not be deterred. I withdrew my request for the repatriation loan, and he left with thanks. I wonder to this day whether that man and his family managed to return to the United States. Somehow, I believed his story about the galleon, far-fetched though it may have been. He did not seem intelligent enough to have invented such a tale, and such wrecks do exist off the Florida coast.

Despite such diversions, I found consular work trying. I particularly detested the bulk of the work, issuing visas for visits to the United States. The United States was, and remains, the destination of choice for millions who wish to improve their economic lot in life. Many applicants who did not qualify for an immigrant visa tried to enter on a visitor's visa, after which they could disappear into our vast country and remain indefinitely. It was the task of the visa officer to determine whether the applicant who professed to want to visit the United States for two weeks was a genuine tourist, or whether he or she actually intended to immigrate. I was strict in these matters, because if one entered the United States on a visitor's visa and subsequently became a permanent resident, that person was delaying the immigration of someone who had openly applied to emigrate to the United States. I did not enjoy sorting through forged documents and barefaced lies.

A Swiss Respite

In August 1965, Hazel came over for a visit. I had encouraged this as a way of helping her deal with her grief. My mother stayed at Hazel's and cared for her three girls; the two boys went to stay with their paternal aunt. Sara Andren had told me that I could not take any vacation during the summer months, and I had alerted Hazel to this possibility. Still, I thought the total change of scene would be helpful to her.

I decided to host a small cocktail party to welcome Hazel and introduce her to some of my friends. I invited Sara and some dozen others. I had ample wine, other alcoholic beverages, cheese, and snacks. Aware that if the party was successful, people might well linger, I had also ordered a large supply of varied sandwiches from the embassy cafeteria. When the guests showed no signs of leaving, I brought out the sandwich trays and we all dug into them.

The party was a success. Hazel had initially been distressed at the thought of it, but everyone loved her, and she relaxed and enjoyed it. The best part (and part of my hidden agenda): Sara was taken with Hazel, and told me the next day that she had rethought her rejection of my request for a week's leave. I could have it.

I encouraged Hazel to research possible trips we might take. I mentioned that there were several travel agencies downtown, a short trolley ride away, near the Metropole Hotel where I had begun my stay in Brussels. While I was at the embassy, Hazel went to work finding a trip for us. She did an amazing job. She found a week's bus trip to Switzerland, all transportation, hotels, and breakfasts and dinners included, for approximately $90 per person! The dollar was strong in those days, but this was still an exceptional bargain. The only catch was that the trip was geared to Belgians, not foreigners, and the guide's lectures would be given in French and Flemish. I assured Hazel that with my French, we could cope, and we signed up.

The trip was delightful. We were the only non-Belgians on the comfortable bus. The guide, learning that Hazel did not speak French, also gave a lot of his spiels in English, while our fellow passengers beamed approvingly. I sensed that they were impressed that two Americans had decided to join their trip. They were unfailingly friendly and kind to us. We stayed at a centrally located hotel in Switzerland, and went out on day trips to various Swiss cities: Bern, Lucerne, and Zurich. The food was good, the scenery beautiful—I took a picture of Hazel walking ahead of me up a high hill, with snow-capped mountains in the background, that I called her "Sound of Music" pose. It was a most enjoyable trip, and a needed respite for me from the consular section.

Antwerp Interlude

My stint in the consular section finally ended. Next was a three-month tour at our consulate general in Antwerp. Being a seaport in the heart of Flemish Belgium, Antwerp offered some different training possibilities for junior officers—work with U.S. ships and seamen, for example. I enjoyed my time in Antwerp. The down side was that because of embassy budget constraints, I could not move to Antwerp, but rather had to commute every day by train. Train service was excellent in Belgium, but the train rides made for long days, which meant that I could not enjoy evening activities in Antwerp. I did stay overnight once with the post's secretary-communicator when there was a social event of special interest.

I learned quickly in Antwerp that my French, which was coming along nicely, was not an asset in that city. I recall one day that a store clerk professed not to understand my French, but when I switched in frustration to English she became quite pleasant and helpful. To this day, language divides that small country into two near-hostile zones—the northern Flemish area, and the southern French-speaking, or Walloon, area. Brussels was officially bilingual; street signs and the like bore both languages.

When my Antwerp duties concluded, I thought that I could chalk off consular duties from my assignment list. This proved incorrect. At one point, when I was working happily in the economic section, I was called to the administrative counselor's office and informed that I would be going back to the consular section to replace Sara for two weeks. I was dismayed, but I had no recourse. Apparently, Sara had been behaving more shrilly than ever with American visitors to the consular section. One outraged businessman had complained to our deputy chief of mission, John McSweeney, and it was one too many complaints for him. He decided that Sara needed a rest, and ordered her to take two weeks' vacation. I was designated to handle the section in her absence.

Sara was chagrined when she met with me to turn over pending cases before she left. She acknowledged that the DCM was right, that she had been uncivil and shrill with Americans seeking her assistance, and was reluctantly willing to do as he had ordered. For my part, I resented being yanked from work that I liked to return to the detested consular section. On the other hand, I was pleased that the DCM and administrative counselor felt that I could handle the section alone. The two weeks passed satisfactorily, and I did not serve in consular again in Brussels.

I retain much admiration for the many competent consular officers in the State Department who carry out their important and frequently frustrating duties so well, performing services for both Americans and foreigners in need of their help. But it was not a specialty in which I was comfortable, and I was grateful when ultimately I was able to pursue political work as my career track.

I Become a Published Author

I finally found myself, after nearly a year of consular work, in a substantive section: the economic section. The economic counselor, Chris Petrow, was a tall, handsome, aristocratic man who could have been selected for the diplomatic service by Central Casting. He was keenly intelligent, dynamic, and very kind to me. His principal economic officer was an Ivy League grad, Bill Harrop, who went on to a very distinguished career with several ambassadorships, including Israel. Bill was brilliant, and his Ivy League speech mannerisms did not conceal a genuinely kind and thoughtful man. I recall on one occasion, when Bill's wife was away, he invited me and another junior officer to his home for a spaghetti dinner that he cooked and served for us and his four lively children.

I was given a most interesting, and challenging, assignment in the economic section. Our new ambassador, Ridgway Brewster Knight, who had replaced MacArthur, had been invited to submit an article to a scholarly Belgian journal. He accepted and decided the topic would be world food production and the steps that needed to be taken to avert shortages in the face of ever-burgeoning populations. The task of writing the article was assigned to the economic section and delegated to me. I was given advice about whom to consult, including the embassy's agriculture attaché, and various publications to review. I was then left on my own to develop the article.

I dug into the material, researched the embassy library, read recent studies on the subject, and produced an article. I was nervous about how it would be accepted—I got a little dramatic in the opening sentences, believing that it was important to grab the reader's attention early on before waxing academic. Bill Harrop liked the article, made virtually no editorial changes, and submitted it to Chris Petrow, who likewise was pleased.

A few days later I was called to DCM McSweeney's office, where he praised the article highly. Subsequently, the ambassador did the same. I was impressed that basically my first draft had been accepted as final, with virtually no revisions. We then had to get the article translated into French, which one of our U.S. Information Agency (USIA) employees did for us. The ambassador was not overjoyed at the translation—he was an elegant man with perfect French, and the translation provided was not up to his standard. But he accepted it, and the article was published in the scholarly journal under my pen name, "Ridgway Brewster Knight."

I enjoyed the substantive work of the economic section, and that of the political section when I finally managed to get assigned to it for a couple of months at the end of my tour. My memory of specific projects during the political section tour is dim. I know I enjoyed the work, but there was nothing as unique as producing an article for publication under the ambassador's name.

Tragedy Finds Me Again

My hazy memory of the specifics of my political section work may have been affected by the fact that my dearly beloved mother became ill and died during that period of my stay in Brussels. In the summer, Mother came to visit me, accompanied by Hazel's oldest daughter, Peggy, and a high school friend of Peggy's. I had great plans to show them what I could of Europe. We had a nice weekend in Paris, where we all enjoyed having coffee at the Café de la Paix near the Opéra Garnier, watching the world go by. Mom was delighted to meet an American woman who had read my brother Charles's book, *Father Coughlin and the New Deal*, about the controversial "radio priest" of the 1930s. We visited Notre Dame Cathedral and the exquisite Ste. Chapelle, and we thoroughly enjoyed our other sightseeing ventures.

We also visited Bonn, and stayed at the apartment of a Foreign Service friend and his wife, Ed and Pat Murphy. I had plans to take us all on the Rhine steamer for a day trip from Bonn to Wiesbaden and return, and get a little of the flavor of that part of Germany. I had also arranged for a trip to the Loire Valley in France to visit the magnificent chateaux.

Unfortunately, mother became ill in Bonn. Not being able to drink the tap water had made her uncomfortable in Brussels and Paris, but in Bonn, at the American residences, she was free to do so. Whatever the cause, she became ill and was unable to participate in the planned activities. I got a German doctor recommended by the embassy to attend to her, but in my view he was worse than useless—he said that perhaps she had gotten cholera, which was totally absurd. I put Peggy and her friend on the Rhine steamer and stayed with mother. After a day's rest, she was able to travel, and I scratched the trip to the Loire Valley and returned to Brussels, a three-hour trip.

Mother recovered as we relaxed around the apartment. I found things for the teenagers to do while the two of us waited for mother to regain her strength. It was not a particularly worrisome time for me—mother did not seem ill. I knew she had suffered from congestive heart failure for some time, but I thought that her illness in Germany probably stemmed from something she ate or from the water she drank—although the water was pure, it was different from what she was accustomed to. I still believe that.

Mother's visit with me relieved her mind about her youngest child, her unmarried daughter. Like virtually all mothers of her generation, she equated security for her daughters with marriage to a good man. That had not happened with me, and I know she worried about me being alone, particularly when I know she felt that she did not have many years left to her. Seeing me happy and successful in my Foreign Service career eased her mind. She told my sister Betty after she got home, "Theresa is really happy there." I think she realized that regardless of what happened to her, I would be able to survive and make a good life.

I hated the fact that mother was alone in the States. I had invited her to come with me to Belgium, but she had declined. I did not push the matter because I also worried that she would be isolated because she couldn't speak French. By the time she visited me, however, I had decided that at least she would have my company in the evenings and on weekends, and this would be good for her. I persuaded her to accept the idea of coming to live with me. I put it in terms of how helpful this would be for me: someone to run the apartment, shop in the neighborhood, cook if she wished, and the like. I stressed how busy my job was, and how wonderful it would be to have someone at home looking out for my interests. To my great pleasure, when she returned to the United States, she wrote and told me that she would accept my invitation.

Not long after her return to New Jersey, however, mother was hospitalized, near death with her heart problem. I flew home and stayed for two weeks, visiting her in the hospital every day. She improved, and several weeks after my return to Brussels, she was discharged from the hospital. She went to stay with my brother Jay and his wife, Marie, who lived closer to our home in Runnemede than my other siblings. Within a day or two of her hospital discharge, mother died peacefully in Jay's home from a pulmonary embolism. Her death occurred on October 9, 1966, one week after my thirtieth birthday. (My father had died on September 25, 1947, a week before my birthday. My birthdays ever since have been a time of mixed emotions for me.)

When mother died, I lost not only my mom but also my very best friend on earth. As the youngest child, I had had more one-on-one time with her than had any of my brothers and sisters, who had married, joined the armed services, or otherwise gone on with their lives a few years after finishing high school. For my part, I lived at home with mom until I left for the Foreign Service at age twenty-six. For several of those years we lived alone. We developed a special relationship. I could joke with and tease mom, and get her to agree to do things that on first blush appeared undoable. We loved to travel together. She was the best travel companion I ever had. Once I had bought my own little car, there was no stopping us. Within a few weeks, we had driven down to Norfolk to visit Ann, my brother Bob's wife, while Bob, a navy pilot, was out to sea. We drove out to South Bend, Indiana, where my brother Charles was getting his master's degree at Notre Dame on a post–air force scholarship. We drove to the West Coast together twice, wonderful trips whose memories I cherish.

I was greatly blessed to have Anna Cecelia Paull as my mother. I miss her still. At high points in my life, such as when I was able to buy a seashore home in Sea Isle City, New Jersey, with an ocean view, or when my career brought me success, I thought of her and wished that she, who loved the sea, and Dad could be with me to share the joy of the moment. In a larger sense, however, they are both still with me.

The embassy was kind to me in my loss. The administrative counselor called me at Hazel's where I was staying and offered to curtail my tour so I would not have to return to Brussels, as my tour would end just after Christmas in any event. I could get a temporary job in the department, and the embassy would pack me out of my apartment. I appreciated the offer, but declined. It was important to me to return to Brussels, to complete what I had started, and move on from there. I returned and got through the last six weeks or so of my tour.

By the time my mother was hospitalized, and I had visited her, I knew that I had been assigned to Saigon as a political officer, preceded by forty-four weeks of Vietnamese language training. I decided not to tell mother about the assignment, knowing she would be greatly worried about my posting to the war zone. I told her only that I expected to get long-term language study in a Southeast Asian language, which would mean that I would again be in Washington for several months and would be able to visit Runnemede frequently on weekends. She was pleased to hear that, and never knew that her youngest child was bound for the Vietnam War.

As I finished my tour, I paid courtesy calls on the heads of section who had helped train me for my new duties. I recall with pleasure the comments of economic counselor Chris Petrow when I bade him farewell. Chris told me that he felt that I would become an ambassador one day. I thought at the time that this was a wonderful thing to say to a fledgling FSO, a great encouragement. I remember his words fondly to this day.

4

To Saigon

Nineteen sixty-seven passed quickly. I found a nice efficiency apartment near Seven Corners in Falls Church, Virginia, in Ravenwood Towers, and began intensive Vietnamese language training. The program called for six hours per day of classroom instruction, in classes of no more than four or five students, plus at least two hours per day in the language laboratory listening to and responding to drills on tape. The Foreign Service method of teaching language was designed to develop speaking and comprehension fluency, and reading skills; we were not expected to learn how to write in the language.

Vietnamese is a tonal language: six tones in North Vietnam, five in the South. Fortunately, I had a good ear and did not have any difficulty in learning the language. I benefited from sharing some classes with students who were less musically inclined than I was. Usually by the time the classes were over for the day, I had pretty well mastered the material and did not have to spend much time in the language lab.

This facilitated the pursuit of my bachelor's degree at night school. While in Chicago at the Passport Office, I had taken some courses at DePaul University. The State Department, which has a program to encourage further education for its employees, paid for these courses. It was not possible to take courses while in Brussels, so I looked forward to resuming my studies while taking Vietnamese. I learned, however, that the department did not want long-term language students in what were termed "hard" languages to take night courses, and thus I could not apply for reimbursement for my expenses.

I quietly registered at the University of Maryland's University College nonetheless and took as full a course of study as I could fit in during my year in Washington. These courses were given at various U.S. military bases in the area. Throughout the next several years as I attempted to complete my bachelor's degree, I took courses at Fort Meade, Bolling Air Force Base, Andrews Air Force Base, and the Pentagon. Eventually I accumulated the necessary credits and received a bachelor's degree from the University of Maryland, with a dual major in history and political science. I would have preferred to have had the degree come from Rutgers University, to which I felt more allegiance than to Maryland, but it was required that the degree be granted from the university at which the last thirty-plus credits had been earned, so I joined my father as an alumnus of the University of Maryland. Dad had graduated from the Maryland Agricultural College, which morphed into the University of Maryland, in 1915.

With the department none the wiser, I earned substantial college credits at night, and learned Vietnamese during the day. At the end of the forty-four-week course of Vietnamese study, I tested at the "3-3" level of proficiency in speaking and reading the language, a level established by the institute to indicate proficiency fully adequate for an officer to pursue one's work in the country concerned. I believe I was the first woman to test at this level. Some students achieve higher grades, of course. A rating of 4 was, I believe, considered to be sufficient for serving as an interpreter in some circumstances. A 5 indicated bilingual ability. But the institute and I were pleased with my 3-3 rating.

Khach San Astor

In January 1968, I flew to Saigon, treating myself en route to brief visits with my brothers in Indiana and Washington State, and to my first of what would become many stopovers in Honolulu. I also took the opportunity to take annual leave en route, and visited Tokyo for the first time and spent a couple of days in Taipei with Elaine

Olson, a USIA friend from Belgium. I found my first exposure to Asia fascinating. I took tours in Tokyo, but in Taipei it was nice to have a friend who knew the area to provide a personal introduction to that interesting city and culture.

I flew into Saigon on January 15, 1968, gulping as the Pan American plane spiraled downward in an unusual pattern developed, I learned later, to foil Viet Cong antiaircraft attacks at Tan Son Nhat Airport. Military personnel, American and Vietnamese, were abundant at the airport and throughout the city. I was met by an embassy staffer and deposited at the Khach San Astor (Astor Hotel) in downtown Saigon, on Tu Do (Freedom) Street, and left to sort myself out.

Downtown Saigon, despite the strong military presence and frequent strategically placed walls of protective concertina wire, was a beautiful, colorful place. The white colonial-era buildings sported dark orange roof tiles. Trees were abundant, their leafy green shading sidewalks. Colorful flowers abounded. A red brick Catholic cathedral was prominent at one end of Tu Do Street. Next to the National Assembly building, the Intercontinental Hotel, favored by the foreign press, offered a large street-level terrace where cooling drinks could be enjoyed in the shade while the busy street traffic—cars and motorcycles but also *xich los*, or bicycle taxis—swarmed by.

I was excited about being assigned to Saigon as a political officer. I strongly supported—and still do—what the United States was trying to accomplish in Vietnam. The country had been divided into two sections as a consequence of the Geneva agreements of 1954, following the collapse of the French effort to retain its colony against a Communist-led insurgency. The North had a Communist government under Ho Chi Minh. The South became a bastion of non-Communists, and the United States was attempting to sustain the South against an ongoing Communist insurgency, which was aided and abetted by the Soviet Union (Union of Soviet Socialist Republics, or USSR) and China. In the context of the times—an expansionist Soviet Union, a China that was funding and supporting Communist parties and insurgencies throughout Southeast Asia— the now ridiculed "domino theory," which posited that if the Communist insurgency in South Vietnam succeeded, Vietnam's neighbors (Thailand, Cambodia, Laos, and so on) would also fall to Communism, made sense to me. The South Vietnamese did not want Communism, and their leaders had asked for U.S. assistance to help them combat the assault from within (the Viet Cong) and without (North Vietnam). I did not, and do not, agree with every aspect of U.S. policy toward Vietnam, but I supported the general purpose, and still do, so I was pleased and honored to be given a front-row seat at the most significant foreign policy venture of that period. This was history in the making, for good or ill, and I was there. I was determined to do my best.

I arrived on a Sunday. After showering and resting, I took myself to the rooftop restaurant of the Astor and prepared to order dinner. Having spent forty-four weeks learning Vietnamese, I placed my order to the Asian waiter in Vietnamese, who responded with a blank stare. I tried again; he still did not understand me. Well, Vietnam had been a French colony, right? So I switched to French. Still the blank stare. Finally, I spoke in English—immediate comprehension. It developed that the waiter was ethnic Chinese, and spoke neither French nor Vietnamese, but could handle English. I later learned to tell the difference between Chinese, Vietnamese, and Koreans (Korea had sent troops to help out in the war), but on that first day, I had assumed the waiter was Vietnamese.

Embassy Duties

The next day I reported to the embassy's political section and began my work. The section was very large—about twenty officers, including several provincial reporters who were based at the four military regional headquarters throughout South Vietnam (and, in some cases, at provincial offices), but reported to the political section. There was a political-military unit, a labor affairs unit, an external affairs unit, and, among other entities, the internal affairs unit. I was assigned to the internal affairs unit, which was charged with following internal Vietnamese political developments. This unit had about six officers, and was headed by a very intelligent, but dour, Ted Heavner. Ted was a superb drafter and thinker. Once a week he met with the ambassador, Ellsworth Bunker, who briefed him on the developments that Bunker wanted reported to

Washington in a highly classified telegram from the ambassador to a limited Washington audience. Ted then drafted the telegram for the ambassador. He helped hone my own drafting skills as he reviewed my cables and memos. He proved to be a fair, somewhat humorless, but solid supervisor. I learned a lot from him.

Don Ferguson, deputy in the internal affairs unit, was a capable, pleasant man. There were three officers following Vietnam's National Assembly: Dave Lambertson, whose career eventually included being ambassador to Thailand; Harry Dunlop, who followed the Senate; and Hal Colebaugh, whose beat was the Lower House. A sharp, young, junior officer, Tim Carney, filled in as needed. (Tim ultimately became ambassador to the Sudan, and played key roles in the United Nations' effort in Cambodia, and briefly in the U.S. effort in Iraq in 2003 and later.)

My tasks were initially somewhat nebulous. I was assigned biographic duties—maintaining up-to-date biographic files on key Vietnamese personalities and writing brief sketches about them for embassy principals. I also was given the chore of reviewing the Vietnamese government's official daily press report, which came out in Vietnamese, French, and English. It was my job to review all three versions of these publications to glean tidbits of interest. There occasionally was much to be learned from these publications, particularly the Vietnamese version, which frequently contained more or different articles than did the other two versions. When I found an item of interest, such as military promotions or hard-line speeches by Vietnam's president, I would prepare a short telegram reporting it.

I also reviewed many of Saigon's twenty-five-odd Vietnamese language newspapers, particularly their editorials, to determine how the various political parties and religious sects were thinking about the war, elections, peace prospects, and domestic issues, such as a proposed land reform program. These newspapers provided a window into the thinking of these publishers: various political parties, key legislators, and religious groups. I frequently took key newspapers to my hotel at night and worked late into the night translating them and drafting a cable about editorial opinion, particularly if it related to U.S. policy. This was tedious work, but necessary in an environment where, despite U.S. war critics' opinions, Vietnam's press was relatively free and public opinion mattered. Newspapers could and did regularly criticize Vietnam's leaders and domestic policies, sometimes in sharp terms. The press could not, however, take any stance that suggested willingness to cede power to the Communists, via a coalition government or other route. Papers that did this risked closure.

The Tet Offensive

Tet, the Vietnamese (and Chinese) New Year's celebration, was usually a three-day holiday, with the arrival of the main holiday itself marked by vivid, and noisy, fireworks displays. Because of the war, the South Vietnamese government had banned the use of fireworks, as the explosions could be confused with military attacks. Nonetheless, Saigon revelers were not deterred, and as the big night approached, explosions of firecrackers were heard frequently outside my hotel window, and the street gutters were sprinkled with pink "snow"—the residue from the long strings of firecrackers strung outside of the shops lining the busy street.

I therefore was not initially alarmed when, at about midnight on the last day in January, loud explosions resounded outside the hotel. But there was something different about these sounds, and I soon concluded that I was hearing major gunfire outside my hotel. I cracked the window blinds slightly and saw armed men running by, shooting rifles. The Vietnamese Naval Headquarters was around the corner, perhaps a block away, and I assumed this was the site of the fight. I got away from the window and considered my options. I was defenseless, unarmed. Should the Viet Cong decide to take over the hotel, what should I do? Speak Vietnamese, or feign ignorance of the language? As the long, sleepless night continued, I decided on the latter, while visions of rough captivity, or worse, ran through my head.

Sounds of a running battle, with sporadic helicopter and heavy-vehicle sounds, continued throughout the night. Dawn finally came, and with it news on the Armed Forces Radio: a major offensive had erupted throughout South Vietnam. The American Embassy had been attacked, with some loss of life. Saigon was in the midst of battles throughout various neighborhoods.

I dressed and went up to the rooftop of the hotel. The sight is etched in my memory. Some of the noise had indeed been more firecrackers—the gutters were incongruously pink with shredded paper residue. But helicopters were flying overhead in the direction of the American Embassy. Gunfire erupted sporadically. A tank lumbered noisily past an intersection a block away. As I surveyed the scene, appalled, a Vietnamese on the rooftop of an apartment building across the street calmly fed his chickens and presented an offering of fruit and flowers to his modest Buddhist shrine. Roosters crowed, oblivious that the battle had already signaled the dawn and aroused any remaining sleepers.

I was joined on the roof by two U.S. Army majors who had just arrived in the country and were temporarily billeted in the hotel. They were in full combat gear, not knowing what to expect. They were astounded to find a young American woman on the roof. We compared notes and shared impressions. The Armed Forces broadcast had told all American personnel to remain in their billets until further notice, but these two were champing at the bit for action. I was concerned about the situation at the embassy.

Because of the Tet holiday, the hotel's rooftop restaurant was closed. The majors noticed that a restaurant a block up Tu Do Street seemed to be open, and suggested that we go get breakfast, not knowing how long the restaurant and its food supply would be available. Flanked by my two majors, I ventured out into the nearly deserted street; we had a pleasant breakfast while automatic rifle fire sounded in the distance.

Returning to the hotel, I turned on the radio again and heard an announcement directing all American employees of the embassy to report to the embassy immediately. All other American personnel should remain in their billets. The embassy was within walking distance of the hotel—perhaps a twenty-minute walk. But should I walk out into those streets, to the main site of the battle? I still heard gunfire, and saw APCs (armored personnel carriers) rolling along the streets. Stifling my concern, I decided that I would walk a block around the corner to an apartment building where two secretaries from the political section lived. Perhaps we could walk together.

I swallowed hard and went to their apartment building. They were understandably worried and excited. Two USIS (U.S.

Information Service) officers who also lived in the building were with the girls. They immediately proposed to drive us to the embassy in their jeep. They were eager to get out on the streets, but had not been authorized to do so. Escorting us to the embassy would give them an excuse to survey the scene. We thought that this was an excellent idea.

The drive to the embassy through the deserted streets of the lovely city was surreal. On this morning, we passed some dead Viet Cong in the gutters as we wended our way to the embassy through the tree-lined streets.

At the embassy itself, the cleanup had not been completed. In the front garden of the embassy, just inside the main pedestrian entrance, four young Viet Cong soldiers were sprawled along the pristine white concrete planters, their blood still vividly red, vying with the bright colors of the flowers. Our USIS escorts snapped photographs, but I deliberately had not brought my camera. It struck me as cold and unfeeling, despite the historical significance.

The Viet Cong, contrary to some press reports at the time, had not penetrated the embassy building itself. They had fought very hard to gain entrance, but had been rebuffed by the marine guards. The Viet Cong had, however, managed to enter a separate building on the compound that housed the consular section. In addition, at least one Viet Cong had entered the house to the rear of the embassy occupied by George Jacobson, the embassy mission coordinator. Our security chief had thrown a weapon up to George, who killed the attacker as he attempted to climb the stairs to Jacobson's bedroom.

My Office Slightly Damaged

When I got to my office, I found chunks of concrete on my desk and typewriter. Apparently the Viet Cong had used mortars to attempt to penetrate the heavy decorative (protective) concrete screen that enclosed the building. It was a startling sight.

But the secretaries and I were a startling sight to our boss, Ted Heavner. Apparently, the Armed Forces Radio directive ordering us to the embassy was premature. There was not a great deal that we all could do while the security situation was being assessed and after-action reports put together. My usual duties were not relevant.

We were permitted to send brief cables to our families informing them we were unharmed. After a few hours, Ted arranged transportation for the three of us. I think we were the only women who had reported to the section that morning (but my recollection could be wrong), and we returned to our quarters. At some point my army major buddies gave me some K-rations.

I don't recall whether I remained at the hotel the next day or whether we reported to the embassy. When I did resume regular embassy duty, an officer picked me up in his car so I would not have to walk. My own car would not arrive for several more weeks.

Sporadic Engagements Continue

What passed for normalcy in wartime Saigon gradually resumed. I recall that some Viet Cong remained holed up in an apartment complex across the street from the embassy, and they occasionally opened fire. For a few days U.S. soldiers bunked in the corridors outside our political section offices. A few times we were directed to leave our exposed offices for the safety of the corridors when shooting broke out. But we worked around all of this. I was surprised at how quickly the extraordinary became ordinary, at how the mind adapts to such stressful situations. For example, fighting continued for some time in the Cholon neighborhood of Saigon. Nightly, helicopter gunships flew over the area and rained bullets on suspected Viet Cong bands. I often had dinner on the roof of the hotel, and while sipping a drink or eating a good meal, I could see in the distance the insidiously lovely patterns made by the tracer bullets from the gunships. Frequently, flares illuminated an area of suspected Viet Cong encroachment; the yellow glow was, in its way, beautiful.

The Tet offensive proved to be a devastating military defeat for the Viet Cong and North Vietnamese. Throughout the South, the Viet Cong infrastructure was exposed and largely destroyed. Psychologically, though, in the court of U.S. public opinion, the story was different. Television coverage of the embassy under attack, of George Jacobson fighting off a Viet Cong soldier on the embassy compound itself, persuaded many Americans that the war was hopeless or already lost. To those of us in the field, who knew the military facts, this was hard to accept. The offensive had been massive, but ultimately it was crushed. The ability of the Communists to launch such a massive attack at all, however, in the face of the huge American presence, very likely helped to undermine the U.S. public's support for the war.

The offensive wreaked havoc on many areas of Vietnam. The ancient imperial capital, Hue, was occupied by the Viet Cong for about a month before being retaken. The Communists slaughtered anyone who had anything to do with the South Vietnamese government—hundreds, possibly thousands, all told—not in military battles but in cold-blooded executions. In one case, they entered a military officer's home and killed his wife, children, pet bird, and goldfish. (See *Tet! The Turning Point in the Vietnam War*, by Donald Oberdorfer.) Included in the carnage were two American employees of the consulate in Hue, who, in violation of diplomatic norms, were executed: a USIS officer (with whom I had studied Vietnamese in Washington) and our young communicator. A political officer from the consulate, Jim Bullington, disguised himself as a French priest and hid out with various Vietnamese friends during the occupation. This cold-blooded slaughter is what we Americans feared would happen throughout the country if the Communists won the war.

Rocket Attacks

As the Viet Cong were pushed out of the city, they employed new tactics: random rocket attacks. Fortunately, the rockets were not very high caliber, but they managed to damage buildings and kill people when they struck. My hotel was hit a few times. At the first sign of incoming rockets, I would either crawl under the bed or take bedding and go into the bathroom and wrap myself in it. The bathroom did not have a window and thus was safe from shattering glass. It was a chilling experience.

The random nature of these attacks was cruel. A couple of blocks from the hotel, each morning an elderly lady improvised a sidewalk stand where she sold fresh French baguettes. French bread went over well with the Vietnamese and Lao, and was readily available in both countries. One morning a small rocket killed this poor woman, scattering loaves of bread on the sidewalk and street. I passed her corner as I was walking to the embassy that morning. Afterward, I seldom passed that spot without thinking of that innocent victim of a harsh ideology's intrusion and attempted takeover of the country.

The Mini-Tet Offensive

At the embassy, my work life assumed a busy, never-enough-time pace. In addition to scanning and reporting on items of interest gleaned from the three language editions of the Vietnamese press, I regularly scanned several Vietnamese language newspapers for hints of the political leanings of the editorial staff. Thanks to the insistence of Deputy Ambassador Samuel Berger, my task of updating our biographic records gained new prominence. I prepared prep cards on various dignitaries for the ambassador and his deputy before key meetings, and on guests attending their dinner parties and receptions. To accomplish all of this, I usually worked through our two-hour lunch break and took newspapers back to the hotel to work on at night, sometimes until 1:00 or 2:00 a.m.

This basic reporting was not simply a case of clipping articles and editorials and sending them in. Their significance had to be placed in context by providing background information and commentary, and occasionally making recommendations for action. I recall that early on in my time in the political section, I prepared a telegram, added comments, and submitted it to the section chief for his review. He scanned it, signed it, and sent it out. I was struck by the fact that what I had written was trusted, not second-guessed or reviewed by additional observers. This made a deep impression on me. I resolved to be even more scrupulous about reporting only facts I could verify, and to be especially thoughtful and balanced in the analysis I offered. Washington had to be able to trust our reporting, and I was determined that mine would stand the test of time.

In May 1968, the Viet Cong made another effort at disruption. Another heavy attack launched in Saigon and in some outlying areas was repulsed, but not without several days of tension, rocket attacks, and fighting in some Saigon neighborhoods. I was still living in my hotel room. This time, however, two officers in the internal unit of the political section, Hal Colebaugh and Harry Dunlap, who shared a lovely house not far from the embassy, invited me to move in with them for the duration of the offensive. This was so much better than sweating out the attacks alone in the downtown hotel. We got along well. I could not help but envy them their very nice living arrangements.

But after the offensive, life in the hotel continued. The political section officers generally shared houses, two or three to a house in a compound with several houses. The political counselor lived in one, and section officers shared the rest. This compound even had a swimming pool in its lovely gardens, where occasionally on Sunday afternoons I swam briefly before the pool was seized by water polo players intent on mayhem: embassy officers and members of the Saigon press corps (including Bob Kaiser, who went on to became a senior editor at the *Washington Post*, and Dan Southerland, then of the *Christian Science Monitor* and later with United Press International and the *Washington Post*). Because I was the first female officer in the political section, the powers that be decided I could not share a house with a male officer. So I languished in the hotel.

I was not the only long-time dweller in the hotel. One evening at dinner in the hotel, I met a woman who worked with USAID (U.S. Agency for International Development). Betty Price became a life-long friend. She was substantially older than I was, and had raised two sons alone after losing her husband to cancer at an early age. With her sons well launched, Betty, who had moved her little boys to the Panama Canal zone to work with the U.S. government there, responded to an appeal for logistics experts from USAID and was assigned to Saigon.

A total of nine months passed before I escaped the hotel. An apartment became available in a building rented in its entirety by the U.S. government for employees. Most of the residents were with USAID, though a first-floor apartment housed a woman officer with USIS. Liz White and I had met at the Foreign Service Institute in Arlington, Virginia, when we were both studying Vietnamese. She was only given a few weeks' training, however, while I took the entire forty-four-week course. We had contacted each other in Saigon and I had been to her apartment, which, although not a house in the political compound, was a thousand times better than a hotel room.

I learned that the vacant apartment, on the third floor, was being readied for a newly arrived labor affairs officer. I was indignant. I went to the head of the political section, Galen Stone, and decried the unfairness of giving this apartment to a newly arrived officer when I had been living in a hotel room for nine months. He initially said that the apartment would not be suitable for my purposes, that the section hoped to find a small house for me. I insisted that I had had it with the hotel and could make the apartment suitable for guests, even though they would have to climb up to the third floor to visit me. I got the apartment, and with fresh paint, some new, simple furniture, and a throw rug or two, it quickly became my Saigon home. My ménage was completed when I hired Chi Hai, a pleasant, competent Vietnamese cook-housekeeper. We got along well. I enjoyed her cooking: excellent Vietnamese, simple French, and basic American cuisine.

Once settled, I invited Betty Price out to dinner. She liked the apartment so much that, when shortly thereafter the apartment across the hall became available, she requested it and became my next-door neighbor. Betty was an excellent cook, who eschewed hiring a Vietnamese maid. She worked normal hours, in contrast to my late nights at the embassy. Quite often she heard me climbing the stairs at 7:30 or 8:00 p.m. and invited me over for a drink on the terrace, followed by a reheated, home-cooked meal. I really appreciated those evenings.

The Vietnam Quoc San Dang

Although my plate at the embassy was overflowing, I chafed at my lack of contact with Vietnamese politicians and officials. I pressed Section Chief Ted Heavner to give me a political party to cover, whose officials I would get to know, whose policies I would learn, whose plans and hopes for the future I would explore. Although the top leaders of the country were military officers, there were several political parties in the country and a functioning National Assembly composed of several blocs. Other officers were assigned to monitor these parties.

Finally, as December approached, Ted informed me he was turning over the portfolio for the Vietnam Quoc Dan Dang (VNQDD) Party to me. The VNQDD was the Vietnamese offshoot of Chiang Kai Shek's Chinese Nationalist Party. Its officials were staunchly nationalist, conservative, and uncomfortable with the role of the military in Vietnam's political life; they were eager for contact with the American embassy. I called on the senior officials and was invited to attend their annual national convention, on Christmas Day in 1968. I had wanted some real political contacts, so I did not complain audibly when I received the invitation. I had an early Christmas dinner and spent the afternoon and evening at the VNQDD convention, trying mightily to comprehend something of what the speechmakers were saying. There were enough written handouts to allow me to put together a cable reporting the convention.

I Become an English Teacher

Several months into my tour, the director of the Vietnam Working Group, John Burke, visited Saigon. His visit in early 1969 proved quite fortuitous for my work in Saigon, and probably helped my career ultimately. I was present at a luncheon given for him by the political counselor. John had served in Saigon a few years before and was well acquainted with some of the key players on the 1968 scene. John said that he had met that morning with Nguyen Van Huyen, the president of the Senate. Huyen had told John that he would like to improve his English. John said he would see how he could help. At the luncheon, John suggested that perhaps I, as the junior member of the section, could give the senator English lessons. Harry Dunlop was assigned to follow the Senate, but I gathered that John, and perhaps the senator, thought that a more junior officer, less well known at the Senate than Harry, should fill the bill. Surprised, but not wanting to miss an opportunity for contact with a senior official and key player in some legislative initiatives that the United States was pressing on President Thieu via the National Assembly, Ted Heavner concurred.

Shortly thereafter, armed with some materials from the USIS English as a Second Language program, I began meeting every morning at 8:00 a.m. at the office of Senator Huyen. He was a courtly southern Catholic, highly regarded in the country as a man of integrity. I was honored to be given this opportunity to get to know him so well. Gradually our English lessons became conversations during which, at his insistence, I corrected any grammatical errors he made and offered suggestions about how to express various ideas. Over time, our discussions took on a political nature. As his confidence in me increased, he would ask me the U.S. positions on certain issues, including some pending legislation. At this time, the United States was eager to see South Vietnam adopt a land reform program, to blunt the Communists' appeal in the countryside. The proposed legislation was entitled the "Land to the Tiller Program." I tentatively asked the senator's opinion of this legislation, and was relieved when he answered me frankly and showed no offense that his English teacher had broached such subjects. From that point on, we discussed the ramifications of the program, which he quietly supported. Our discussions touched on possible legislative amendments, the timetable for attempting passage, prospects for passage, and the like. The program was not universally welcomed in the assembly, as it was designed to take land from wealthy landowners, with compensation, and distribute the land in smaller increments to rural farmers, giving them more of an incentive to resist the Communists. Staunchly anti-Communist, Huyen helped get the program approved in the assembly. Our morning sessions continued throughout my tour in Saigon, and our political discussions gave the embassy a valuable window into the thinking of this influential man and of the workings of the senate and the assembly as a whole. Likewise, the senator's daily contact with me gave him ready access to U.S. views on subjects of concern to him.

The Return of Big Minh

Being the junior officer in a large political section (twenty-plus officers, counting our provincial reporters) had certain advantages, as evidenced by my growing professional relationship with the third-ranking official in the country, Senator Huyen. In the summer of 1968, a political development of some import occurred when Duong Van Minh—"Big Minh"—one of the generals who overthrew and murdered President Ngo Dinh Diem in 1963, was allowed to return to Vietnam from exile in Thailand. This was a move the United States had been pressing on President Thieu: to allow more political activity, even from individuals he believed to be left-leaning. Big Minh was probably the most popular of the generals who participated in the coup against Diem, and his return was big political news.

The embassy wanted to establish early contact with Minh and to record his arrival. But how could this be done without sending an incorrect signal to Thieu that the United States secretly supported Big Minh? This was resolved by sending a thoroughly nervous me to the airport to meet Big Minh's plane upon its arrival in Saigon. I was instructed to make my presence known to Minh, but not be too obvious a member of the welcoming entourage.

There was a large group of political operatives welcoming Minh. A few were senators, formerly generals and co-conspirators with Minh, including Senator Tran Van Don, whom I had met at the Senate. He spotted me and struck up a casual conversation. When Minh arrived and was surrounded by welcomers, I seized my moment and introduced myself, identified myself as an embassy officer, gave him my card, and said I would welcome an opportunity to meet with him. He nodded noncommitally, and I made my escape.

A few days later I called Minh's residence and asked if I could call upon him. He agreed, and I went to his large, comfortable home in downtown Saigon for our first meeting. I asked his impressions of the current situation, inquired concerning his future plans, and otherwise probed his political intentions. He was responsive, glad to be back in South Vietnam, but somewhat short on specifics. Nonetheless, the cable I wrote reporting our conversation apparently was widely read, because a few weeks later, our ambassador to Laos, Bill Sullivan, visited Saigon and asked to meet with the writer of the Minh cable. He had also served in Vietnam years earlier, knew Minh, and wanted an update. I liked Ambassador Sullivan. This was the first of several fruitful encounters I had with him throughout my career.

A few weeks later, the powers that be decided I should contact Minh again for an update on his activities since settling into life in Saigon. I did so, and we had another comprehensive discussion of his activities and plans. I wondered how long this former titan would be willing to discuss serious matters with a junior officer—and a woman, at that—and it was not too long before the political counselor learned through other channels that while Big Minh had enjoyed his discussions with Miss Tull, he believed that he merited contact with a more senior American official. Minh then became the occasional guest of the political counselor at dinner, and my one-on-one meetings with perhaps the key player in the downfall of Ngo Dinh Diem ended. It was a fascinating exposure to a complicated, difficult-to-fathom, Vietnamese political figure.

Interesting Fringe Benefits

The workday in Saigon was long and frequently intense. My duties often involved working at home after hours, translating articles and gleaning grist for our apparently eagerly awaited reporting. I frequently worked through the lunch hour, forgoing the charm of the Cercle Sportif, a restaurant and club left over from the French era that was very popular with my diplomatic colleagues. But I enjoyed the work and the sense that I was part of an important foreign policy undertaking.

Work was not the only element of my life in Saigon. There were occasionally very interesting fringe benefits. In addition to my contact with Big Minh and Chairman Huyen, leading scholars and journalists came to Saigon and sought the views of us young political officers. One evening a few us had dinner under the stars with the noted reporter Robert Shaplen and compared views on Vietnam developments.

One Thanksgiving, Deputy Ambassador Samuel Berger at the last minute invited a few of us to his home for dinner. Although we had other plans, junior FSOs did not, in that era, at least, turn down invitations from ambassadors; we all accepted. The highly regarded columnist Joseph Alsop was Berger's houseguest. Conversation at dinner was fascinating. To our surprise and pleasure, the deputy ambassador excused himself after dinner and asked if we junior officers would stay and keep Alsop company. We three young FSOs remained with the distinguished journalist for perhaps an hour, and, in response to his questions, shared our impressions and opinions on the state of the war and political developments. This was a heady experience for a young FSO just a few years removed from her secretarial position. After this discussion, the three of us proceeded to another Thanksgiving dinner, this one given by one of our colleagues, which we all had agreed to attend several days before getting the deputy ambassador's impromptu invitation.

Musical Opportunities

Saigon introduced me to another welcome addition to my life—the opportunity to sing in a competently led choral group. One night not long after the Tet offensive, I was working after hours in my embassy office when Don Ferguson, deputy chief of the internal affairs unit, came by and said he was leaving to practice with a newly formed choral group. He insisted that I accompany him. This proved to be the beginning of several enjoyable musical experiences for me in Saigon.

The choir I joined was nondenominational, directed by the wife of a USAID officer. She introduced me to the joy of singing Handel's "Messiah." I sang second alto. We performed in Saigon and at a U.S. Army base in I Corps, where we were warmly welcomed by soldiers straight from the field. The director also formed a madrigal group with about a dozen of us. I thoroughly enjoyed the challenges of performing madrigals before audiences at the USIS-run Vietnamese-American Association.

I met a talented young American woman, Nan Nall, a fledgling opera singer, who was with Special Services, an organization whose purpose was to develop entertainment for the troops. She and a colleague became aware of the musical groups in Saigon and decided to try to stage an opera. I had taken a few voice lessons from Nan. She decided I was capable of singing the role of the mother in an abbreviated version of *Hansel and Gretel*. She and her colleagues found other cast members among the groups with which I had been singing. Nan played Hansel, the young wife of a USAID officer sang Gretel, and a British clergyman sang the role of the wicked witch. The father, my "husband," was a young Chinese member of the clergyman's choir, who had a remarkable bass voice for a man of slight stature and build.

Nan organized a small children's choir, and after much rehearsal, we were unleashed on Saigon. Several free performances were given to Vietnamese schoolchildren, and a couple of paid performances were given in the evening. Ambassador Ellsworth Bunker, General Creighton Abrams, and the prime minister of Vietnam, Nguyen Van Khiem, attended on opening night. The audiences were receptive. The schoolchildren avidly followed the action of what was probably their first opera, and the evening audiences were generous with their applause.

For me, the experience was exhilarating. Before Saigon, I had enjoyed singing and was generally regarded as having a pleasant voice. But I did not know *how* to sing. Nan's lessons opened a new level of singing for me, with proper breathing and use of the diaphragm. With these lessons, I, a comfortable second alto, morphed into a passable mezzo-soprano, singing in *Hansel and Gretel* the B-flat just below high C.

Thus Saigon marked my debut not only as a full-time political officer but also as an opera singer. *Hansel* is a memory I treasure, although I wisely didn't opt to give up my day job. I took my love of choral music with me from Saigon to my subsequent Washington and overseas assignments. It deeply enriched my life.

A Siamese Friend Joins My Household

During the mini-Tet offensive, Beverly Dunn, an embassy communicator, informed me that her two Siamese cats, bought from the Bangkok Sunday Market, had conspired to produce kittens. She promised me one, a beautiful little seal point whom I named Mai Thai (a play on the name of the cocktail—she would be my "Thai," my Siamese cat). While I lived in the hotel, Mai Thai, once she was weaned, was taken in temporarily by Hal and Harry, with whom she resided comfortably until I got my own apartment.

Mai Thai took to the apartment and its third-floor balcony with aplomb. I soon got over my concern that she would venture too far out on the balcony and test her nine lives, although I never allowed her to be on the balcony unless I was with her. She quickly became my good friend and companion, greeting me affectionately when I returned from work, accommodating herself to my schedule.

Unlike some (perhaps most) cats, Mai Thai seemed to enjoy company. She never fled the living room when guests appeared, but would eye them curiously and frequently settle herself in the middle of the floor on an Oriental rug I had acquired on a trip to Nepal. Vietnamese traditionally do not like cats and generally do not have them as pets, but my Vietnamese guests seemed (or, at least, feigned) to be fascinated by the beautiful creature with her penetrating sapphire eyes.

In addition to companionship, Mai Thai performed two valuable functions: she was my informal rocket attack early-warning system, and a keen exterminator. Shortly after she joined me in the apartment, I was still abed on an early Sunday morning when suddenly Mai Thai leaped on my chest, yowling. Before I could react, I heard the nearby explosion of a couple of rockets. Mai Thai apparently, with her more acute hearing, had heard the shrill whistle of the incoming missiles. We both took refuge in the windowless bathroom until the short-lived barrage concluded. After that, whenever Mai Thai leapt on me as she had before the explosion, we both skedaddled to the bathroom.

I also called on my fearless Siamese (who weighed six pounds at most) to rid me of the occasional massive flying roaches that regularly share just about everyone's living quarters in Southeast Asia. These roaches, the size of silver dollars, had wings, making it more difficult for squeamish me to catch them. A technique I developed once Mai Thai arrived, and after I had seen her proudly march into my bedroom carrying one of the massive insects in her petite little mouth, was to corner the critter, cover it with a wastebasket, and call in my personal exterminator. She never failed.

Unfortunately, Mai Thai also enjoyed catching, and toying with, the small lizards that frequented the walls and ceilings of residences, onomatopoeically called chinchooks. The chirruping of these little creatures, about six to eight inches long, sounded similar to the name by which they were known. These are not geckos, as some have suggested; we had geckos in Vietnam, but not in my apartment (just in the gardens, and once in the water pipes of our apartment building). Geckos were larger, perhaps a foot or more in length, and were beige with reddish spots. At dusk and in the early evenings, they would call out for mates with their remarkably powerful voices—"geck-o, geck-o"—which gradually diminished in loudness. Outdoors, at some gatherings I attended, conversation ceased while the gecko called out. If he called "geck-o" seven times in a row without a break, it was regarded as good luck for the listeners. The chinchooks performed a useful service in the tropics, eating mosquitoes and other small insects. Once I had become accustomed to their presence on my walls and ceilings, I appreciated their service, although I did not show much gratitude when one of them fell on my bed or on me. But I would not have troubled them.

For Mai Thai, however, chinchooks were great fun. She would emerge from a corner into which a hapless chinchook had dropped, with her prey dangling from her mouth. She would release it, and quickly seize it again with her paw as it attempted to scoot away. Occasionally, she would be left with just a piece of the tail in her possession, as these remarkable creatures could, and did, easily regrow that portion of their anatomy. Be assured that I always tried to help the chinchooks escape her clutches—but not always successfully.

Hal Colebaugh had also acquired a kitten from Beverly, and when his male and Mai Thai matured, we brought them together. Mai Thai thoughtfully gave birth to only two kittens, for which Hal and I quickly found welcoming homes among the American diplomatic community. Most likely because of the inbreeding, one of the kittens had a slightly crooked tail. He was a smart, feisty male, and the crook made him even more engaging. I thoroughly enjoyed observing Mai Thai as a mother, teaching her young how to stalk and pounce, swatting them when they misbehaved, and carrying one of them by the scruff of the neck back into the living room when he had slipped out on the balcony (forbidden to them). No human mother could have made it any clearer to her young that this behavior simply would not be tolerated.

I enjoyed observing the kittens so much that I was gently accused by their prospective families of hogging them, delaying their departure from my clutches. So I reluctantly surrendered them. By all accounts they became happy, cherished Foreign Service cats, living all over the world with loving families to a ripe old age.

Mai Thai wandered around the apartment, puzzled, for a few

days, looking for her kittens, but she adapted quickly to their loss. These were her only kittens; I decided to have her spayed. She was a very small cat, and I did not want to push my luck, or hers, with additional pregnancies. She gave me a great deal of pleasure in Saigon and stayed by my side until her death, seventeen years later, fittingly enough in Laos, where I was serving as chargé d'affaires.

Home Leave and Return to Saigon

I had comfortably settled into the political section and into my apartment, despite the unnerving aspects of the war around us. My work with Senator Huyen had proved valuable. When Harry Dunlop's tour of duty was ending, I was offered the job of assuming his responsibilities for covering the Senate, while continuing my morning meetings with Senator Huyen. My eighteen-month tour of duty ended in July 1969, and I agreed to take home leave and return to Saigon for an additional year, with my principal duty being following the Senate.

I left Saigon on July 20, 1969. As we were approaching the Tokyo airport, our pilot announced that Neil Armstrong had just walked on the moon. I had a couple of hours between flights in Tokyo, and was pleased to see that the airport officials had placed numerous television sets in waiting areas so that passengers could observe this historic event. I watched, mesmerized, as the astronaut walked on the moon.

I had arranged to meet my sister Hazel and her three youngest children at my brother Bob's home in Oak Harbor, Washington, in time for his retirement ceremony from his career as a naval aviator. On the way back to the States, however, I decided to see a bit of Alaska. I booked a flight to Fairbanks along with a two- or three-day tour. On the flight to Anchorage, I developed an excruciatingly painful ear infection, which perforated the eardrum. The doctor who treated me strongly advised me not to fly for at least two weeks. I felt miserable, and a few days' recuperation did not seem particularly onerous. I reluctantly cancelled my Fairbanks arrangements and relaxed in a less-than-first-class hotel, the best I could find on short notice.

A problem remained: how to get to Whidbey Island in time for Bob's retirement ceremony without flying? Fortunately, I learned that a tour group was staying at a nearby hotel. I sought out the tour guide and arranged to ride with the group on their bus as far as Skagway, where they would join a cruise ship for a trip down the Inland Waterway to Vancouver. The guide could not guarantee me a berth on the ship, but I learned that the Alaskan Ferry System had boats with bunks that regularly made the run from Skagway to Prince Rupert, Canada.

I enjoyed my few days with the bus tour group. We saw Mount McKinley and other strikingly beautiful natural sights in Alaska. I recall spending the night in Valdez, a small, unprepossessing little town which, we were assured, would become a major player in Alaska once the Alaska oil pipeline, for which Valdez would be the terminus, was completed.

Unfortunately, when we reached Skagway, there were no rooms available in the inn—the cruise ship was booked to capacity. I bid farewell to my traveling companions and booked passage, with a bunk, on the Alaska ferry. It took the ferry a good two days to make it to Prince Rupert. It was an interesting trip through incredibly beautiful scenery. The snow-clad mountains seemed to come down just about to the water's edge as we traversed the waterway. I could not leave the ferry at its interesting stops (including Sitka, whose Russian onion domes looked so enticing), as the ship was stopping only to disgorge and take on passengers. "One day," I promised myself.

The bunk in my ferry cabin was a wooden frame with a thin mattress, but with clean sheets. My bunkmate was a seventy-something retired professor from the University of Fairbanks. I took the upper bunk in deference to her age, which she appreciated, but she was hearty and very interesting. She was a source of considerable local information for a first-time visitor to Alaska.

From Prince Rupert, I boarded another ferry to Victoria, on Vancouver Island, Canada. This short ride was followed by yet another brief ferry ride from Victoria to Vancouver. From there, I took a bus to Everett, Washington, a quick ride from Oak Harbor. Bob picked me up at the bus station there, and I arrived in time for his ceremony.

A moving military ceremony marked Bob's retirement with the rank of commander from a naval career he had begun during

World War II. After a few days' stay with Bob, Hazel and I and the children (Barbara, Bob, and Michael) began our automobile trip back to the East Coast.

We started by driving down the West Coast to California. We saw beautiful Crater Lake in Oregon and drove down scenic Route 1 in California to San Francisco and Los Angeles. We then headed across the country, stopping at Las Vegas, the Grand Canyon, Bryce Canyon, Mesa Verde, and other scenic highlights. It was a great trip. We had little time for sightseeing in the final leg of our trip because of the delays during my Alaskan adventure. We ate up the miles so I could make it east in time to join my sister Betty and her husband Jack at their Long Beach Island apartment for a week.

Before returning to Saigon, I had consultations in Washington for a few days. Interest was high concerning prospects for passage of the Land to the Tiller law, and possible additional political liberalization.

Covering the Senate

I enjoyed my work reporting on the Senate in Saigon. My relationship with Senator Huyen grew closer and even more rewarding. For a first-tour political officer, I felt confident that I was making a contribution to our effort in Saigon, encouraging the strengthening of democratic institutions in South Vietnam. When our policy was challenged by critics, I argued that the people of South Vietnam were not being offered a choice between Nguyen Van Thieu and Thomas Jefferson. The choice was between Thieu, who, under U.S. pressure, was attempting to develop a more democratic system of government while simultaneously fighting a war, and a Communist system that promised vicious totalitarian rule. There was no free press in Hanoi, and no National Assembly struggling to develop a land reform program. A ruthless land takeover following the Communist ascendancy in North Vietnam had claimed tens of thousands of lives. I was convinced that the U.S. effort in Vietnam had valid goals, and I was comfortable attempting to help achieve them.

South Vietnam's Land to the Tiller bill was passed, signed into law, and implemented. It gave title to land that tenants had been tilling for some time and increased these former tenants' stake in a non-Communist Vietnam. It also offered fair compensation to the landowners who had a portion of their holdings taken for this program. National Assembly elections, hotly contested, were held during this period. Covering them was exciting. Chairman Huyen was among those reelected.

Meanwhile, as the year went on, the security situation improved. By the time the summer of 1970 arrived, I was able to drive with my friends to Tay Ninh Province, on Vietnam's border with Cambodia, and visit the Cao Dai sect's temples and savor their tasty vegetarian food—the soybean pork chop would have fooled a pig. We also managed a day trip to Vung Tau, a seaside resort on the South China Sea. This proved to be a bit ambitious because, on the way back to Saigon, we ran into a firefight. Our driver floored the gas pedal while the rest of us ducked down in our seats, bullets whizzing overhead, as the Army of the Republic of Vietnam (ARVN) and the Viet Cong fought it out. I recklessly took a picture, which turned out well.

Back to Washington

It was soon time to consider my next assignment. I was delighted to be contacted by the director of the Vietnam Working Group in Washington, Freeman Matthews, asking if I would be interested in replacing the officer who followed internal Vietnamese politics for the group. This person was also deputy director of the Working Group, a position for which I was too junior, but I was very pleased that I was wanted for the internal politics position. I accepted with pleasure and bid on the job. I was finally assigned to the position after State's byzantine assignment process had run its course. I left Saigon in September 1970, eager to take on my new responsibilities.

Initial Disappointment in Washington

When I joined the Vietnam Working Group, Freeman Matthews had completed his tour and had been replaced by James Engle. Jim was a pleasant man, but older in his ways than most of my male colleagues, and he did not take a female political officer very seriously. He assigned me projects that his competent secretary could have handled—rearranging the small office library, consolidating files, and so on. I performed these chores, assuming that with time he would understand that my position involved more substantive duties. To my dismay, I learned that he was recruiting another officer to cover my duties. I confronted Jim with my knowledge of this situation, and my dissatisfaction with the way my duties were evolving. I told him calmly that if he preferred to bring someone else on to do my job, I would immediately seek a transfer to another office.

Engle was startled at my reaction and reluctant for me to seek a transfer. He assured me that I would keep my position, and that if the officer he was recruiting joined the office, it would be in another capacity. Only partially mollified, I decided to see how the situation developed before seeking a change of assignment.

Fate ultimately intervened on my behalf. A senior department official, a political appointee, wanted to make an orientation tour to Asia. Jim was assigned to arrange it and accompany him on this trip. Upon its completion, the official asked for the continuation of Jim's services, and Jim left the Vietnam Working Group. He was replaced by Josiah Bennett, a capable officer of the old school, but one who had no difficulty in working with a female officer. Belatedly, the job turned into the one I had been assigned, one that I was eager to undertake.

My two years with the Vietnam Working Group were filled with interesting developments, long workdays, and some personal satisfaction. I had saved enough money in Saigon for a down payment on a home. After visiting single houses in the Washington suburbs and contemplating the commute, I bought a one-bedroom apartment in Potomac Plaza Terraces, at 24th and H Streets, Northwest—a ten-minute walk from the State Department. The apartment worked out beautifully. I could work until 7:00 p.m. or so and still make a Kennedy Center concert or dinner with friends. In bad weather, I was the reliable person who could walk to work during snowstorms—a mixed blessing, but one that my superiors appreciated.

Two of the many interesting experiences and challenges of my work with the Vietnam Working Group stand out particularly in my memory: briefing Secretary of State William Rogers and appearing before a House of Representatives committee chaired by fire-eating Representative Bella Abzug, a virulent opponent of the Vietnam War.

I Brief the Secretary of State

South Vietnam was preparing for a presidential election. Duong Van Minh, the coup general whom I had met in Saigon, was believed to be contemplating running against incumbent Nguyen Van Thieu. The United States, which wanted a contested election, feared that Minh would back out. An uncontested run by Thieu would encourage American critics disdainful of South Vietnam's efforts at democratic practices.

As the election approached, interest in Washington heightened about the South's electoral practices. Joe Bennett and I were summoned to the office of William Sullivan, the deputy assistant secretary of state in the East Asian Bureau, to discuss this. Sullivan would be briefing Secretary Rogers the following morning on the Vietnamese elections and the constitutional requirements for it prior to Rogers's meeting later that day at the White House with President Nixon.

Knowing the details of the Vietnamese constitution was part of my job, and I fielded Sullivan's questions at some length. Shortly after Joe and I returned to our offices, I got a call saying that Sullivan wanted me to accompany him to his meeting with the secretary. I was delighted and told Joe Bennett about the request. Shortly thereafter, Bill, conscious of protocol and not wishing to snub Joe, called and asked him to attend also.

I was nervous but confident as I accompanied Ambassador Sullivan into Secretary Rogers's beautiful office on the exalted seventh floor of the State Department. The heads of the bureaus of intelligence and research and policy planning were also in attendance. When Sullivan introduced me to Rogers, the secretary smiled graciously and said, "Oh, you've brought your secretary with you." Sullivan said instantly, "No, Mr. Secretary. Terry Tull is the department's expert on the Vietnamese constitution. I thought she should be with us." The secretary accepted this explanation and invited me to sit beside him.

Sullivan took the lead in introducing the topic at hand—the Vietnamese election, and the possible ramifications if it were uncontested. Initially, the secretary posed his questions to Sullivan, but Sullivan deferred to me as the expert, and Secretary Rogers began putting his questions directly to me. Secretary Rogers was interested in both the constitutional and political ramifications of an uncontested election. It was a treat for an officer of my rank to be discussing an issue of critical importance to the United States with the secretary of state, and I still savor the memory.

This experience increased my already great respect for Ambassador Sullivan. It demonstrated his self-confidence, his ability to delegate details, and his willingness to share the spotlight with juniors. It was not his job to know what article 7 of the Vietnamese constitution said; that was my job. Instead of pretending he knew this arcane matter, he brought me to the meeting. His refusal to pretend detailed knowledge he did not have impressed me, and I took this lesson with me. As my responsibilities grew, I was always able to defer to the knowledge of the officers who worked for me and allow them the opportunity to shine when their expertise was called for.

Belling Bella

Bella Abzug was a feisty Democratic member of Congress who represented Brooklyn. She was known for her spectacular hats— she was rarely seen bareheaded—for her outspoken championing of women's rights, and for her opposition to the Vietnam War. As the Vietnamese election approached, she contacted Bill Sullivan and demanded that he appear before her committee to discuss the elections and U.S. policy regarding them. Sullivan demurred, suggesting that Abzug should be briefed by the department's expert on these elections, Terry Tull. Abzug refused; she wanted a higher-level official, specifically Sullivan. He told me later that he had wondered aloud to the representative about how it would appear if it were to be known that she had refused to receive a female State Department officer, even though that officer was the person best qualified to address her concerns. Abzug relented, and I was fed to her lions.

I appeared before her committee prepared to be devoured, but also determined not to be intimidated. I would be polite, but I would not grovel. I recall a fairly packed committee room with several members of congress in attendance and Bella presiding, wearing a striking signature hat. The questions were uniformly hostile, and I answered them as well as I could. Abzug and the other members wanted me to change U.S. policy toward Vietnam, which was beyond my pay grade. I doubt that the committee received much information, though I offered a lot of it concerning the technical details of the election process and the constitution. Nor did their opposition change my conviction that what the United States and the South Vietnamese were attempting to pull off was far preferable to the totalitarian Communist dictatorship in North Vietnam. I was personally convinced that Big Minh would not subject himself to a free election. His skepticism in this regard was understandable, although I believe the National Assembly and provincial council elections had been fair. My impression of his persona was that he felt he should be, in effect, given the presidency, and not have to endure the indignities of any election, free or otherwise.

When the session was over, I found myself in the elevator with Bella Abzug. We exchanged greetings, and I recall her saying something along the lines of "There was nothing personal about all this"; I accepted her peace offering. Subsequent press reports, of course, quoted her as saying that Theresa Tull had been "totally unresponsive" to the committee's concerns. Bill Sullivan thought that this was just fine.

5

Back to Vietnam

During my tour on the Vietnam Working Group, we had been disappointed, if not surprised, when Big Minh decided at the last minute not to challenge Nguyen Van Thieu for the presidency of South Vietnam, alleging that the election would not be fairly conducted. Thieu ran unopposed, to much criticism in the United States. Meanwhile, however, the Paris Peace Conference on Vietnam had been in progress for some time, bringing together the North Vietnamese, the South Vietnamese, and the United States in an attempt to bring about an end to the war. I had wanted to be assigned to the Paris talks, but instead had gotten the Vietnam Working Group job, which for me was a good assignment nonetheless.

It was a troubled time in the United States; opposition to the war had escalated. While I was on the Vietnam Working Group, a massive antiwar protest took place, with the organizers' goal "to shut down Washington." I was frightened when I walked to work that morning, passing crowds of hostile hippy-like protesters who were trying to block traffic and prevent anyone from entering the State Department. Some even stood in the middle of the street and grabbed keys from the ignition of vehicles whose drivers had thoughtlessly left their car windows down. The keys were then flung as far as the protester could manage. I was determined not to be deterred from reaching the department and my work on the very policy the protesters were screaming obscenities against.

President Nixon cracked down hard on the protesters, arresting them by the hundreds and dispatching them in some cases to RFK Stadium. His actions were later condemned as excessive, but this was no peaceful protest: it was menacing. I had no sympathy for the thugs who protested that day. On other occasions, in the course of speaking engagements throughout the country, I encountered many young people who were opposed to the Vietnam policy, but they expressed their opposition in peaceful, legal ways. I respected their right to disagree with the policy.

But my time with the Vietnam Working Group was coming to an end. In filing my bid list for future assignments, I requested Southeast Asian area studies at a university to solidify my Southeast Asian credentials. To my great satisfaction, I was selected for this program. I researched the leading universities with an emphasis on Southeast Asian studies. My choices came down to Cornell and the University of Michigan. Michigan offered a master's degree in the specialty, but Cornell expected students to proceed to a doctorate. I preferred to take my chances at earning a master's degree in the one year at Michigan. I already had met one time-consuming requirement for the degree: proficiency in a language of the region—in my case, Vietnamese.

I obtained the assignment, but one afternoon I received a puzzled call from personnel. They had noticed that I was being assigned to graduate school at Michigan, but they could find no record of my bachelor's degree. I assured them that I would be receiving my bachelor's from the University of Maryland in January 1972, and would not leave for Michigan until the late summer. They believed me, and my orders were issued. Since entering the Foreign Service with about seventy-five college credits, I had been taking night courses wherever possible. Finally, in January 1972, I received the hard-won degree from Maryland, where my father had earned his degree in 1915 when the school was still the Maryland Agricultural College.

College campuses were not very welcoming to State Department officials during those divided times. Nonetheless, I was so delighted at the prospect of attending college during the day, with no other obligations—as opposed to working all day and attending night school for years, as I'd done before—that I was determined not to be disturbed by student opposition to me or to Vietnam policy. I need not have worried. I had no difficulties establishing my place among my fellow graduate students. Any discussions we had regarding Vietnam were civil and straightforward. I recall one professor, who taught a history course, informing us about his trip to Hanoi over the Christmas break. He said straightforwardly that he had been surprised at how carefully targeted the U.S. bombing had been there; he did not see much damage at all to non-defense-related targets.

I enjoyed my academic year in Ann Arbor. The course work was interesting, the professors top-notch, and my fellow students engaging. I felt almost like I was on vacation; all I had to do was attend class. The department paid all of my expenses, including a per diem rate, which was enough to cover the cost of my one-bedroom apartment just off the campus. I joined a "town and gown" choral group and had the unique experience of singing some beautiful music in Hebrew. The group also sang at a concert at which Van Cliburn was the guest soloist. I took a few lessons in sight-reading from one of the professors, and enjoyed it thoroughly. Personally, I took advantage of Ann Arbor's proximity to South Bend, Indiana, to spend some holidays with my brother Charles, his wife Mickey, and their family there. Charles had accepted a teaching position at the University of Indiana's South Bend branch.

I was determined to earn a master's degree while I had the chance. The program involved writing a substantial thesis. I selected as my topic the Mekong Committee, which comprised the riparian countries of the Mekong River. The Mekong Committee planned to encourage regional economic development by harnessing the power of the Mekong River to a huge dam to produce hydroelectric power. I contended in my thesis that the Pamong Dam offered a chance for peaceful cooperation and economic development for North and South Vietnam, as well as Laos, Thailand, and Cambodia. Research into the subject was an interesting task. The writing portion of the work diminished the vacation aspect of my sabbatical, but I completed the paper to favorable comments from my faculty adviser. I had a straight "A" average in all my classes, and left Ann Arbor in June 1973 in happy possession of a master's degree in Southeast Asian studies.

Although I had gained admission to the Foreign Service through the regular examination process without having earned a college degree, I had subsequently completed the bachelor's degree requirements and had gone on to earn a master's degree from a prestigious university as well. This not only gave me personal satisfaction but also increased confidence in my professional life.

Assignment Da Nang

In January 1973, the Paris peace talks produced an agreement—the Paris Peace Accords. The United States would withdraw all of its troops from South Vietnam, the North Vietnamese would do likewise, and peace would reign. The United States was permitted to have fifty military personnel in the country to provide logistical support to help coordinate U.S. military assistance to the South, which would continue under the agreement. The United States would also send a number of peace accord monitors to South Vietnam. Some of my Foreign Service friends were soon off to Vietnam to carry out this chore.

I had hoped that having obtained my Southeast Asian master's degree, I would be able to leave my Vietnam days behind me. I particularly wished to be assigned to Indonesia, a country that had long fascinated me. I was offered an excellent position, but it was in Vietnam once more: deputy principal officer at the American Consulate General in Da Nang. During the war, there was a large office in each of the four military regions in South Vietnam called CORDS (Civil Operations and Revolutionary Development Support) headquarters. These offices, which were staffed by USAID officers, military personnel, some Foreign Service and other personnel, oversaw the nonmilitary U.S. effort in South Vietnam—rural development and other aid activities—and monitored the progress of the war for the U.S. government. With the Paris agreements, these CORDS offices were converted into traditional diplomatic establishments, specifically, consulates general. In each military region, each consulate general had provincial offices. In Military Region I, where Da Nang was the seat of the consulate general, there were provincial offices in Hue, Quang Nam, and Quang Ngai.

Disappointed at not getting an assignment other than Vietnam, but gratified at being offered a substantial position with significant management responsibilities, I accepted the assignment and headed again for Vietnam—this time, to the northernmost region of South Vietnam, the region in most danger should the North Vietnamese break the Paris agreements. I thought there was a fighting chance that the agreements would hold long enough for South Vietnam to develop enough economically to be able to afford to defend itself—oil was rumored to be available in the South China Sea. Meanwhile, I was ready to do my best to promote that effort.

An Inauspicious Beginning

In August 1973, I found myself once again in Vietnam. After brief consultations in Saigon, I boarded an Air America flight to Da Nang on a Sunday morning. We had not gone far when it became apparent that there was a serious mechanical problem with the plane. The copilot rushed to the rear of the plane to check something out, then rushed back to the cabin; this sequence was repeated. I noticed that we were flying in a huge circle. In an excited voice, the pilot informed us that we had to return to Saigon, but he intended to use as much fuel as possible before he attempted to land. A mechanical problem made it imperative to abort the flight. A few passengers (by and large Vietnamese) expressed their fears aloud—not quite screaming, but talking excitedly, almost keening.

I looked out of the window and prayed. I remember thinking that, all told, I had had a good life, albeit a somewhat short one. I had achieved entry into a career that was intellectually satisfying and within which I had achieved some recognition for competence. I had a large and loving family who had supported me. I prayed that they would not have to face my premature death from a plane crash.

Our fuel apparently almost used up, the pilot brought the plane in for a rough, yet safe, landing in Saigon. The plane was unable to taxi to the hangar gate, but after some moments a bus came planeside and we were driven to the waiting room. Several hours later, another plane was found and, swallowing my qualms, I boarded and proceeded without further incident to Da Nang.

Military Region I Daily Briefings

Paul Popple was the consul general in Da Nang. My new boss was a diminutive career officer of considerable intelligence. He had served previously with Ambassador Graham Martin, who knew Paul had not been an enthusiastic supporter of the U.S. effort in Vietnam. Nonetheless, he wanted Popple to take on the challenge of heading up the I Corps consulate general and to serve, I intuited, as a kind of devil's advocate—not afraid to speak truth to power, to tell it like it was.

Popple was determined to put a clear civilian stamp on the former CORDS headquarters establishment. The consulate general had retained its provincial offices in Hue, Quang Nam, and Quang Ngai, but with a reduced staff of USAID officers. Through Dan Leaty, the officers' very capable and pragmatic Da Nang–based boss, Paul instructed the officers to report to me as his deputy. This did not go down well at first with these war-hardened USAID workers. They initially resisted my authority, which I attempted to wield very lightly. For example, they resented being asked to write reports on political and economic developments and submit them to me for editing and clearance. Eventually, they accepted the situation—particularly when the situation took a turn for the worse in 1975.

To emphasize that a new civilian era had begun in I Corps, Popple abandoned his CORDS chief predecessor's practice of attending the daily military briefing at I Corps Headquarters in Da Nang. He advised me that he had arranged with the commanding general, Lieutenant General Ngo Quang Truong, that I would attend the 8:00 a.m. briefing Sunday through Friday. Popple himself would attend the Saturday briefing and would meet privately with the general afterward.

I felt honored to be given the opportunity to attend these morning briefings, in which the I Corps senior staff informed the I Corps commander of significant military and related developments that had occurred throughout the region during the previous twenty-four hours. The general seated me at his immediate right, making clear by this gesture that I was welcome and a serious participant in the American presence in I Corps. I immediately saw the great respect that the I Corps officers had for this man, whose reputation for courage, leadership, strategic and tactical brilliance, and unquestioned personal integrity was widely known in both Vietnamese and American circles. If the general had any reservations about having a relatively young American woman attend his daily military briefings, he tactfully concealed them.

I concluded that General Truong had fully accepted me as a colleague when Quang Ngai province experienced serious flooding, which was reported at the daily briefing. After the briefing, the general invited me to accompany him on an inspection tour of the affected area. I obtained permission from the consul general to make the trip, and soon was flying down to Quang Ngai province in a helicopter piloted by the I Corps commander. In Quang Ngai we climbed on top of a tank and toured the area. I had not had time to change into slacks before the trip. I can still see the startled looks on the Vietnamese farmers' faces when we rolled by—not only appreciation that the commander had come to see what they needed, but also surprise and near astonishment that he was accompanied by an American woman in a flowered dress!

Attending these daily briefings helped me develop excellent relationships with General Truong and many of his senior staff. Over time, these relationships produced useful information. I recall the CIA's senior military analyst observing to me wryly toward the end of our stay in Da Nang that I was obtaining better information than he was about the military situation—a high compliment from a retired army colonel I admired.

Whither Peace Prospects? A Grim Assessment

Paul Popple was concerned about prospects for peace in Vietnam under the terms agreed in the Paris Peace Accords. He was determined to convert our USAID provincial officers into reporters, assessing prospects for South Vietnam's survival. He instructed me to work with the officers to develop an outline for assessing all aspects of the current situation in I Corps and analyzing what the findings meant for the future of a viable non-Communist South Vietnam. I met with these officers and elicited their inputs on areas that we should examine.

The military situation was important. The North had left several divisions in South Vietnam, in violation of the Paris accords, and had significantly expanded its logistics base. The economic situation—investment, new construction, health care, refugees, and a whole range of indicators—also warranted attention. I polished this input into an outline for a proposed airgram (a dispatch that was not sent telegraphically to the department), ran it by the USAID officers, incorporated their fixes, and put them to work.

I received the provincial officers' input just before the Tet celebrations of 1974. I spent the Tet holidays at the consulate general, analyzing raw data, combining assessments, and melding the officers' separate reports into a comprehensive overview of I Corps one year after the Paris accords. The material these officers had assembled was disturbing. The military reality was negatively affecting construction and business activity, and refugees were an increasing burden. Despite General Truong's excellent leadership and the good work of much of his staff, the reluctant conclusion drawn by the officers, which matched my own growing concerns, was that I Corps would not be able to hold up against a concerted North Vietnamese military offensive, an event that we felt would most likely occur.

I presented the finished airgram to Popple after Tet. He took his time reviewing it; prodded by me for his reactions, he said he did not fault the conclusions. But he said that Ambassador Martin would not approve the piece for transmission to Washington. The consulates general were not permitted to communicate directly with Washington; all communications had to be sent first to Saigon for approval. If granted, the cable or airgram would then be forwarded to Washington. This clearly was an effort by the ambassador to ensure that all elements of the mission sang with one voice concerning the situation on the ground in Vietnam.

The consul general did approve the airgram, with minor editorial adjustments, and took it to Saigon on his next consultation trip. As he predicted, the ambassador would not approve the piece for forwarding to Washington. Embassy political-military counselor Al Francis initially vetted our work. He had served with the ambassador before and was regarded as his fair-haired boy. He was very capable, intelligent, and a true believer in the Vietnam effort. Paul Popple and I believed strongly that we had a duty to report the situation as we saw it. Ambassador Martin and Al

Francis were probably concerned that my balanced but negative assessment would resonate badly on prospects for continued aid to Vietnam. Clearly, it would contradict the ambassador's views, which I have no doubt were more positive than those of Da Nang's consulate general.

In any event, the airgram languished in my files in Da Nang for some months. I was always too loyal to "back channel" or "bootleg" copies of my work to friends in the department. Perhaps this was a failing on my part. In early 1975, when the situation on the ground was not going well, a senior officer with the Vietnam Working Group visited the country to take soundings. I told him of our misgivings, and he wondered why we had not reported them. I pulled out my airgram, which he read avidly, and said it was exactly the kind of reporting that should have been submitted. He may have taken a copy of it with him when he left; I did not take it with me from Da Nang.

A New Consul General Is Appointed

At some point during 1974, Paul Popple received an unexpected appointment to serve as the deputy head of the American Institute in Taiwan. For Popple, this was an advancement in his career. For Ambassador Martin in Saigon, it provided an opportunity to replace his devil's advocate with an officer more attuned to Martin's own strong views about the correctness and viability of U.S. policy toward Vietnam—Al Francis.

I swallowed my reservations about how the consulate general and I could work with an officer who, in his role in the clearance process for cables and airgrams in Saigon, had revealed less enthusiasm than we felt for reporting negative developments to Washington. But the duty of a deputy is to support the chief, while giving him or her the benefit of the deputy's best judgment and advice. I resolved to support Al's efforts to the fullest extent possible. We developed a good working relationship, which grew closer over time to one of mutual respect.

Al had served in I Corps earlier in the war and was acquainted with some of the senior Vietnamese officers posted there. After his initial introductory call on the I Corps commander, Lieutenant

General Truong, I advised him that his next call should be on the deputy corps commander, Major General Hoang Van Lac. Al, who was not strong on protocol, insisted instead that he go down to Quang Nam province and call on the commander of the ARVN Third Infantry Division, General Nguyen Van Hinh, whom he had known during his earlier service in Vietnam. I strongly advised against this breach of protocol, knowing it would offend General Lac and could be embarrassing for the third division commander. Al would not be deterred. To his credit, several weeks later, he volunteered to me that this had been a mistake on his part; he recognized that he should have followed protocol and called on the deputy commander before venturing to meet with subordinate generals.

Babysitting a Spy Plane

It was a beautiful Saturday morning, nearing noontime. Al had plans to go to Hue for the weekend to visit our provincial office and meet with senior ARVN commanders. An urgent phone call came in from Utapao Air Base in Thailand shortly before he was scheduled to leave. The caller was speaking about a serious problem in veiled terms I could not understand. I gave the call to Al, who was familiar with the language being used. Al told me that a U.S. reconnaissance plane, an SR-71 (known familiarly as the Blackbird) based in Utapao, had encountered serious mechanical difficulties and was planning an emergency landing at the Da Nang airfield. The presence of a U.S. military plane of any kind, let alone a "spy" plane, in Vietnam was clearly a violation of the Paris accords. Yet we could not risk the life of the pilot. The plane would land—at noon, in full view of the crowd at the airport preparing to fly to Saigon for the weekend on an Air America flight. Another U.S. Air Force plane, bearing repair parts, mechanics, and a fresh pilot, was also on its way to Da Nang.

Al called the commander of the Vietnamese Air Force in I Corps, General Khanh, to alert him about the imminent landing of the forbidden plane. He instructed me to follow him to the airport. I directed our two capable political officers, Gerald Scott and David Harr, to make haste for the airport as well. We arrived minutes after the sleek black aircraft. which seemed to be mostly wings, had touched down on the tarmac. It was taxiing down the runway as we approached the strip. An agitated General Khanh, whom I fortunately knew quite well, was on the scene to greet us. He insisted that the repairs had to be completed as quickly as possible. He made a hanger available for the plane, which, to my relief, was large enough to conceal the entire plane. Shortly thereafter, the second plane arrived. At the same time, the small jet plane that the consulate general had at its occasional disposal was prepping to take Al to Hue. I wondered whether he would abort his plans.

He did not. Al gathered the group of some ten or twelve air force personnel in the hangar and advised them sternly that he was expected in Hue, and that in his absence, I was fully in charge. My orders were to be followed without question. Under no circumstances were any of the visitors to leave the hangar without my permission. He then boarded the small plane and left the situation in my hands.

The repair work took several hours. I sent one of our political officers out to buy food for the air force personnel, a couple of whom could barely conceal their excitement about being in Vietnam after the Paris accords. They accepted my authority and worked hard. At one point, I asked if they would like to have souvenirs of their clandestine visit. Either David or Gerald, our political officers, then went downtown and bought several small sculptures made from marble from Da Nang's Marble Mountain. These mementos were well received.

General Khanh appeared periodically and anxiously asked about the progress of the work. I assured him it was going well, and that our personnel and their aircraft would not remain on Vietnamese soil a minute longer than necessary. He was helpful logistically; there was a gasoline shortage in Da Nang at that time, and my official car's gas tank was dangerously low on fuel. I did not welcome the thought of running out of gas in the middle of the night heading home from the airfield. General Khanh arranged for my car to be fueled at the air base tanks.

Night fell, and it became clear that the work would not be completed in time to allow an evening return to Thailand. The airmen would remain at the airfield working on the plane, with the expectation of a dawn takeoff. The two reconnaissance plane pilots (the pilot of the injured aircraft and his replacement) needed sleep if they were to be able to fly the plane safely home in the morning. I invited the two pilots to spend the night at my residence. I left Gerald and David at the airfield with the repair crew.

The two pilots were wearing bright orange flight suits. I asked them to slump down in the seats of my car as we drove through the dark streets, to minimize the risk of detection. I had alerted my cook-housekeeper, Chi Hai, to have a late dinner ready for us, which we all devoured. Then the two pilots retired for well-deserved sleep. I slept fitfully.

By dawn we were back at the airfield. The mechanics had done a masterful job; the plane was ready for takeoff. The pilots and repair team were very appreciative of the consulate general team's efforts. Gerald, David, General Khanh, and I stood in amazement as the SR-71 roared briefly down the runway, took off almost vertically at what seemed to be right angles from the earth, and soared skyward. I have never, before or since, seen a takeoff like that. The repair plane left shortly afterward, and the United States was once again abiding by the terms of the Paris Peace Accords. Gerald, David, and I headed home to rest after an exhausting but most stimulating experience.

A couple of nights later I went to my favorite seafood restaurant in Da Nang. When I emerged from my car, the deaf and mute parking attendant ran over to me. Using his hands excitedly, he mimicked the dramatic takeoff of the plane. I laughed and nodded. Who else had seen that incredible dawn sight, I wondered? To my great surprise, however, no journalist picked up the news that an SR-71 had visited I Corps. To my knowledge, this news was never reported.

Al returned from Hue on Monday morning. I reported on our handling of the aircraft and its crew, and he told me about his visit to Hue. The fact that he had trusted me and the others on the staff to deal with this situation helped to overcome some of the reticence some of us had felt about his assignment to Da Nang. It was a good lesson in management, which I had occasion to emulate several months later as Da Nang was falling to a North Vietnamese invasion.

A Marine's Last Wishes

Several months later, in early 1975, I received a letter from an officer on the Vietnam Working Group with an unusual request. A twenty-eight-year-old ex-marine, unable to adjust to the civilian world, had ended his life. His suicide note, left for his sister, asked that he be buried in I Corps, as close as possible to the spot where he had been very happy. While serving with the marines in I Corps, he had been encamped close to an elementary school. He and his fellow marines had enjoyed playing with the children, giving them little gifts. He wanted to be cremated and to have his ashes buried near that school. His sister had contacted her congressman, whose staff had approached the State Department. She also had asked that a woman bury her brother's ashes, if possible. My Vietnam Working Group colleague wanted to know whether I thought, given the war situation, the Vietnamese would be responsive to this request.

I was certain, given the respect Vietnamese give to their ancestors and the care they give to family burial plots, that the Vietnamese would be very touched by the desire of this young marine to be buried among them. I approached General Truong, who agreed instantly to the request. I informed Washington that we had approval, and that I was willing to undertake the burial.

Around this time, I acquired a new secretary, Elizabeth Montagne. I was out on an appointment one morning when the diplomatic pouch arrived from Washington. Liz was sorting out the items addressed to Al and me. She came upon a carefully wrapped cardboard box, about ten inches square, and put it on her desk. She read the label, and exclaimed to Al's secretary, at a nearby desk: "This says the box contains cremated remains, and they're for Miss Tull!" The other secretary, busy typing a cable, said casually, "Oh, yes, Miss Tull is expecting that. Just put it on her desk." (Liz told me later that she wondered at that point what she had gotten herself into by volunteering for Da Nang.)

Per General Truong's direction, I met with his deputy, General Lac, to make final arrangements for the burial. General Lac, from information I had provided about the marine's service, had pinpointed the spot where the young man had been encamped with his unit. Unfortunately, the North Vietnamese, who had never respected the Paris accords, had taken that ground. But General

Lac located an elementary school across the river from the marines' encampment and decided that was a fitting place for the burial. A few days later, on a dreary, rainy Saturday morning, I flew with General Lac by helicopter to a site several kilometers from the chosen school. Our USIA officer, who had a consular credential, accompanied me so he could properly witness and document the burial. We drove by jeep over pockmarked, muddy roads to the schoolyard.

The school was near the bank of a narrow river. I could hear the sounds of fighting in the near distance as we performed our task. Although General Lac had a soldier do most of the digging, I insisted on personally removing a couple of shovelfuls of earth from the hole to involve myself literally in the burial process. I placed the box of remains in the earth, paused for a moment or two of silent prayer, and the soldier filled in the small grave. As we left, I looked across the river and wondered how long this site would be in ARVN hands. I was comforted by the fact that it was probably unlikely that the North Vietnamese, should they succeed in taking over the region, would destroy the school. Our troubled marine would rest in peace, soothed by the laughter of children at play.

The Military Situation Worsens

The military situation throughout Vietnam worsened in early 1975 as the North Vietnamese grew even bolder in their violations of the Paris accords, for which, ironically, Le Duc Tho and Henry Kissinger received the Nobel Peace Prize. From my attendance at the I Corps morning briefings, I was fully aware of the fighting, which was increasing throughout the western part of the region. At the same time, the U.S. Congress was failing to provide the continued economic and military logistical assistance that had been promised to the South Vietnamese to persuade them to accede to the Paris accords.

In late January 1975, the North Vietnamese captured a provincial capital in the Mekong Delta. No effort was made to recapture this psychologically significant town. This failure convinced me that South Vietnam would not survive long.

I was scheduled to depart Da Nang at the end of February 1975, upon the conclusion of my eighteen-month tour of duty. As I was mentally preparing for my departure, Consul General Al Francis fell ill. It became evident that his illness was serious and required treatment in the United States. I urged Al to leave, saying that I would postpone my departure from the post until his return. He reluctantly agreed to accept medical evacuation to the United States and got approval for an extension of my stay. I had received orders to report to the State Department's Bureau of Intelligence and Research to work as an analyst on Southeast Asian issues. A few weeks' delay in departing would not affect this assignment.

Three CODELs

I became the acting principal officer at the American consulate general in Da Nang at a crucial time in the denouement of U.S. involvement in Vietnam. I was in charge for approximately three weeks. During one two-week period, we hosted three congressional delegations (CODELs): one delegation of staff only, two of members and staff. These delegations allegedly were intended to give congressmen a firsthand look at the situation in the country so as to encourage them to vote in favor of the assistance South Vietnam needed.

General Truong cooperated wholeheartedly in our effort to expose our congressional visitors to the realities of the situation in I Corps. On one occasion, the general agreed to take the most influential of our CODELs on a tour of some of the sensitive areas in the region. That morning, I had learned at the I Corps briefing that fighting at one location had been intense, and at least one South Vietnamese helicopter had been shot down. In late morning, General Truong personally piloted the visiting congressmen and me by helicopter to check out the situation. At one point I looked down and saw that we were flying low over the spot where the ARVN helicopter had been shot down just hours before—its wreckage was visible beneath us. The general caught my eye, with a twinkle in his. I read his glance and said, "General, I know where we are." He smiled, and we were soon out of this particularly hazardous area. The congressmen were oblivious to the danger.

The delegation was impressed by what General Truong and his people had accomplished in I Corps. One of them, who had served with the U.S. Marines in the region, told me that when he was in I Corps, the peaceful rice paddies we were then flying over had clearly been in Viet Cong hands, and had not been as richly cultivated as they were at this time. Nonetheless, the congressmen held out little hope that the United States would provide the aid needed to stave off what ultimately became the major, final invasion by the North Vietnamese of the South, in blatant violation of the 1973 Paris Peace Accords.

The admiration of all three of the visiting CODELs was to no avail. Congress shortly thereafter cut vital assistance to Vietnam.

Evacuation Plans

In preparation for my departure, I arranged for my personal belongings at my residence to be packed one morning in mid-March; I remained at home while the packing was being done. The phone rang. It was General Truong's chief of staff, Colonel Dang, asking whether the general could use the consulate general's small jet plane for a quick trip to Saigon, where he would meet with President Thieu. I said I would check to see if the plane was available and get back to him as soon as possible. The officer who scheduled the use of the plane assured me that it was available, and I communicated that to Colonel Dang.

As soon as I arrived at the consulate general, a senior officer came to my office and showed me a report he had just prepared for dispatch to Saigon. It reported that President Thieu had decided to strengthen the defense of Saigon to create an enclave there, and possibly in a few other key cities. To do this, he had ordered General Truong to dispatch some of his key troops to Saigon immediately. The marine division, based north of the Hai Van Pass in the northern part of Military Region I, and the airborne division, based in Da Nang, were to be redeployed to Saigon. The ARVN First Division, based north of the Hai Van Pass, would be redeployed to the Da Nang area. The northern part of I Corps would be denuded of troops—in effect, that territory, which contained the former Imperial capital, Hue, would be ceded to the advancing North Vietnamese troops. General Truong had requested an urgent meeting with President Thieu to object to these redeployments.

I was stunned. I had sensed that collapse was near, but these redeployments, in my view, would not create safe enclaves for the continuation of a shrunken Republic of Vietnam. They would instead cause the immediate collapse of I Corps and, rapidly thereafter, the loss of the entire country to the North Vietnamese. I doubted that General Truong would be able to dissuade Thieu from this plan. My thoughts immediately turned to preparing for the evacuation of Consulate General Da Nang.

Emergency Evacuation Plan: Worthless

Every diplomatic and consular establishment of the United States has a plan for the emergency evacuation of staff, dependents, and foreign national employees. I had already reviewed the plan for Da Nang (a portion of the overall embassy plan) and had determined that it would be worthless in the current situation. The plan described a simultaneous evacuation of the embassy and all of its outlying posts, not the collapse of the country in phases, as now seemed imminent to me. Nor did the plan make adequate provision for the evacuation of our Vietnamese employees—as I recall, it made absolutely no provision for such evacuation. Abandoning our employees to the North Vietnamese and Viet Cong was simply not acceptable. The slaughter by the North Vietnamese in Hue of any Vietnamese who had cooperated with the Americans was too fresh in my mind to allow me to neglect their fate.

I convened a meeting of key consulate general section heads— consular, the provincial office chief, my two political officers, and a CIA representative—and cautioned them to keep our discussions absolutely secret. I filled them in to the extent I felt I could about what I anticipated to be the looming I Corps collapse, and said we had to design a new evacuation plan. In my own mind, I had already decided that we should evacuate all of our formal Vietnamese employees and their spouses and children. Given the large size of Vietnamese families, I reluctantly decided that we could not offer to evacuate parents and siblings and their families. I did not initially disclose my thinking to the staff, but asked them to consider the matter carefully, share ideas among themselves, and to come up with an estimate of the numbers we might have to evacuate under different scenarios. I said we would meet the next day to review our thinking.

Meanwhile, General Truong returned empty-handed from his brief expedition to Saigon. I learned almost immediately through our CIA station that Thieu had refused to reconsider his redeployment plans.

When the planning staff met with me the next day, I shared this information with them. We talked through various scenarios about local national evacuation, and reached agreement on the plan I had privately decided would be appropriate: we would offer evacuation to Saigon to all of our Vietnamese employees, their spouses, and children. We concluded that we could not offer evacuation to the several hundred guards on the consulate general's payroll—principally ethnic minorities who guarded (unarmed) all of our facilities and houses—as they were not as closely identified with the work of the consulate general as the formal employees. We agreed that we should begin a phased evacuation, beginning with the few dozen American spouses and dependents at the post. Thereafter, we would quietly phase down our operations, beginning with our constituent posts, which were most exposed. To avoid panicking the Vietnamese military and civilian population, with potentially dangerous effects on our efforts and personnel, we would keep a skeleton staff at these posts as long as possible.

I then turned to my secretary and dictated a cable to Saigon, outlining my conviction that the planned withdrawal of key military units from I Corps would result in the collapse of the region to the North Vietnamese. My staff had estimated the air assets we would require to begin the evacuation; I requested these assets and the authorization to begin the evacuation. I included the recommendation that U.S. naval assets be positioned in the South China Sea to handle what I assumed would be a massive refugee outpouring from South Vietnam. It was at this point, as I noted at the beginning of this book, that Mary Francis, Al's wife, who had been hosting a coffee for consulate general wives, came to my office bearing treats for my secretary and me. I opened a fortune cookie and read its prescient observation: "You've come a long way, baby."

I signed the cable, but before dispatching it, I took it to the CIA station chief for his information. I did not want to risk battling a difference of opinion with Saigon should he not agree that the situation was grave and required immediate action. He read the cable and suggested that I add a sentence saying that he had reviewed the message and concurred with my recommendations.

I authorized the cable to be sent and reflected that, given Ambassador Martin's optimistic outlook, I might well be on the next plane to Washington, disgraced. Fortunately for us all, however, Martin was in Washington at that time getting dental work done (and, I have no doubt, attempting to shore up congressional support for the fading effort in Vietnam). His deputy, Wolf Lehmann, was chargé d'affaires. He immediately approved my requests. The very capable USAID staff in the provincial offices and in Da Nang began putting our evacuation plans in motion.

I called on the beleaguered General Truong and informed him of our decisions and our plans to begin evacuating our staff, including Vietnamese and their families. At the recommendation of our provincial officers, I asked his permission to include in our evacuation the ARVN military personnel who served at our provincial offices as interpreters. He agreed. We discussed the situation at length. I was sadly confident that my grim analysis was correct, and that I Corps would not hold once the marines and airborne divisions had departed, and that the loss of I Corps—particularly of Hue, the beautiful former imperial capital—would trigger the collapse of the entire country.

The next several days passed in a blur of activity. Our American dependents were evacuated to Saigon. Gradually, our Vietnamese employees and their families, almost all of whom seized the opportunity to leave, began the trip to Saigon. As I recall, the embassy assigned a C-47 airplane and a helicopter exclusively for our use. The USAID provincial officers performed splendidly. This was demonstrated in one instance when they rebuffed the demand of a bullying U.S. Army colonel who wanted to use the helicopter for his own survey of the situation. I had resisted allowing this officer to visit Da Nang on his long-planned trip, and had been assured that he understood that he would get no logistical support from the consulate general and would not be able to leave Da Nang. He had come in any event, and almost immediately he had begun demanding the use of our evacuation helicopter. Unfazed by his pressure, the USAID officer said that Miss Tull had forbidden our air assets to be used for anything except staff evacuation. The colonel huffed and said he would see about that, but he had the good sense, apparently, to give it up; he did not approach me.

The problem we faced in Da Nang was that, except for a very few people, most of the Americans in the U.S. embassy and mission in Saigon did not comprehend that the end was nearing. Despite the loss of the provincial capital in the delta and the collapse occurring in II Corps Central Highlands, and the fact that we had begun a quiet evacuation of personnel from Da Nang, many of these people apparently were going about their usual business. I was particularly angered by a high-handed phone call from the head of USIS in Saigon, who practically ordered me to make one of our helicopters available to the director of the Imperial Museum in Hue for the removal of the valuable porcelains and other antiques from the museum. I explained that we had to use our helicopter to evacuate personnel. He persisted, indignantly, and was angered when I finally told him that our air assets would be used for people whose lives could well be in grave danger soon, and not to carry antique pots. He blustered and I finally said I was too busy to continue the conversation.

Maintaining a Provincial Presence

As the military situation worsened, I became increasingly concerned about the safety of our American personnel who worked in our provincial offices. After consultation with their Da Nang chief, I instructed these officers to come to Da Nang in the evenings, and to return to their posts in the mornings, situation permitting. Their daylight presence facilitated the evacuation of personnel and helped to prevent a panic.

Meanwhile, my own departure prompted certain protocol activities. General Truong, in appreciation for my support, and in recognition of the U.S. contribution to Vietnam over the years, awarded me a Vietnamese medal at a simple ceremony following a morning briefing at I Corps. He was initially nonplussed as he moved to pin the medal on me, as he would have done with a man, but thought better of it and handed the medal to me instead. I was deeply moved to be so recognized.

General Truong and his wife later hosted a farewell dinner for me as days in Da Nang grew fewer. On this particular day, we were finishing up the evacuation of our people from Quang Ngai province. In Quang Ngai, there was a group of antiwar American Quakers, who were assisting the Vietnamese in health-related activities, providing prostheses for people who had lost limbs. Someone in the consulate general had contacted them and offered evacuation. They had thus far declined. David Harr called me late in the day from Quang Ngai. I was in the consulate general, dressed in an attractive long dress preparatory to attending General Truong's dinner. David was very concerned because the Quakers had again refused to take advantage of our offer to help them leave. I told him to try once again—to tell them that this was their last chance, that we would not be taking the helicopter to Quang Ngai again, as our evacuation there was finished. If they still refused, David was to return to Da Nang, knowing that we had done our best to provide for these Americans. They refused, and ultimately spent some time in detention when the North Vietnamese took over the province.

As the North Vietnamese troops grew nearer to Hue, the population responded by "voting with their feet." A mass exodus began, with people abandoning their homes and livelihoods and fleeing by any means down the Hai Van Pass to what they hoped would be a more secure situation in the Da Nang area. At one point I was approached by Don Oberdorfer, a *Washington Post* reporter whose work I respected, about the possibility of getting transportation to Hue. I authorized his passage to Hue on our helicopter, in the forlorn hope that his reporting of how the people of I Corps did not wish to live under Communism might help generate more U.S. support. At a minimum, he would tell an accurate story of what was happening. He was grateful for the lift.

The same evening of the Truong dinner, we were also just about completing our drawdown from our office in Hue. I went to the Truong residence, carrying my two-way radio and getting reports from our officers in Hue. I asked the senior officer there to come to the general's residence when he returned to Da Nang to report to us both on the deteriorating situation. General Truong, of course, was in constant communication with his own aides, but he welcomed the report from a fresh source.

Shortly before dinner was served, Mrs. Truong took me aside and quietly asked me whether, if the Communists took over the country, I would take their children to the United States. I looked at this beautiful woman for a moment and said that I would. At dinner, I was seated to the right of General Truong. Across the table from me was our CIA station chief. I decided to confirm once more that the situation was as grave as I thought it was. I said to the general, in Vietnamese (because I did not want the station chief, who did not speak the language, to know about this new development yet), that his wife had asked me to take their children to the United States if the country was taken over by the Communists, and that I had agreed. He looked at me for a long moment and then said, "Thank you very much." I needed no further confirmation. The next day I told the station chief what I had agreed to.

Francis Returns; I Go to Saigon

A few days before the final collapse, a still clearly ailing Al Francis returned to Da Nang. My replacement as his deputy, Brunson McKinley (another Graham Martin protégé), had already joined us in Da Nang. Al must have wanted me out of the way, because he asked me to spend some time at home working on a report I was preparing about the status and role of the Catholic Church in I Corps. I am sure he knew, as I did, that this was a fruitless exercise. He then began to reverse some of my decisions. He had our American staff stay overnight in the provinces, and I recall that he joined them himself in Quang Ngai one memorable night; they barely escaped capture when the North Vietnamese came precariously close to their quarters. This venture was short-lived; Al then proceeded with the evacuation, thinning down our remaining staff. I left, saddened, for Saigon on what I think was the final scheduled flight of Air America. Al, Brunson, and most of the men remained behind for Da Nang's final chaotic hours as a free entity.

In Saigon, I stayed initially in the apartment of a USAID officer, a friend of my good friend Betty Price. Betty had retired after a tour of duty in Vientiane, Laos; I had visited her there briefly early in my Da Nang tour. Betty and I had planned the trip of a lifetime, to begin at the conclusion of my Da Nang tour. She would meet me in Saigon, where she would stay with this USAID friend. We would then take a lengthy trip that would, in effect, take us around the world, if we counted our Pacific crossing to get to Vietnam.

We would go to Thailand, Burma, India, Nepal, Kenya, Tanzania, Egypt, Iran, Greece, and the United Kingdom, and then fly to the United States across the Atlantic, thus completing our trip around the world. The new situation, including my pledge to take over custody of General Truong's children, had put this trip on hold. Betty had already proceeded to Saigon to await my arrival.

Her friend had done me a most thoughtful favor. In the early days of the decline, she had had business in Da Nang. I had allowed the trip, knowing that she would not leave the city. I asked her to lunch at my home, and she met my treasured Siamese, Mai Thai. When she reported to me upon the conclusion of her visit, this lovely lady, a calm, competent professional, asked if I would like her to take Mai Thai to Saigon with her, so I would not have to bring her myself when I left. Unspoken, but understood between us with that chemistry that sometimes communicates itself between people, particularly women, was the conviction that my own eventual departure might well be disorganized, if not worse. I gratefully accepted her offer, and Mai Thai preceded me to Saigon.

I Backstop Da Nang

The embassy was attempting to provide resources to Da Nang to further the evacuation. The situation deteriorated rapidly. The embassy's mission coordinator, George Jacobson—the man who had been cornered in his residence by a Viet Cong during the Tet offensive—was coordinating relief efforts to Da Nang and also to II Corps, which was also succumbing to North Vietnamese attacks. George consulted with me frequently about the logistical requirements for Da Nang. I ended up helping to backstop the final Da Nang evacuation with George, advising on possible landing sites for helicopters, talking on the phone with an increasingly exhausted Al Francis, and contributing what I could to the effort on the basis of my experience at the post and knowledge of the city. I spent two evenings on Easter weekend, 1975, on the couch in the ambassador's office, snatching a few hours rest between phone calls and consultations with Jacobson. Then it was over. The North Vietnamese overran Da Nang on March 29. Al had left, finally, on a Vietnamese naval vessel. I learned later that General Truong had waded out to make his way to a naval vessel and, exhausted, had been assisted to the boat by some of the ARVN military fleeing with him. He, too, was on his way to Saigon.

Ambassador Martin Returns

Ambassador Martin returned to Saigon just as the evacuation of Da Nang was winding down. I learned later that he had commented in Washington that I had "overreacted," and that he would put things right when he returned. He was still in denial that the decades-old U.S. effort to prevent a Communist government in South Vietnam had failed.

I met with the political counselor, Josiah Bennett, after Da Nang's collapse. I had worked with Bennett when he became director of the Vietnam Working Group in Washington. I told Joe that I did not think the rest of Vietnam could last more than thirty days. I stressed the psychological impact on the general populace of the loss of the imperial capital, Hue, to the North Vietnamese. He quietly agreed.

Arrangements for the Children

I was devastated by the deteriorating situation, and I knew I had made a major commitment to the Truong children. I wanted to confirm that the Truongs still wished me to take the children. I learned that the general was resting at an ARVN military hospital in Saigon. Al told me that the ambassador had forbidden his officers to contact him or other senior ARVN officers without his express permission. I sought an appointment with the ambassador and told him my purpose in wishing to visit the general. Ambassador Martin told me that there were rumors that General Truong was considering a military coup against President Thieu. I recall telling the ambassador, "Unfortunately, sir, he is not the type to do that." Truong was that rare Vietnamese general, a nonpolitical, fighting general. I knew he would never allow himself to participate in such a plan. If startled by my impolitic remark, the ambassador hid it and gave me permission to visit Truong.

It was an emotional meeting. He looked so exhausted and frail in his hospital pajamas. To my surprise, he embraced me; we both knew what he had been through, and what the loss of Da Nang entailed. To my question, he said that he and his wife were most appreciative of my willingness to take their children. I said that I would try to get them visas if he could give me their passports. He said that President Thieu had visited him, and he had told Thieu that the only thing he wanted was passports for his children. Thieu had promised to provide them.

Meanwhile, I had cabled my brother Bob and his wife Ann and asked if I could send them three children for whom I was assuming responsibility. Bob was a retired naval carrier pilot, supportive of our efforts in Vietnam. Bob and Ann had a large family of their own (nine children), all but two of whom were adults. They were comfortable financially, and lived in a lovely, large house in the country on Whidbey Island, Washington. They had on one occasion hosted a teenager from Colombia under Rotary Club auspices, so I knew they would be comfortable hosting "my" children until I could return to the States and claim them. I did not know when I would have to leave Vietnam—Ambassador Martin was becoming concerned about the deleterious effects that the presence of saddened American personnel from the now closed consulates general were having on embassy morale—and I wanted to ensure that if I left before the children, they could be sent directly to Bob and Ann's safe haven.

Bob and Ann responded immediately that they would, of course, accept the children. I told them I was going to abandon my planned two-month trip with Betty Price and would return directly to the States to claim the children as soon as they arrived in Washington State. Bob insisted that I take my trip. He said that my life would be changing in unimagined ways by suddenly becoming a single mother, and I should take and enjoy the trip while I could. The children would be fine with him and Ann and their two children who remained at home. Betty was already in Saigon, and I decided to accept this kind and generous offer.

Visas for the Children

President Thieu kept his commitment, and General Truong received passports for the three children they were surrendering to me: Trinh, fifteen years old; Tri, eleven; and Tram, nine. Trinh and Tram were girls, Tri a boy. I had met the Truongs' three-year-old son, Thien, briefly, and was willing to take him too, but Mrs. Truong was reluctant to part with her youngest, her baby, and also thought that the three children would be enough for me to handle.

Vietnamese passports in hand, I called on our consul general in Saigon. I explained that I was planning to take the three children to the United States to care for as my own. If the situation in Vietnam should improve, they would return and rejoin their parents. In the meantime, I would be completely responsible for their care and expenses; they would not become a public charge. The consul general said quietly that this sounded like B-2 (visitor) visas to him. With much gratitude, I left the passports with him for processing.

I met with the Truongs and the children at their Saigon home on a Sunday afternoon. I had prepared a letter I wanted both parents to sign, giving me custody of the children. I also gave them a letter listing my brother's name, address, and other particulars. When flight arrangements were made, the Truongs were to inform Bob and Ann, who would meet the children in Seattle.

I had seen the children briefly on a couple of occasions in Da Nang. After dinner at the Truongs, the children had emerged and played beautifully on the piano, particularly the two girls. They had bowed to the guests' applause and withdrew. Now these three children in front of me were soon to be mine. They were very attractive and polite, and spoke no English. They would undertake this journey into the unknown because their parents wished them to do so. It would be a wondrous experience for all of us, in many ways.

Mrs. Truong and I discussed details: what should she pack for the children? I said she should not pack many clothes, as the children would want to acquire American clothes. I did say they should bring warm sweaters, as it was chilly in Washington State. Mrs. Truong subsequently knit each of the children a heavy sweater. Her packing, I learned later from my brother and sister-in-law, was exquisitely thoughtful. She had included a Vietnamese-English dictionary, some favorite Vietnamese language books, the children's music books, some recordings of Vietnamese music, a couple of treasured Chinese-style bowls, some jewelry for the girls, and other items to help the children remember their heritage.

I was ordered to leave Saigon before the children got out. I left in the middle of April. I was able, before leaving, to ship Mai Thai on Pan-American Airlines to my brother Jay in New Jersey. I was devastated by the fast-moving developments, and decided to proceed to Pattaya, a seaside resort in southern Thailand, for a few days' rest. Betty Price decided to remain in Saigon a few days longer to keep her USAID friend company until she, too, was ordered to depart. We agreed to meet in Bangkok to finalize our plans for our trip.

My time in Pattaya was spent, I realized at the time, in mourning for all that was lost in Vietnam. I was completely disheartened that the United States had abandoned its ally after persuading the South Vietnamese to accept a flawed peace agreement, with promises we probably knew we would not be able to keep. I was deeply saddened that the 50,000-plus U.S. lives and the hundreds of thousands of Vietnamese lives lost in Vietnam, on both sides of the conflict, had only resulted in what would be a despotic Communist regime. I worried about the fate of the Vietnamese officials who could not escape the country; I feared another Hue Tet-style massacre. I spent some time by the pool, reflecting on all that had occurred during my time in Saigon, in Washington working the issue, and in Da Nang. I wept.

6

A Memorable Journey to Foster Parenthood and a New Assignment

Betty and I embarked on our trip with heavy hearts. At various stops, I checked at U.S. embassies for information about the fate of Vietnam. From phone calls with my brother Bob, I was relieved to learn that the three children with whom I had been entrusted had safely reached Oak Harbor, Washington. When the final collapse of Saigon came, I cabled an offer to sponsor General Truong and his wife for residence in the United States. The situation was uncertain for a time. Then I learned through my contacts that various U.S. military officers had come forward to offer their sponsorship. Ultimately, it was Lieutenant General Cushman, then commandant of the Command and General Staff College at Fort Leavenworth, Kansas, who extracted General Truong, his wife, and two remaining sons from refugee camps. Once I learned that they were accounted for, I settled in more comfortably for a most interesting trip.

The Trip Begins

After recuperation time in Thailand, Betty and I set off for a few days in Burma (Myanmar). A friend of mine, Matt Ward, was consul in Mandalay, and after visiting Rangoon we flew north, checked into a hotel, and went to call on him. Matt insisted that we move out of the hotel into his lovely residence immediately. A friend of his, a prince of the Karen people of Burma, was also visiting, and he took us around beautiful Mandalay. It was a delightful respite.

The morning of our arrival, Matt informed us, other Foreign Service friends had headed downriver by ferryboat to Pagan (now Bagan), an ancient site along the Irrawaddy River known for its proliferation of thousand-year-old Buddhist temples. Betty and I were already booked to fly there, and we were happy to link up when we arrived with my other Foreign Service friends, who were visiting from their station in the Philippines. Pagan was fascinating—a flat plain alongside the river, dotted with what seemed to be hundreds of ancient temples and stupas. A year or so later, massive floods destroyed many of these temples; we were fortunate to have visited when we did.

The Taj Mahal

From Burma we flew to New Delhi, where we hired a car and driver to take us down to Agra to visit the Taj Mahal, an exquisite mausoleum built by Mughal emperor Shah Jahan in memory of his third wife, Mumtaz Mahal. It was a few hours' trip from the airport by car; because we wanted to see the Taj by moonlight, we booked an overnight stay. We were again very fortunate—we did see this marvelous monument to love by the light of a full moon. I had wanted to see the Taj Mahal because it was on everyone's list of the wonders of the world, but I had no idea that it was as beautiful as it actually is. This is no mere tourist attraction; in the understated words of the *Michelin Guide,* it is "worth a journey."

From Agra, we returned to New Delhi for a couple of days. We found it terribly hot and, to our uneducated eyes, unnoteworthy. We were more than ready to leave for our visit to Kashmir, the small mountain redoubt that was the subject of a territorial dispute between India and Pakistan. It was then in Indian hands, although Pakistan claimed it, and the Kashmiris themselves most likely would have opted for independence.

A Houseboat in Kashmir

Again, we were fortunate to visit when we did. I had heard about the delights of staying on a houseboat on Dal Lake, a huge body of water in Srinagar, Kashmir, and that is what we did for close to a week. It was a Shangri-La existence, peaceful, beautiful, pampered, far removed from the horrors of the lost war I had recently left behind. It was not high season for the houseboats, so we had ours to ourselves. We each had our own small room, with a tiny shared bath. There was a pleasant little dining room for lunch and dinner. But the place where we stayed most was on the deck, in comfortable lounge chairs, with elaborate rugs if we wished to use them to fend off the chill. Our maître d', who cooked and took excellent care of our every need, brought steaming cups of tea to the deck for us. We sipped the tea and drank in the view of the blue lake and the surrounding snow-capped mountains while we waited for breakfast to be served.

Throughout the day, boats visited us offering lovely wares for sale. I bought several beautiful embroidered cashmere shawls from one vendor. We went into town one afternoon for sightseeing and jewelry shopping, where I bought some unset stones. Most proved to be just fine, but one alleged sapphire ring I bought was subsequently found to be fake. The tiny diamonds surrounding it, however, proved to be worth the purchase price of the ring.

We took a few other brief excursions throughout the valley and on the lake, but nothing too elaborate. Principally, we relaxed in one of the most beautiful spots in the world, totally indulged by our maître d'. It was a memorable interlude. In recent years, serious fighting has broken out in Kashmir between India, Pakistan, and Kashmiri rebels, turning Srinagar, with its gorgeous lake and mountains, into a war zone.

An African Photo Safari

From Kashmir, we flew to Bombay. The following morning we were to fly to Nairobi, where we planned to take a photo safari of African game parks. Our hotel was nice, but in general we did not like what we saw of Bombay, a large, dirty, overpopulated city. Foolishly, Betty and I decided that we would go to mass before leaving for our morning flight to Kenya, so we left before dawn to walk the several blocks from the hotel to a Catholic church for a 6:30 a.m. mass. We literally had to step over dormant bodies on the streets, some of which I doubted would ever move again. The sidewalks and streets near the curbs were filled with people sleeping, and worse. We were approached by beggars but refused to respond. We made it safely to church, but acknowledged that we had taken an unnecessary risk in doing so—two unescorted Western women, walking those tortured streets before daylight.

We arrived in Nairobi in late afternoon and checked into the Hilton Hotel, where I called a Foreign Service friend, Kay Gilstrap, who was concluding her assignment in Nairobi. She invited us to join her and some friends right away for dinner, after which, before dusk fell, they took us to a wildlife park on the outskirts of Nairobi. I was excited to encounter giraffes ambling at will as we drove around the preserve.

The next day we went to the embassy to follow up on my inquiries concerning the Truongs, where I met another Foreign Service friend, a woman who had entered the service with me in 1963, Gwen Coronway. She wanted us to move out of the Hilton and stay with her. (Foreign Service hospitality is commonplace— we hadn't stayed with Kay only because she was moving out of her apartment the day after we arrived.) We declined, as we would be leaving on a safari in a day or so, but at her urging, we agreed to stay with her upon our return from the safari. Kay and Gwen recommended a travel agency the embassy had found reliable, and we arranged our trip through it.

We engaged our own car with a driver/guide. We took off on a seven-day trip that proved even better in reality than it had been in my imagination—for years, I had dreamed of visiting the great game parks of Africa. The vastness of the Great Rift Valley; the beauty of the plains; the magic of seeing huge herds of gazelles, zebras, wildebeests, and elephants thundering freely across the plains; the sight of lions casually lounging in the sun with their mates and cubs, one young adult draped across the branch of a dead tree; a leopard darting in and out of sight in a wadi; the beautiful array of colorful birds—these sights combined to make a truly incredible journey. And at day's end, a comfortable game lodge would suddenly materialize, and we would be plied with good food, good drink, and the amenities one would expect in a major city—how delightful!

I don't recall our complete itinerary. I know we crossed the Serengeti and visited the incredible Ngorongoro Crater. En route to the Ngorongoro Crater, our car experienced its second flat tire; a previous flat had required the use of the spare, which now, of course, was also flat. We had not seen a car on the road the entire day. Our capable driver/guide seemed concerned, but calm. Betty and I, experienced travelers (or oblivious ones, perhaps) settled down on a blanket under one of the few trees near the road and awaited rescue. Time passed. To our fascination, a group of Masai warriors and their families and cattle approached us. We found these tall, thin, dignified people, with their arresting attire and beadwork, fascinating. Our guide was less delighted than we with their presence. He spoke with them and encouraged them to keep some distance between them and us. We then heard the unique barking of hyenas, and saw a group of these unpopular animals a hundred yards or so from us. This disturbed our guide, prompting him to reassure us that he was confident a car would come and get us out of our predicament long before nightfall, when, even as I knew, the hyenas could be a real problem.

Saved by the arrival of a car! After a couple of hours under our tree, a small car made its way over the lonely road. Our guide waved it to a stop. The occupants were an elderly American couple who were wending their own way, *sans* guide, on a safari to some of the major game parks. They kindly welcomed us, and our guide took over the driving, which at times was quite difficult—when crossing not quite dry streambeds, for example. We were moving along nicely when this car, too, got a flat tire, doubtless caused by the rough road. Our host was grateful that our strong driver/guide was with him to change the tire—he said he had not thought about that detail, and doubted that he would have been able to do it.

On our way again, we finally pulled into the lodge at the rim of the Ngorongoro Crater after nightfall. We were relieved to see an oasis of civilization again. Our driver, poor man, arranged to return to our abandoned car with the means to replace the damaged tire and to retrieve our luggage, which he had left locked in the trunk. I think he gave the Masai some presents for looking after it in our absence.

Betty and I checked into our cabin, freshened up, and prepared to go to the main lodge for drinks and dinner. As we were leaving, we saw a notice on the wall of our room saying that to go to the lodge after dark, we should call the desk for an escort. We could see the main lodge from our front door, and decided that we could find it on our own.

We enjoyed a good meal and a couple of drinks, and began to leave the lodge to return to our cabin. A lodge employee stopped us, and called for an escort. We said it wasn't necessary, that we could see our cabin clearly. But he insisted, and our escort, a small African carrying a large pole, led the way back to our cabin. En route, I asked him why he had to escort us. "Because of the buffalo," he said. "What buffalo?" I asked. He turned his flashlight on and pointed it down the incline by the side of the road. Dozens of pairs of large eyes gleamed in the night. The African buffalo, we were told, is a very ferocious animal. The next night we called for an escort before going to dinner.

We thoroughly enjoyed our African adventure, which incorporated game parks in both Kenya and Tanzania. Upon our return to Nairobi, we accepted Gwen's invitation and stayed in her lovely apartment a few days, relaxing, seeing a movie or two, enjoying her company, and generally recharging our batteries.

Egypt: Cairo, Pyramids, and Memphis

Our next stop was Cairo to see the Pyramids. We had been hesitant about including Egypt on our itinerary, as U.S.–Egyptian relations had been sour under Nasser and were only recently beginning to improve. Still, how could you make a trip around the world and not see the Pyramids? We were glad we had overcome our qualms. We were warmly received at the airport, where the officials had not seen too many U.S. travelers in recent years. Our taxi driver was delighted to have Americans in his cab again, he said. Throughout our brief stay (three nights), we were treated well. We enjoyed seeing the Pyramids—I had not realized that they were so close to Cairo. Our hotel was a small *pensione*-type place, comfortable but not as conveniently located as we might have wished, so we spent a fair amount of time at a large old hotel on the banks of the Nile—a classic hotel of the British era, which still had tremendous charm. Its rooftop restaurant offered fine views of the Pyramids. We booked our tours from this hotel, and used it as our home away from home.

The main Cairo museum was dusty, but offered a treasure trove of Egyptian artifacts.

At the Pyramids, we were offered the opportunity to climb down into one of them, to see the paintings on the walls of the tomb. Betty, who was much shorter than I, scrambled down. With my height and claustrophobia, I passed on this adventure. I also declined to mount one of the ubiquitous camels offered to tourists for rides.

We also took a day trip to Memphis, where I did enter some tombs to see the ancient hieroglyphics on the walls. I learned more about Egypt's interesting past. At the conclusion of our brief stay in Cairo, Betty and I agreed that we should have allocated more time to this most interesting country. But we were awaited in Tehran, where my good friend Liz White was working with the USIA.

A Friend in Iran

Liz made us most welcome. Her house was lovely. After being on the road for several weeks, it was relaxing to settle in once more to an American home. During our exploration of Teheran, Betty and I had dinner at a hotel near the mountains on the edge of the city. The city impressed us—I particularly remember being awed by the Iranian crown jewels—and we generally found Teheran to be an attractive, interesting place. We had planned to visit Isfahan and Shiraz, cities noted for beautiful mosques, but changed our minds. Betty had visited these cities several years before, and I could not work up the necessary enthusiasm to leave our comfortable accommodations to travel alone to these places—I could always come back, I thought. This was a mistake; a few years later, the Islamic Revolution took over Iran and turned it into a place hostile to Americans and inhospitable to women.

Greece, London, and Home

From Iran, we flew to Greece, where we spent a delightful several days, principally in Athens, from which we took day trips to such places as Delphi. We also took a ferry to Mykonos, a beautiful island of white buildings, and spent a couple of nights there to give us the flavor of the Greek Islands. We thoroughly enjoyed Greece. The last stop on our journey was London, where we spent a couple of days enjoying the theater and the wonderful street life of that great city before bidding each other farewell. I crossed the Atlantic Ocean, completing the trip around the world that I had begun in August 1973, when I crossed the Pacific to take up my post in Da Nang.

I Become a Single Mother

I learned en route home that General and Mrs. Truong had made it safely to the United States. I knew, however, that they would need assistance making a life for themselves and their children in the United States. General Truong had a reputation for being an honest, incorruptible general—an unfortunate rarity among Vietnamese generals. I knew that my instincts about him were correct, and that there would be no Swiss bank accounts at his disposal. He and his family had gotten out of Vietnam with very little more than the clothes on their backs. They needed help, which I assumed would be forthcoming now from General Cushman, who had become General Truong's sponsor.

When I arrived back in the States, I called General Cushman to make arrangements, I thought, to transfer the three Truong children staying temporarily with Bob and Ann in Washington State to his care, inasmuch as he had sponsored the general and his family. I assumed that as a three-star general, his income would be more than sufficient to take on the entire Truong family, and I surmised that he would be better situated than I to help find suitable work for the Vietnamese general to help him settle into life in the United States.

General Cushman explained, however, that he had seven children, two or three of whom were currently in college. He fully intended to help General Truong, but he did not see his way clear to taking custody of the three children I had spoken for. In addition, he said that General Truong was eager to see these children in my care. He invited me to visit with them all at his residence at Fort Leavenworth, and I agreed to do so on my way to Oak Harbor to attend the wedding of my niece, Susie. The children at Bob and Ann's were excited about the wedding, and wanted to stay for it.

I accepted General Cushman's invitation. General Truong's

warm reaction when we met again, and his manifest gratitude that I had gotten his children out of Vietnam, made it clear that I should keep the children, not General Cushman. Cushman ultimately took the Truong's oldest son, Diep, into his household for a year or more of schooling, and together with other U.S. generals helped General Truong find initial employment with the Defense Department writing historical accounts of aspects of the Vietnam War. I proceeded to Oak Harbor for the wedding, in the meantime getting acquainted with my three children, whom I had seen only at a distance on two or three occasions, and generally briefly, as they played the piano for their parents' guests.

The children had settled beautifully into Bob and Ann's warm and loving household. Trinh, a lovely fifteen-year-old, was the leader, and the other two accepted her leadership. Tri, aged eleven, was a good-looking boy who rarely smiled but seemed content. Tram, a diminutive nine years old, was a China doll beauty and a near prodigy on the piano. All of the children had studied piano. Trinh played beautifully, and Tri played at it, but Tram's talent was exceptional and gave great pleasure to Bob and Ann, and later, to me.

A Fearless Solo Journey

I learned that the children had left Saigon on a Pan American flight technically under the wing of a foreign national, a former CIA employee. The impression I got from the children, however, was that they were very much on their own. They changed planes in Honolulu and arrived at the Seattle airport late at night. Bob and Ann were there to meet them, armed with a letter from me and also signed by the general authorizing them to claim the children. But these children simply got off the airplane and Bob and Ann spotted them and assumed they were the three charges they had come to pick up. Anyone could have collected the children, apparently; there was no supervisory presence at all.

Bob and Ann took the children home to Oak Harbor, about a two-hour drive from the airport, arriving at their large, comfortable home about 2:00 a.m. As Bob and Ann told it, Tram spotted their piano immediately and climbed up on the bench and began playing

Beethoven beautifully. Tri discovered their television set, and Bob and Ann obligingly turned it on and let him enjoy it as the three children wound down from their adventure. Thoughtfully, Bob and Ann put all three children in one large bedroom for company, to lessen the strangeness, although the house had bedrooms enough for each to have a private room. This arrangement worked nicely, and was continued throughout the children's approximately three-month stay in Oak Harbor.

The next day, Bob and Ann took the children shopping and got them warm down jackets, blue jeans, and other essentials of a child's life in the United States. The three settled in quickly, aided, I am sure, by the cool-headed Trinh's confident acceptance of their new life. Ann told me that the morning after their arrival, she found Trinh in the kitchen, attempting to prepare breakfast. Apparently, her mother had told her not to be a burden on her host, to pitch in and make herself useful.

The children's introduction to the United States was eased by the fact that two of my brother's nine children, teenagers Chris and Anne, were still living at home. They readily accepted the children. Trinh was soon riding Anne's prized horse. Tri enjoyed riding Bob's tractor-type lawn mower. And they all were looking forward to the wedding of older sister Susie, planned for the early summer.

In the middle of one night in late April, the household was awakened by a telephone call from Guam. It was the children's mother, who had been airlifted out of Saigon in the massive effort by the U.S. defense attaché's office to evacuate Vietnamese who had been closely identified with the U.S. effort in Vietnam. The children were ecstatic to hear their mother's voice and to know that she was safe. Subsequently, they learned that their father, too, had made it out of Vietnam.

Vice President Ky's Intervention

When I agreed to take the children to the United States, it was with the understanding that they would be mine forever if their parents did not make it out of Vietnam. Knowing General Truong's dedication to his duty, I did not think he would leave. If he stayed behind, I assumed the North Vietnamese would execute him. I was making a lifetime commitment to those children. It was with great joy that I learned that the Truongs had escaped, for their sake and for the children's.

After President Thieu had fled the country, he was replaced by General Duong Van ("Big") Minh, the coup leader with whom I had initiated embassy contact after his return from exile in Thailand; Senator Nguyen Van Huyen, my dear friend, agreed to stay as vice president. This interim government, however, lasted only a week, abolished when the North Vietnamese took over the city. After the chairman of the Joint Chiefs of Staff, General Cao Van Vien, left Vietnam, General Truong was the most senior military officer left in the country. He attempted to make plans for the final defense of Saigon with the fragments of the Vietnamese military that remained.

On April 30, 1975, as the North Vietnamese tanks were beginning to roll into Saigon, General Truong told me, Vice President Nguyen Cao Ky went to military headquarters and, in effect, ordered Truong to leave the country with him. He said that he had a place on his helicopter for Truong, and that the American ambassador, Graham Martin, was at that very moment leaving the country—in short, it was over and Truong must leave. Truong accepted this as an order and boarded the helicopter, which Vice President Ky flew directly to the U.S. destroyer *Blue Ridge*, which was accepting refugees off the coast of Vietnam. Without Ky's intervention, I am confident that General Truong would have remained in Saigon, to either face execution or prolonged detention in a so-called reeducation camp.

I Find a Washington Home

The children and I thoroughly enjoyed Susie's wedding, and our few days together made us much better acquainted. Bob and Ann insisted that the children should stay with them until I had found a suitable home for us all in Washington. At that point, I owned a one-bedroom apartment in Foggy Bottom that was within convenient walking distance of the State Department, but it couldn't accommodate the four of us. I continued to rent it out, which paid the mortgage. I found and rented a large, homey, unpretentious house in northwestern Washington, on Ellicott Street, just off

Wisconsin Avenue a few blocks from the Maryland border. I got my belongings out of storage and set about replacing the goods I had lost in Vietnam (my household effects never made it out of Da Nang). I bought beds and linens for the children, dishes, kitchen equipment, and so on. When the house was ready, Bob and Ann put the three saddened Truong children—once again these youngsters were being thrust into the virtually unknown—on a plane to Washington.

The children loved Bob and Ann and their life in Oak Harbor, but they quickly adapted themselves to life in our house in Washington. I did not want to leave the children alone all day while I worked, so I invited a couple of nieces and nephews, in shifts, to come stay with us in Washington. This kept the children company and continued their introduction to the ways of teenage Americans. Michael McLane, my sister Hazel's sixteen-year-old son, came down from Pennsylvania for two weeks, as did Mary Tull, my brother Charles's daughter from South Bend, Indiana. The young people got along very well together.

English Lessons

The children had made good progress in learning English during their three months in the United States. Their mother had given them an excellent Vietnamese-English dictionary, which they consulted regularly to help make themselves understood. I initiated English drills, which we tackled after dinner, based loosely on the Foreign Service Institute method of language study. I would hold up various objects and say, for example, "I have two pencils," and then ask the children, in rapid succession, to correct my statement by substituting the appropriate word— "three," perhaps, or "books," depending on the context.. They caught on quickly and enjoyed the game. One evening I was tired and said we could skip the drills, but they asked if we could do it anyway.

I Find a School

I had hoped to enroll the younger children at St. Ann's elementary school, which was just a few blocks from our home. Trinh, I thought, could be admitted to a Catholic high school in the general area. My inquiry at St. Ann's proved fruitless, however; the school was fully booked, apparently, and administrators were not inclined to make any exceptions or reduce the tuition for three Vietnamese refugee children. I was reluctant to enroll them in the public school system. As I was grappling with this problem, I came across an article in the *Washington Post* reporting on the efforts of Gaetana Enders, wife of FSO Thomas Enders, who had been deputy chief of mission at our embassy in Cambodia, to assist Cambodian refugees. The article mentioned that Mrs. Enders was on the board of trustees of the Washington International School.

I called the somewhat flamboyant lady (she was minor Italian royalty, and played the part) and told her about the children's and their father's background, and our current situation. I explained my desire to get the children enrolled in a good, safe school, and told her that my finances were limited to the salary I was earning as a midlevel FSO. Mrs. Enders was immediately responsive. She said she would call the International School on my behalf. Not long thereafter, I was called by the principal of the school, who agreed to take all three children and to charge the faculty rate for their tuition, a substantial savings over the regular tuition. I took the children to meet her, and we agreed to begin some intensive English language lessons at the school before the beginning of the school year.

Thus began the children's most enjoyable, fruitful experience at the Washington International School. Not only was this a fine school, it was also just a short bus ride away, followed by a walk of several blocks through a good neighborhood near the Washington Cathedral. The school offered instruction for kindergarteners through high school seniors. This meant that all three children went to the same school, leaving home at the same time in the mornings, shortly before I left for the State Department, and returning home about 4:30 p.m.; they were alone only until I arrived home at 6:15 p.m. I instructed them to always return from school together. If one of them had an after-school activity, the others were to do homework in the library or otherwise occupy themselves until the time when all three could undertake the homeward journey together. (Ignorance is bliss—the children were so good that I only learned several years later, through their amused confession, that they occasionally observed this instruction in the breach.)

Shortly after the children arrived from Washington State, my sisters Betty and Hazel, eager to meet the children, brought my well-traveled Siamese cat to Washington, D.C. They kept Mai Thai on a leash until I returned home from work. When I released her, she made a thorough inspection of the house and found it to her liking, making herself immediately at home. She also took easily to the children, as if she had always lived in a busy household. Trinh, and particularly Tri, were very fond of Mai Thai; Tram liked her, but was disinclined to hold her. When we all adjourned to our little family room at the rear of the house to watch television, however, they all urged Mai Thai to choose their lap from which to enjoy the show. She was an equal opportunity pleaser, bestowing her favors whimsically—and occasionally, on weekend nights when bedtime was later, seemingly attempting to encourage an earlier bedtime by leaving the room, heading for the stairs, and returning, disappointed, when no one followed her to bed. We all believed she made a beautiful, delightful addition to our household.

The Good Doctor

I encountered several kind people during the course of caring for the children. To enter them into school, I had to arrange physical examinations. I chose a doctor on the State Department's recommended list who lived in our general part of the city, made the appointment, and took the three children to the doctor's office. I did not seek favors from him, but simply said they needed physicals to enter school. He was quietly intrigued to learn that this young woman was presenting three Vietnamese refugee children for examination. Was I married? No. Did I have health insurance for the children? No. They were my foster children, I said, and they could not be covered under my health insurance. How had I acquired custody? I explained that I had been in Da Nang at the collapse and knew their father.

The doctor examined all three children and gave me certificates of their good health for the school. When I inquired about the bill, he said that he would make a deal with me: if I promised to call him the moment any of the children got sick, without fail, he would treat them without charge. But I had to promise that I would not hold back on any needed care. I accepted this kind offer immediately. He said that he had been troubled by the fall of Vietnam and had been wondering how he could be of help, and I had presented him with an opportunity. He also insisted that I should come to him if I got ill, and directed me to begin taking a strong multivitamin pill myself because the children would be bringing home germs to which I, as a single woman, had not been regularly exposed.

I deeply appreciated this kind offer. My finances were stretched as it was, having added three children to my household, and it was an unexpected relief to know that I had good medical care available for the children, if needed. Fortunately, they enjoyed good health, but I did have to take Tram to him once for a stomach ailment, and later he helped Trinh with an eye infection. After treating it himself, he asked me to take her to a specialist to follow up his treatment. This specialist also declined to give me a bill for his services.

I enjoyed the children, and we grew close. After a few months, their parents relocated to Falls Church, Virginia, when the general was engaged by the Defense Department. They rented a small apartment for themselves and their oldest and youngest children, Diep and Thien. It was reassuring to me to know that they were nearby. We saw them frequently. One afternoon is burned deep into my memory, and gives ample evidence of why these people merited assistance. I was invited to a wedding of a Foreign Service friend, and was reluctant to leave the children alone for the afternoon and evening. The Truongs agreed to come over while I was gone. While I was dressing for the wedding, I heard the sound of a lawn mower; it was General Truong, mowing our small front yard. When I came downstairs, Mrs. Truong was on her hands and knees, scrubbing our kitchen floor. They had come from the top of one society to the virtual bottom of another. They were a class act, accepting their fate with dignity and determination. Before long, Mrs. Truong studied to be a hairdresser and worked for several years at this profession. General Truong, upon the completion of his Defense Department assignment, studied computer operations, and he gradually rose through the ranks of that field, from operator to systems analyst.

The children were "my children" for two full years, during which time the Truongs settled into their new lives and jobs. When my two-year tour in Washington was completed in 1977, the children rejoined their parents, who were now better able to provide for them. I continued to pay tuition at the International School for the children. Trinh and Tri graduated from there. Transportation became a problem (Falls Church to Northwest Washington is awkward to manage by public transportation), so Tram transferred to a high school in Northern Virginia when she completed the eighth grade; she did well there. I also paid for Tram's piano lessons, which the other two children had discontinued. It was hard to leave them, but in fact, I did not. They remained, and remain, a wonderful part of my life. Thanks to them, I am the only single woman I know who has five grandchildren—three children of Trinh's and two of Tram's. Tri married only in April 2005, and has not yet made a contribution to this cause.

I Become an Intelligence Analyst

When I was first assigned to be an analyst of Southeast Asian developments in the State Department's Bureau of Intelligence and Research (INR), I was very disappointed. I would have preferred a more action-oriented position over a heavily analytical one. As events unrolled in Vietnam, however, and I accepted responsibility for the three children, the INR assignment looked increasingly like the type of job a brand-new single mother of three should have. I could count on the hours being more or less regular, within the normal eight-hour workday, with occasional early morning and Saturday work. But I was reasonably confident that at day's end I could leave the department at a reasonable hour—before 7:00 or 8:00 p.m., that is, as had frequently been the case when I had worked with the Vietnam Working Group. Fortunately, I was right.

My portfolio in INR was limited to the Philippines, Australia, New Zealand, and the South Pacific islands.

As it developed, the INR assignment proved worthwhile. I had to focus on the big picture, drafting extensive analyses of Southeast Asian issues, rather than dealing with the daily crises faced by a State country desk officer. For example, I prepared a detailed assessment of the Soviet Union's attempt to penetrate the South Pacific, including efforts to obtain fishing rights and deeper relations with some smaller states, in an area of previously almost exclusive American influence. I also produced studies on the Muslim insurgency in the Philippines, among other issues. This work sharpened my analytical and drafting skills, and it taught me to cull through large quantities of daily intelligence reports each morning, to select the key items that I would take to the East Asia and Pacific bureau, where I daily briefed a deputy assistant secretary. (On weekend duty, I briefed the assistant secretary.) These officials frequently solicited my opinion about developments and the possible policy implications of the intelligence I was reporting. These encounters broadened my contacts in the bureau, in which I hoped to spend the bulk of my Foreign Service career.

The work also introduced me to the broader U.S. intelligence community—including the CIA, the Defense Intelligence Agency, and the National Security Agency. We officers in INR often drafted terse intelligence items, which were included in the nightly reading sent to the president or in his daily briefing notes. My bosses in INR were seasoned professionals, both civil service and Foreign Service, and although demanding were pleasant to work with. The two years passed quickly; I settled comfortably into the work and into my role as foster mother to three fine children.

My Service in Vietnam Recognized

Al Francis felt strongly that the work of those of us in Da Nang who had organized and run the massive evacuation deserved recognition. He encountered strong resistance from Ambassador Graham Martin, who told Al he did not believe in rewarding "failure." Al persisted, however. He asked me to write nominations for awards for two of the officers who had worked for me in Da Nang, Gerald Scott and David Harr. Al nominated me. Nothing was heard, and I assumed the matter was a dead issue.

Jimmy Carter was about to be inaugurated as president of the United States in late January 1977. My brother Charles was planning to fly in to spend a couple of days with me to attend the inauguration, for which I had obtained standing-room tickets on the Capitol grounds. Two days before the inauguration, on a bitter, snowy, morning, I received a phone call at my desk in INR. "Miss Tull, there is going to be an award ceremony about Vietnam in

the secretary's office this afternoon at 2:00 p.m. You are invited."
I thanked the caller for the information, but inwardly noted that I
was busy and might not attend.

A couple of hours later, the same person called. "Miss Tull, I
don't think I mentioned that you will be receiving an award this
afternoon from the secretary. You are welcome to bring your family
with you."

I was annoyed at the lack of notice. Given the snowy condition
of the streets, I hesitated to get the children out of school, doubting
that I could arrange for a taxi to bring them to the department. And
Charles, who would have loved the event, was coming in the very
next day. With a little advance notice, some of my brothers and
sisters in New Jersey and Pennsylvania might well have opted to
come down for the ceremony. But it was now about noon, and I
was due in the secretary's office at 2:00 p.m. I managed to convince
a nearby hair salon to fit me in so that at least my hair would look
good for the occasion.

Secretary of State Henry Kissinger spoke warmly to the half
dozen or so of us gathered in his office. He praised our efforts ef-
fusively. In speaking about the fall of Vietnam, his voice broke, and
tears were clearly visible in his eyes. This man had won the Nobel
Peace Prize for his negotiation of the Vietnam Paris Peace Agreement, concluded just four years before this date. Witnessing his
emotion on this occasion made me suspect, despite my cynicism,
that he had not anticipated the total withdrawal of U.S. support,
and the massive invasion of the North Vietnamese armed forces,
that had put an ignominious end to the decades-long effort to prevent South Vietnam from being taken over by a Communist regime.

For my work in developing and organizing the evacuation of the
consulate general in Da Nang, I was presented with a Meritorious
Honor Award. I welcomed having my work recognized, but the
level of the award itself was disappointing. Al had nominated me
for a Superior Honor Award, which ranks above the award I was
given. But I appreciated the effort that Al had expended to persuade
the ambassador to accede to even this level of award (although the
male officers were more generously recognized). Several years
later, a feisty female FSO brought a lawsuit against the department
alleging, with some justification, discrimination against women

officers. The suit noted, among other things, that female FSOs had been slighted in the distribution of service awards. I joined the suit, which the plaintiffs won, and my award was upgraded to the more appropriate Superior Honor Award, which now hangs in my den. The department belatedly added a small cash token (under $300) to the award. But it took a lawsuit. Still, I did receive the initial award from the hands of the secretary himself, and the photo marking the occasion also hangs in my den.

Charles arrived the next day, chagrined to learn that he had just missed the ceremony. He was present in the State Department lobby, however, when Secretary Kissinger bade an emotional farewell to the department, which compensated somewhat for missing the award ceremony. And we enjoyed the Carter inauguration the next day. My brother Jay joined us in the afternoon to watch the inaugural parade.

Papua New Guinea; Senators Mansfield and Glenn

My responsibilities in INR included being the analyst for the Philippines, Australia, New Zealand, and the Pacific Island nations. A highlight of the assignment was the opportunity afforded me to visit my "parish" for a nearly four-week tour. General Truong, by that time established in Falls Church, came to our home and stayed with the children while I was away.

My trip included stops in the Philippines, Australia, and Papua New Guinea. In Papua New Guinea, I had the pleasure of spending a few days in the company of Senator Mike Mansfield of Montana and Senator John Glenn of Ohio, the first U.S. astronaut to orbit the Earth. When I landed in Papua New Guinea, I discovered that our very small embassy was at that exact same time hosting a visit by Senator Mansfield, the outgoing Senate majority leader, and Senator Glenn. The embassy did not have the staff to arrange completely separate schedules for both of our visits, so to the extent feasible I was folded into the senators' schedule. I attended all of their embassy briefings and social events, including a dinner hosted by the prime minister of Papua New Guinea.

Both senators were excellent representatives of Congress and of their country. They asked pertinent questions at the embassy briefings, and clearly were interested in the answers. They knew where they were and what the issues were for the fledgling country, only recently independent. This attitude was in marked contrast to some congressional delegations I encountered during my thirty-three years with State—some of these visitors were clearly bored and seemed interested chiefly in what exotic shopping might be available in the country they were honoring with their presence.

Mansfield and Glenn were interested, pleasant, and courteous, and they treated me as an equal colleague. I valued my exposure to these fine gentlemen. Although Mansfield was by far the more important of the two in terms of congressional power, for the people of Papua New Guinea, John Glenn was the star. Young people lined the roads as we traveled from point to point, waving and cheering, "John Glenn!" Glenn acknowledged the crowds cheerfully, and the notoriously quiet Mansfield did not seem to mind the attention his junior colleague was receiving.

The life of Senator Mansfield, who died in 2001 after gaining additional distinction as a long-serving U.S. ambassador to Japan, was a remarkable success story. I learned from his obituaries that he had joined the U.S. armed forces during the First World War, and ultimately served in the army, navy, and marine corps. Settling in Montana, his young wife recognized his intellect and encouraged him to go to college. He developed a great interest in Asia, and became a professor of Asian studies in Montana before running for Congress. A Democrat, he was a bitter opponent of the Vietnam War, an issue on which I strongly disagreed with him. But he was universally recognized as a person of staunch integrity. I regard my brief experience with him, and with Senator Glenn, as one of the quiet bonuses of my Foreign Service career.

Next Assignment: Consul in Cebu

In 1977, I was again looking for an onward assignment. I optimistically felt that I was ready to become a deputy chief of mission at a small embassy, which I thought would be excellent training and experience. I managed to make the short list for a few embassies, but the DCM is one of the few positions that (at that time) the ambassador may fill at will, and in that era, when a woman FSO was still a bit of a rarity, I was not selected.

Failing a DCM slot, I wanted to serve in Indonesia, a large country that fascinated me. No luck. I ultimately was selected to serve as consul in Cebu, in the Visayan Islands of the Philippines. This proved to be an interesting and, for the most part, enjoyable experience. Although the post was small, it was *my* post. The embassy was several hundred miles away; I would be largely on my own, with responsibility for monitoring developments and representing the United States in the entire southern half of the extensive Philippine archipelago.

The children rejoined their family, and I prepared to depart for the Philippines. Again, family tragedy intervened. My sister Hazel's daughter Peggy, a high-school Spanish teacher in Tampa, Florida, was gravely ill with breast cancer. I visited her for several days at her home in Tampa, and later during her final hospital stay. As Peggy's situation worsened, I summoned Hazel, who was then at work in Pennsylvania (she couldn't stay with Peggy indefinitely and still keep her job), and told her that she should return immediately to Tampa. She did so, accompanied by her daughter Susan. I bid a last farewell to Peggy, returned to Washington, and departed for Manila. Shortly after my arrival, in mid-August 1977, I was notified that Peggy had died at age twenty-eight after a valiant struggle with the hated disease. I felt that I could not return for the funeral, having done what I could for my beautiful niece while she was living and having said my goodbyes. I opted instead to invite Hazel to visit me in Cebu once she felt up to it. On this sad note, I completed consultations in Manila and flew to Cebu to begin my tour as consul at one of our historically oldest consular offices. A U.S. consular presence in Cebu was begun, I believe, in the late 1790s.

7

Consul in Cebu

Cebu City is situated on the island of Cebu, in the Visayan Islands of the central Philippines. It is a bustling, crowded city of shops, houses, industry (copra processing, beer production), and tourism. The consul's pleasant residence was on a hillside overlooking the city and the sea.

My consular district included all of the islands from the Visayas southward to the tip of the southernmost island, Zamboanga. The many islands of the district each had their distinctive flavor, and I visited most of them during my tenure. The largest island is Mindanao, then—and now—the site of an ongoing Muslim insurgency.

The principal purposes of the consulate were to show the flag; to provide basic consular services, including nonimmigrant visas (all immigrant visas were handled at the embassy in Manila); and to report on political and economic developments in the consular district. As consul, most of the "showing the flag" duties and reporting fell to me; a young vice consul did consular work. When time permitted, he also did some reporting. Eight Filipino nationals worked at the consulate. Marisol Putong, a widow from a distinguished Cebuano family, was an invaluable resource who had guided many fledgling consuls through the intricate protocol of Cebu life. Her family's beachfront home on Mactan Island (where explorer Ferdinand Magellan was killed in battle with native Indians, ending his planned circumnavigation of the globe) provided many Sunday afternoons of beach and snorkeling fun.

There also was a USIS office in Cebu. The USIS officer operated a library and arranged speaking engagements for USIS-sponsored academics, scholars, and occasionally entertainers. The Peace Corps also had a presence in the district; I enjoyed cordial contacts with the director, who was Cebu-based, and with volunteers when they returned to Cebu from the field. The young volunteers welcomed the good meals my excellent cook provided for them on occasion.

As soon as I had made the acquaintance of the principal officials in Cebu, I set out on trips to other islands in the district. Negros Oriental and Negros Occidental were the center of the Philippine sugar industry. I paid an early visit to Bacolod, the capital city on Negros Occidental, where I met officials and toured sugar plantations and centrals (mills). Riding for miles on country roads with sugar cane on both sides of the road dwarfing the car made clear the important role sugar played in the Philippine economy. The contrast between the opulent residences of the sugar plantation owners and the stark poverty of the sugar workers made grimly apparent the vast class differences in that element of Philippine society.

Everywhere I went, I was greeted warmly and plied with huge feasts. The trips provided opportunities for wide-ranging discussions on the political and economic situation with officials, businessmen, clergymen, and private citizens. When in Bacolod, for example, I occasionally met with Bishop Sin (later Cardinal Sin), who subsequently played a major role in the People's Power revolution that forced Marcos from office. It was clear that President Marcos did not enjoy deep support. I visited Leyte on October 20 for the commemoration of MacArthur's liberation of the Philippines, and made several trips to Mindanao. I frequently gave speeches at Rotary and occasionally Kiwanis and Lions Clubs throughout the islands, where, to my bemusement, I would sometimes be introduced as "Our consul from Cebu." There remained a solid underpinning of affection for the United States in the Philippines at that time.

Official Inspection: Will Cebu Be Closed?

I was informed when I initially arrived in Manila that the embassy, and Consulate Cebu, would soon be undergoing an official State

Department inspection. One question the inspectors would be examining closely was whether it was worthwhile, at a time when budget cutbacks were needed, to continue to operate the consulate. I was encouraged to make the best case possible for retaining the consulate.

Preparing for the inspection was arduous and time-consuming, but I was glad that the inspection was coming at the beginning of my tour rather than near the end. Any problems found could not fairly be blamed on me, and I could benefit from recommendations the experienced senior officers would make. Although I felt initially that the massive preparation materials for the inspection did not really apply to a small consulate, I made the decision that my entire staff and I would act on the assumption that they did. We completed everything as thoroughly as possible.

The preparations were complicated by the chargé d'affaires' visit to Cebu the preceding Saturday. He and I differed, it developed, about why Cebu was a post worth keeping. I insisted that the representational aspects of the job had been very time-consuming but worthwhile, but he insisted that all of that could be done by visits from the embassy, and I had to be able to justify the post on the basis of consular output. So I went into the inspection with a somewhat negative outlook, convinced that the purely consular services were only a part of what Cebu was all about.

A team of nine inspectors descended on Manila. The senior inspector, Ambassador Brandon Grove, and two others visited Cebu. Fortunately, they came out exactly where I had on the value of the post. They didn't miss a trick, and their probing and poking proved to be quite an experience. But they ended up with a very favorable report stressing the point of view I had taken—that the post performed invaluable service as a U.S. presence in the district. They were very complimentary to me personally. Ambassador Grove told me that a major embassy could not have done a better job preparing for the inspection, and said that in his opinion I was ready to be a chief of mission. I treasured that comment, coming from so distinguished an officer and at such a relatively early point in my career. After his departure, he took the extra step of writing a highly laudatory letter about me for my personnel file. And the inspection report saved Cebu; to keep Cebu in operation, the department reduced the embassy's staff by two officers and cut a minuscule amount of its massive budget.

Consular Cases

Within my first several weeks in Cebu, the consulate, presumed by most distant observers to be a quiet little post, was presented with several unusual American citizenship protection cases that would have challenged a large embassy. Although my principal duties were representation and reporting, I had to play a large part in resolving these cases. My vice consul, Richard Hermann, a very capable twenty-five-year-old on his second assignment, was dedicated but needed higher-level backing in his dealings with the Philippine authorities. Following are samples of these cases.

- We handled the estate of a deceased naturalized U.S. citizen, who died on a neighboring island. The principal component of this estate was a beautiful twenty-eight-foot sailboat. It was stolen after his death, but recovered after I got the Philippine constabulary general in the area cranked up. We had to bury the boat's owner, arrange payment for the interment and for his hospital bills, get an appraisal to determine the boat's value, sell the boat, and transmit the proceeds to the estate's heir, a sister in Denmark. Pending the sale, we had to protect the boat from vandals and thieves. I had my vice consul drape the cabin doors with red tape imprinted with the consular seal. It did the trick, and eventually the boat was sold and turned over to its new owners.

- An American medical student with a history of mental illness— which had required hospitalization in the United States—had nonetheless been sent by his father (a doctor) to Cebu to study medicine. The student apparently stopped taking his medication and began roaming the streets, threatening passersby. He was arrested and brought to our attention. The young man agreed to our suggestion that he return to the United States for treatment. His family, clearly not interested in having their mentally ill son near them, insisted they could not afford to pay for his repatriation. Despite the fact that the father was a doctor, he could not be compelled to assist his over-twenty-one-year-old son. So the consulate worked with the State Department to provide funding and to hire an attendant to accompany the obviously disturbed young man to the States. My kind vice consul kept the young man overnight in his own home to ensure that he would not go roving and terrorize the Filipinos again. Several months later, we were shocked to learn that the young man had returned to Cebu. His family had paid off the loan to the State Department to enable him to get his passport back, and dispatched him back to his studies. Some of his fellow students informed us that they were attempting to keep an eye on him, but they thought his prospects for regaining his mental health were poor.

- About this same time, a U.S. citizen was murdered in Mindanao in a dangerous, remote area. I was asked to try to obtain justice for his murder. I pressed the Philippine authorities on the case, but insecurity in the area, where the Muslim insurgency was very active, precluded my going personally to the scene. To my knowledge, the murder was not solved.

We Get a New Ambassador

In mid-January 1978, our new ambassador, David Newsom, made his first visit to my consular district. I met him in Iloilo, on the island of Panay, where the ambassador had been invited to attend a local fiesta. Ambassador Newsom had previously been ambassador to Indonesia. He and his wife, Jean, were both warm and friendly. My job was to smooth the way for the ambassador and to brief him on local developments. I ended up spending two entire days with him and his wife.

A week later, the ambassador and his wife came to Cebu for two days on his first official visit. They were my houseguests. It was a good visit, and he was pleased with it. The party arrived by defense attaché aircraft at 10:00 a.m. and were met with full military honors at the airport. I took the men on courtesy calls to the mayor and governor, and then it was lunch at my house for the ambassador's party and the official Americans in Cebu—a total of ten at a formal sit-down lunch. He paid courtesy calls on the military in the afternoon, at which time he was tendered additional military honors (including the review of troops), and then he visited the consulate and the USIS branch office.

At 6:30 p.m., I gave a reception in the ambassador's honor, complete with receiving line. At 6:35 p.m., I had the ambassador in the receiving line, and about twenty guests had already made their appearance in this society where lateness to social functions is usually a given—but not one of the five waiters I had hired for the occasion had shown up. My staff coped beautifully until the waiters did arrive, having been delayed for lack of transportation. The reception, for 250 people, was a success.

The next day we visited Peace Corps projects in the morning, and the USIS officer gave a lunch primarily for press and university contacts. In the afternoon, we visited San Carlos University, one of the oldest in the Philippines (established in 1595 as a school, although not initially at the university level). We then toured a copra processing plant, which had a nice American, Bill Bartels, as its vice president for manufacturing. In the evening, the governor and mayor hosted an official dinner for the ambassador at a local Spanish club.

The following day, we flew south to Davao, in southern Mindanao, where we spent a few hours touring a banana plantation, among other things. The next day, we flew to Cagayan de Oro, in northern Mindanao, visited the governor and the local army general, and toured Del Monte's pineapple cannery. We then drove up to the Del Monte plantation where the pineapple is grown and sampled fresh pineapple cut for us in the field—delicious.

On Friday, I flew to Manila with the party and was the Newsoms' houseguest in their beautiful home. On Saturday evening, the ambassador took me to dinner with then Foreign Minister (General) Carlos P. Romulo. Mrs. Newsom had flown to Baguio with a visiting State Department interior decorator, so the timing was good for me—the ambassador asked if he could bring me in lieu of his wife. It was very interesting to meet Romulo, whose statue I had seen in October at the commemoration of the landing of U.S. troops in Leyte; he is depicted with General MacArthur ("I have returned") and a couple of other generals, wading ashore in the liberation of the Philippines from the Japanese.

I have very fond memories of Ambassador Newsom and his wife. He was unfailingly kind and courteous to me. Traditional diplomacy requires that certain courtesies be afforded ambassadors, which sometimes conflict with the courtesy true gentlemen show ladies. I always tendered him those diplomatic courtesies—such as having him precede me through doors, up steps, and so on; rising when he entered the room; and standing until he sat— all of the traditions established to show respect to the personal representative of the president of the United States. Ambassador Newsom accepted this in clearly official, public circumstances, but in less official cases, he would smile and say, "I think you're not my consul now, you're a lady," and insist that I precede him. As his houseguest, he did the rising when I entered the room and did his best to make me feel comfortable. We discovered a common taste in the English musical act Flanders and Swann, and he and his wife and I found ourselves singing "The Hippopotamus Song" ("Mud, mud, glorious mud, nothing quite like it for cooling the blood") while being driven home from the governor's official dinner for him in Cebu.

Decent Interval Recognition

About this time, I learned from a Washington visitor that I was briefly mentioned, and relatively favorably, in the just released controversial book about the collapse of Vietnam called *Decent Interval*, by former CIA analyst Frank Snepp. Snepp was hard on most of the people whose performance he commented on, but he noted my role in planning and executing the evacuation of Da Nang. I was troubled, however, because Snepp suggested that the Da Nang CIA station chief, who in Da Nang had agreed with me that beginning the evacuation was the right thing to do, had privately criticized this move behind my back.

I Am Accused of Intervening in Support of Opposition Candidates

Cebu was a center of opposition to the Marcos martial law government, to the extent that any place in the Philippines could be so viewed in the clamped-down atmosphere of that government.

In the spring of 1978, however, elections for the National Assembly were planned, and oppositionists in Cebu put forth candidacies. With the advance approval of the political counselor in Manila, I made contact with the leading opposition candidates to ascertain their views. I had frequent contact with the government officials and candidates, but it is incumbent on U.S. officials to maintain channels to oppositionists as well, to know their views, and to have contacts with them should they, in a free election, become the incumbents. To me and to the political counselor, this was standard practice for political officers.

In March, my sister Hazel arrived in Manila to begin a three-week visit to the Philippines. I met her at the airport, and we settled in at the beautiful Manila Hotel, which had been General MacArthur's headquarters at one time. I had arranged a boat ride out to Corregidor with the defense attaché. When I went to the embassy, I was informed that Ambassador Newsom wished to see me. I was shocked to learn from the ambassador that President Marcos had complained to him that the American consul in Cebu was interfering with the forthcoming election. Newsom questioned me thoroughly to satisfy himself that my actions, fully approved in advance by his political counselor, were proper. He was satisfied and said he would so inform Marcos.

Although I had had annual leave approved for the period of Hazel's visit, the ambassador asked me if I would first make another trip throughout my consular district to take the pulse regarding the forthcoming election. I had no choice but to agree, but I did not want to abandon my sister to a week alone in Cebu. I assured him that she was discreet. He had no problem with her accompanying me.

Hazel and I flew to Cebu, where I hastily arranged a trip to some of the key islands. We flew to Iloilo on Panay, and then we were picked up and driven to the province of Antique, a three-hour ride over mountains and near the sea. Antique's bright, young, dedicated, mildly oppositionist governor Evelio Javier showed us his province and entertained us as his guests. We stayed in a nipa house on the beach, where the absence of industry treated us to the most beautiful canopy of stars I have ever seen. The next day, we returned to Iloilo and took a three-hour ferry ride to Bacolod in Negros Occidental, where I visited officials and other contacts. Outside official circles, there was uniform dissatisfaction with the continuation of martial law and some doubt that the elections would be free of fraud. When I returned to Cebu, I wrote reports on my travels, which I took to Manila. I was then free to relax with my sister.

We first went to Hong Kong for a few days, Hazel's first visit there. The vibrancy of that lively city, the fine restaurants, and the variety of the shopping made a nice change from the provinces of the Philippines. Returning to the Philippines, we joined forces with a dear friend, the personnel officer in Manila, Claire Moore, and rented a Land Rover for a drive to the Banaue rice terraces in northern Luzon. It was a fascinating trip. These are steep terraces, manmade some 3,000 years ago and cultivated ever since, in deep mountain valleys—strikingly beautiful, and a tribute to human ingenuity and endurance.

From Banaue, we went by car to Baguio, an eleven-hour, difficult ride through the hills. Baguio was a treat, cool and beautiful. We stayed in the ambassador's summer residence, enjoyed our cocktails in a living room complete with a Gilbert Stuart painting of George Washington. The Japanese surrender in the Philippines at the end of World War II was signed in that house, which had been General Yamashita's headquarters during the war.

A Change of Ambassadors

Ambassador Newsom's tenure in the Philippines proved to be brief. He was called in mid-1978 to higher duty in Washington, assigned to serve as under secretary for political affairs at the State Department, the highest position a career FSO traditionally holds. His replacement, Richard Murphy, proved to be as capable and personable as Newsom.

Rotary Club Dilemma

I went to Manila for consultations in mid-July and met Ambassador Murphy. My visit was timed to so that I could accompany him to his first public speech in the country, at the Rotary Club in Manila. The Rotary Club's practice (at that time) of forbidding female membership posed a problem for American diplomats. Shortly after taking office, President Jimmy Carter issued an order that henceforth the Lyndon Johnson ban on federal officials attending or participating in or belonging to groups that discriminate on the basis of race would be extended as well to those that discriminate on the basis of sex. Officials should not condone such practices by their presence. However, the American ambassador to the Philippines traditionally made his public debut by speaking at a luncheon at the Manila "mother" club of the Philippine Rotary, to which five cabinet members belonged.

To deal with this dilemma, the embassy sought an exception to this ruling, on the grounds that the ambassador would be bringing along staff to "integrate" the gathering. Thus Miss Tull, the consul in Cebu, accompanied the ambassador to the Rotary Club luncheon for his speech. I doubt that the Manila Rotarians got the message; if the ambassador wished to bring a woman to the luncheon, they, too, would make an exception and allow it. I enjoyed the opportunity to get to know the new ambassador and to hear his presentation on the U.S. view of U.S.–Philippine relations.

The Rotary Club's female exclusion policy was a problem for me in Cebu, too. I was the first American consul to be denied membership in the club. Before my arrival, our USIS officer had been invited to join, so the consulate, through him, had contact with these business and official community leaders. With embarrassment, the Rotarians asked me to join the female auxiliary of the Rotary, the Inner Wheel; I declined, explaining that it was not possible to be a member in any way of an organization that discriminated against women. They next offered membership to my vice consul, but I declined to grant permission for this, citing the Carter prohibition. (I did not make an issue of the USIS officer's membership, although it violated the Carter policy. It would have been awkward for him to quit, and it would have brought even more friction into our relationship. He was considerably older than I, and his personal rank was higher than mine, but I as consul was the senior U.S. official in the district, which I sensed he sometimes found chafing. I decided not to add a Rotary membership challenge to our improving relationship.)

I thought that I should continue the traditional consul's role of speaking at Rotary, Kiwanis, and Lions Clubs and other organizations that discriminated against women. These clubs provided valuable venues throughout the many islands of the consular district, and gave a welcome platform for the American consul to discuss U.S. policies to an influential audience. Shortly after arriving in Cebu, I had sought an exception to the Carter prohibition on these grounds, and said that I would insist, when I accepted a speaking invitation, that the clubs invite their female auxiliaries to the speeches, so that I would speak to an integrated audience. I was authorized to proceed on these grounds, and I made countless appearances before various such groups. Still, it galled me that this American-founded club still discriminated against women. But the Philippine clubs were simply following the orders of their American mother club, which then and for several years thereafter forbade membership to females.

The Murphys Take Cebu

In late July, I had the pleasure of welcoming Ambassador Murphy, his wife, and his thirteen-year-old son to Cebu for their introductory visit. Arranging suitable schedules for them was a challenge for the two bachelor officers at the little post. Finding activities, and a host, for the boy prompted my vice consul at one point to suggest, tongue-in-cheek, that he could perhaps teach the boy to do visa interviews, if all else failed. This did not prove necessary. Marisol Putong's sister-in-law took the boy in tow and showed him a fine time.

The visit went well. I dusted off the schedule we had arranged for Ambassador Newsom's visit just several months earlier, including the courtesy calls, dinners, and reception for 250. The ambassador—tall, handsome, personable, and young (forty-eight years old)—wowed Cebu. He had a fine voice, an asset in the music-loving Philippines. He made himself at home at my piano. The women fell in love with him, teenagers wanted his autograph, and mucho-macho Filipino men looked up at his towering height and boyish manner and told me in stage whispers, "You've got a good one there." I wholeheartedly agreed.

One of the things that new ambassadors like to find out at constituent posts is how well the embassy's administrative section supports them. The ambassador got a firsthand look at a major deficiency in this regard during his visit. In March, the air conditioner in my official sedan broke, and the administrative section was responsible for ordering the part to fix it from the States. But the part never came. I prodded them frequently, by phone and at least twice in writing, but one excuse or another followed each inquiry. In early July, I visited Manila and told the new administrative counselor about the problem, reporting that I wanted the air conditioner operative by the time of the ambassador's late July visit. But visit day dawned, and despite further entreaties, the air conditioner was not yet functioning.

Despite his previous service as ambassador to Syria, Ambassador Murphy had not developed a taste for the humid variety of heat in Cebu, particularly as encountered in a large U.S. sedan painted black, an excellent color for retaining heat. He was game about it, but clearly distressed, as I had been since March. Came the magic moment when he asked the question: "How is your support from the admin section?" I made all of the positive noises I could, not wishing to bite the hand that controlled the pipeline of necessary supplies: "Usually, it is very good," and "They are quite helpful," but, yes, there was this unusual problem of the sedan's air conditioner part, which I had requested in March. I confessed that I had been tempted to write to my brother-in-law in the States and ask him to mail me the part; the ambassador opined as we made our way down a breezeless country road en route to a Peace Corps project that, indeed, that would have been a fine idea.

The poor man left Cebu sniffling—not from sorrow at leaving our sweltering vehicle, but because of a severe head cold he attributed to frequent changes of temperature, moving from air-conditioned to non-air-conditioned habitats. A few weeks later, I met the ambassador's secretary in the embassy courtyard. She promptly told me, away from overhearing ears, about the ambassador's return from Cebu. She said that the usually gentle, mild, good-humored man had come into his office from the airport dripping from his head cold and, hardly bothering to say hello, told her to get an immediate answer from the administrative section about "when Terry Tull can expect to receive the air conditioner part for her car, which she told them about in March." "Pin them down," he instructed. He wanted a report with a firm statement in an hour. She said that she wanted to laugh, but wisely decided against it; rather, she relayed the ambassador's demand to the administrative counselor. In August, I saw the ambassador again when he visited Dumaguete and Iloilo, in my district; almost the first thing he asked me was whether the air conditioner had been fixed. It had, by then. Cebu's administrative needs thereafter received closer attention.

Ambassador Murphy visited cities in the consular district on several occasions. On each such visit, I either met him at the city or, on occasion, he picked me up in the defense attaché's aircraft in Cebu. I thoroughly enjoyed working with him. He was a fine representative of the United States, and a warm human being. After the Philippines, he went on to serve as ambassador to Saudi Arabia and as assistant secretary for Near Eastern and South Asian affairs, with great distinction.

Exotic Zamboanga

The assignment in Cebu offered me the opportunity—actually, the requirement—to visit widely throughout the consular district in many interesting places. None held quite the allure of Zamboanga, on the southern tip of Mindanao. Because of the Muslim insurgency and the frequency of kidnappings for ransom in the area, the ambassador had forbidden official Americans to visit the city. Because my duties required it, I was granted an exception, and early in my tour, having made careful arrangements with the Philippine military authorities in the region, I paid my first visit.

My hotel was at the harbor's edge. The colorful array of boats in the water seemed to spring from an earlier century, with their colored sails and painted designs on the prow to ward off evil spirits. I sat at the outdoor bar drinking in the scene as I enjoyed a predinner cocktail, savoring this very "foreign" flavor of the Foreign Service.

The senior Philippine military official in Zamboanga, a gregarious admiral, was a gracious host for my official program. He insisted on providing me with an armed military escort for my daytime activities. After a full day of official activities, my guards deposited me back at the hotel. After dinner, however, I hired a taxi and went off on my own to meet with a well-known opposition figure in Zamboanga. I was nervous, and perhaps a bit frightened, about venturing off in the dark in a kidnapping-prone area to meet a known opposition figure, but meeting oppositionists came with the territory. The taxi located his residence without difficulty. I was greeted by a gray-haired man sensibly dressed in a sarong, accompanied by several other curious men. I was looking forward to an interesting discussion of the local political situation, but the first thing out of this significant oppositionist's mouth was a query about how to go about retaining his U.S. green card (permanent resident status identification). Once this topic was disposed of, the discussion turned to the political situation. He was, predictably, adamantly opposed to the Marcos regime; a few years later he was murdered in what was widely viewed as a Marcos-directed political assassination.

Santa Cruz Mission

In May 1978, I had the opportunity to visit a unique site: the Santa Cruz Mission to the T'bolis, in Mindanao. I flew to Davao City, where I connected with the Peace Corps director for the Philippines and his Cebu deputy. We then went in a four-wheel-drive vehicle to the remote location that was home to the T'bolis.

The T'bolis were a fascinating hill tribe almost overlooked by anthropologists because, until recent years, they had been nearly inaccessible at their home on beautiful Lake Sebu in South Cotabato Province. It took us about six hours of very rough driving to even approach the mission, which is situated in a beautiful mountain valley. A very difficult ride up a trail, fording several streams, ensued—fortunately, it had not rained recently, or we would have had to abandon the Land Rover and proceed several kilometers on foot. We arrived after dark, unfortunately, but luckily there had been enough light during our trek to enable us to see the gorgeous Lake Sebu around which the T'bolis traditionally made their home. (They had been gradually losing their land to settlers from the Visayas—a development reminiscent of our own country's expansion westward, in which Native American tribes, like the T'bolis, were supplanted.)

The Santa Cruz mission was run by Passionist priests from the United States. Father Charles Adams was our host, and a very considerate one. He installed me and the Peace Corps director in his modest nipa house and found space for the remainder of our party in the dormitory. The mission runs a clinic, school, and crafts department, and had recently constructed a corn and rice mill to help the T'bolis find a cash crop to help them better resist outsiders' incursions on their land. We had a fascinating talk over dinner on his porch, where the utter silence of the place cast its spell.

In the morning, Marsh Thompson, the Peace Corps director, decided nothing would do but that, after mass, he take a side trip to another mountain valley. I decided that I was quite content where I was, as did our Cebu Peace Corps representative. We spent a wonderful day at the mission. For all of us, our day started with a T'boli mass. The tribespeople gathered at the nipa church, the women and little girls in their distinctive attire—beautiful woven blouses, cummerbunds, and skirts, decorated with elaborate beadwork. In their hair, the women often wore beaded ornaments, and they decorated their arms, waists, and ankles with bells and brass or silver bracelets. They literally jingle when they walk—the bells make a light, pleasing, chiming sound. The women all seemed beautiful, and even the young girls wore makeup, including lipstick and eye shadow, but not commercial products—they used natural materials.

The mass was in the T'boli language, which Father Adams employed very well. Drums and gongs, with exciting rhythms, provided the music. Singing was chantlike and distinctive. In lieu of a sermon, Father Adams said a few words and opened the floor to discussion, with the elders of the tribe encouraged to address the congregation. Perhaps a half dozen people spoke—reminiscent of a tribal meeting, I suspected. Finally, the senior datu (chief) of the group was encouraged to speak, and did so in a rousing manner to everyone's obvious satisfaction, even though he was four times married and obviously not a Catholic. At the offertory, three exquisite little girls, dressed alike and jingling like fairy musicians, performed a delicate T'boli dance at the altar as the collection was taken. The service was very beautiful and moving.

The lazy members of our party then retired to a relaxed lunch on Father Adams's porch overlooking the valley and lake, while the energetic ones roared off on their further and, to me, foolish explorations. With paradise at your feet, why drive away? I wanted to savor what I knew was one of the rarer experiences of my life.

After a sensible rest, Father Adams took me and the Cebu Peace Corps official for a stroll through the mission and nearby village. The peace of the place was almost overpowering. He decided we should call on the head datu, which we did. We climbed up a ladder into the datu's nipa longhouse and stepped back in time hundreds of years.

The house was large, as befitted the head datu, but it consisted of one room. There was no furniture, only handmade mats. We reclined on the floor, resting our backs against kapok-filled pillows. There was not much light in the room, just enough to see comfortably if you did not plan to try to read. A couple of kittens wandered around, and in a corner a chicken pecked at some corn. On a slightly raised platform to my right, a man about forty years old (an unidentified relative of the datu) used a combination of fingers and toes to prepare abaca for the tie-dye mat weaving for which the T'boli women are known. Three women busied themselves in various ways: one climbed into the house bearing water in a bamboo container; two worked quietly and steadily making simple floor mats; and in a corner an older woman stirred from a nap, drew herself up into a sitting position, stared briefly at us, and began chewing betel nut, her red teeth showing that this was a common pastime for her. We learned that she was the datu's sister. In the meantime, perhaps ten village children wandered into the house (well, they could not exactly wander up a ladder, but they straggled up in twos and threes to observe the strangers). They obviously were welcome, and grouped themselves as they pleased on the fringes of our group.

It was an hour frozen in time for me, reclining on that mat watching the old datu with his face out of *National Geographic* chatting in T'boli with our priest interpreter, and sharing cigarettes with him. He told us some of the tribal customs: for instance, he said he usually fed thirty to forty people at dinner, because anyone who stopped by at that time expected his datu to feed him—it went without saying. At one point, Father Adams told him jokingly that he was putting up five Americans, "and they eat a lot." The datu scolded him, telling him he should not say such a thing. Father Adams explained to us that he had expected a rise from the datu, because for the T'bolis, who barely have enough to go around, it is the height of insult to suggest that someone takes more than their share or is greedy. If we were to attend a T'boli feast, he said, one person would be designated to dish up the food and would do so in equal portions; there would be no seconds, as he would distribute the food the first time until it was gone. To suggest that you were still hungry when you had eaten your portion was just unheard of. He said that the T'bolis usually had enough, but never had excess. It is very much a subsistence economy.

The afternoon grew darker. One of the women opened a trapdoor window, and there in that special light of the late afternoon was framed a spectacularly beautiful view—the valley, water buffalo quietly grazing, and the gemlike Lake Sebu glistening in the setting sun. It is one of those moments that is seared into my memory. I knew at the time that I was being treated to a glimpse of something few Westerners experience. I thought of Shangri-la. I understood why Father Adams, of Brooklyn, New York, was spending his working life among the T'bolis.

Before we left, I noticed that the datu's latest wife was working at her loom, weaving the tie-dyed abaca matting into a distinctive wall hanging. I arranged to buy it upon its completion, which could take as long as three months for a ten- to fifteen-foot creation. Our bargain held, and the weaving arrived in Cebu some months later.

As night fell, we had dinner and an evening nip of some of the Scotch we had brought along, accompanied by a little singing when Father Adams was persuaded to bring out his guitar. Quiet talk followed, about T'boli-settler problems and Philippine army abuses against nearby Muslims. Afterward, more music, another scotch, and we were off to bed, knowing that the morning would see us board our jeep for the ride back to the twentieth century. The journey, the experience—unforgettable.

A Mindanao Adventure

The embassy strictly controlled travel to Marawi City in Mindanao, the heart of an area continually troubled by an insurgency of Muslims seeking independence, or at least autonomy, from the Philippines. Kidnappings for ransom were common in the area, and a diplomat would make a prize catch. Still, I was keenly interested in seeing this beautiful region and assessing the situation on the ground.

I had the good fortune to meet an American couple who were Lutheran missionaries, the Robert McAnises, working among the Muslims in Marawi City. I hosted them on one of their R&R (rest and recreation) visits to Cebu, and they invited me to come to Marawi City and stay with them. I got approval from the ambassador and the Philippine military to make the trip. The general in Cebu told me that his counterpart in Marawi City had insisted on meeting me with a military escort at the airport in northern Mindanao to conduct me to Marawi City. I had no choice but to accept this provision, although my missionary friends observed resignedly that traveling the roads near Marawi with a Philippine military escort was tantamount to painting a target on one's back.

We timed the visit so that I could fly to Mindanao with the McAnises in February 1979. When we arrived at the airport, there was no sign of a military escort. We waited fifteen or twenty minutes, then decided to proceed on our own to Marawi City in vehicles provided by the missionaries' aides. After riding without incident for about twenty minutes, traffic suddenly came to a halt. We heard gunfire ahead of us near the road. We sat for a while, feeling like sitting ducks, and finally a Philippine military officer approached and asked us to wait a little longer. He explained that a Philippine military detachment heading for the airport had been ambushed, but reinforcements had arrived and the situation would soon be under control. Not long thereafter, we were allowed to proceed. I learned subsequently that one young soldier had died—a young man en route to the airport, I felt certain, to protect me on my trip to the city.

The delay made me late for a ceremony that the Philippine colonel in charge of Marawi City was attending at a stadium, to which I had been invited. I went to the stadium, late, and told the colonel the reason for the delay. He sought additional information, and later confirmed to me that it was my intended military escort that had been attacked. For the rest of my official program in Marawi City, he insisted on having me accompanied by armed military. When I asked to visit the central market, he concurred, but sent me there in an armored personnel carrier. As I walked among the stalls, I was escorted by two machine-gun-toting soldiers. The colonel did not intend to lose the American consul on his watch.

The World Gets Smaller

I was the houseguest of the friendly missionaries in their nipa home near Lake Lanao, the beautiful lake around which Marawi City clusters. I had told them I hoped to have the opportunity to meet with an American scholar on Philippine Muslims, the Reverend Peter Gowing, author of books on the Mindanao Muslims and a professor at the university in Malawi. They told me that this man rarely met with U.S. officials for fear, perhaps, of harming his credibility with his Muslim friends and contacts. My friends knew him well, however, and said that they thought they could lure him over for dinner with me that evening. They would not surprise him with my presence, but they offered him the rare treat in that Muslim area of gin and tonics, made from supplies they had purchased in Cebu. To my pleasure, the professor accepted and appeared at cocktail hour.

There we were, sitting in a nipa house along the shores of Lake Lanao, the outdoors silent except for the call to prayers of a Muslim muezzin, in an area where the ambush of my military escort had brought home very clearly that the Muslim insurgency was very much alive. Enter the reluctant professor. Introduced to me, he puzzled briefly over my name: "Tull? Tull? Do you happen to know a Bob Tull?"

Yes, I replied, my brother's name is Bob.

"Was he ever in the navy?"

Yes, I said again, he was a career naval officer, a carrier pilot.

The professor shook his head. "Well, I served on the USS *Greenwich Bay* with him in the Persian Gulf. I was the ship's chaplain. We shared a cabin."

We were all astounded by this coincidence, which, aided by

our missionaries' good gin and tonic, made for a most enjoyable and, ultimately, fruitful evening. The professor, his suspicions of U.S. officials abated because of my family connection, shared his impressions of the state of the insurgency and other matters of interest with me, enabling me to flesh out our understanding of this troubling issue.

I awoke early in the morning to the muezzin's call to prayer. As I lay in bed reflecting on the peaceful setting, the bugler at the Philippine army camp awakened the troops to greet the morning, in perhaps accidental competition with the muezzin's chant. I wondered whether these two strikingly different ways of rousing one's followers would ever be able to exist harmoniously together. As I write this many years later, that outcome seems increasingly unlikely. The insurgency has worsened, and it is most likely being supported by Al Qaeda.

When I returned to Manila, I wrote a comprehensive airgram about my visit and attempted to paint a word picture for readers in Manila and Washington who had not experienced this beautiful but troubled place, where Muslim culture lived uncomfortably under martial law dictated by non-Muslims. Several weeks later, I received a strong commendation of the report from Washington end users in the intelligence community.

Assessing the Marcos Regime

As my knowledge of the area and the general situation grew, I became convinced that the Philippine populace, at least in the Cebu consular district, was growing increasingly restive under the martial law regime of Ferdinand Marcos. Marcos had been elected president twice, which is the constitutional limit in the Philippines. As his second term neared its end, Marcos declared martial law, contending that was necessary to combat multiple insurgencies. A Muslim insurgency raged in the south, and a small Communist insurgency was present in Luzon and on a few islands in the center of the country. He had ruled through martial law for some time, and no end was in sight. As my experience deepened and my convictions grew, I wrote a comprehensive report concluding that soon the Filipino people would have had enough of Marcos and martial law. They would tolerate neither the suppression of the opposition nor the pervasive role of Marcos and his associates in the economy. If they were deprived of electoral means to effect change, I could envision the people taking to the streets. This report was submitted by the embassy to the department in an airgram.

At some point, this message was either given to or discussed with a reporter in Washington, I am certain, because it was cited in a book critical of the Marcos regime, *Waltzing with a Dictator*, by Raymond Bonner. I was cited as a lone voice predicting the eventual collapse of the regime. I was disturbed when I read the book, because although the names of my sources were not mentioned, a careful reader of the book—and I am confident there were many of these in the Marcos entourage—could have concluded from whence my negative conclusions arose. Sources speak with diplomats in the expectation that their confidences will be respected and their identities protected. I worried that people who had trusted me might suffer as a consequence.

My prediction about the people taking to the streets eventually came to pass. In 1986, the peaceful People Power revolution pushed Marcos from power. Before this occurred, however, Marcos's principal opponent, Benigno Aquino, had been assassinated at the airport in Manila following his return from the United States (I had met with him in New York). The charismatic young governor of Antique, Evelio Javier, had been slaughtered in his home. The aging Zamboanga oppositionist with whom I had met during my first visit to that exotic city had been gunned down by Marcos's thugs while riding his motorcycle in Zamboanga.

Photo Gallery

With Lt. Gen. Ngo Quang Truong, Military I Corps Commander, in Da Nang, Vietnam, July 4, 1974, at the Consulate General's Independence Day reception.

With Lt. Gen. Ngo Quang Truong, I Corps Commander, Maj. Gen. Hoang Van Lac, his deputy, their wives, and senior members of Consulate General Da Nang staff, in late 1974.

My "foster children," Tri, Trinh, and Tram, outside our home in Washington, D.C., on July 4, 1976.

Ambassador to the Philippines David Newsom, center front, visits a cocoanut oil plant in Cebu, the Philippines, in 1977. On his left, William Bartels, the American plant manager.

With Governor Javier in Antique province, the Philippines, 1978. Javier was later assassinated in the run-up to the People Power Revolution that unseated President Ferdinand Marcos.
(Photographer, Hazel Tull McLane).

July 4th reception in Vientiane, Laos, 1986. My toasting partner is the Lao Vice Foreign Minister.

With Lt. Col. Joseph Harvey and his deputy, in Pakse, Laos, January 1984, arriving to conduct the preliminary site survey for the first joint crash site investigation in Indochina since the communist takeover in 1975.

As Ambassador to Guyana, with President Ronald Reagan in the Oval Office, June 1984.

Breaking ground for the new U.S. Embassy in Georgetown, Guyana, with Foreign Minister Rashleigh Jackson, November 1987.

With Guyana's President Hugh Desmond Hoyte at a July 1990 reception in Georgetown, Guyana.

The Sultan of Brunei, Hassanai Bolkiah, is a dedicated polo player. At a match in 1994 against a Citibank-sponsored team, I awarded trophies to the winning team. Here we share a light moment.

8

To the Human Rights Bureau

In mid-1979, it was time for another transfer. Ambassador Murphy had asked me to consider transferring to the embassy's political section, where I would head a small unit following internal Philippine developments. I was pleased to be asked, but I was not enamored of the prospect of two more years in the Philippines. I enjoyed the near autonomy of the Cebu assignment and hesitated to become a small part of a huge embassy operation. I tried again, unsuccessfully, to get an assignment as a deputy chief of mission, which the Foreign Service inspectors had urged me to do. Failing this, I was delighted to be promoted to FSO-3 near the end of my Cebu assignment and to be assigned to a year of study at the National War College in Washington. The assignment to this prestigious institution suggested that, despite the lack of a DCM appointment, my career was on track. I packed up, put Mai Thai in her travel cage, and set off for another tour in Washington.

Fort McNair

My academic year at the National War College, situated at historic Fort McNair on the Anacostia River in southeast Washington, was a very interesting experience. It was good to settle back into my own Foggy Bottom apartment again after spending two years with the children in a rented house in northwest Washington and two years in the Philippines. And after my very active Cebu assignment, it was relaxing to be relieved of such responsibilities and stimulating to take part in a classroom experience with the cream of the U.S. military crop of potential generals and admirals.

The class of approximately 130 officers of colonel or equivalent rank consisted of some 100-plus military officers from all services and about 25 to 30 civilians from branches of the U.S. government who dealt with foreign affairs, including a few State Department officers. There were five women in the class, two from State, and one each from the navy, army, and air force. We were assigned to seminar classrooms of approximately a dozen officers each, where we spent the bulk of our class time reading deeply in foreign affairs, military history, and current events, and discussing our conclusions under the guidance of a capable professor. In addition to the readings required of all students, we were offered a choice of elective classes, a certain number of which we were required to take. All students also had to prepare a major thesis. Because I knew little about OPEC (Organization of Petroleum Exporting Countries) and wished to know more, I did my thesis on that consortium, whose production and pricing of oil were so important to the United States and to the world economy. In addition, we were treated to frequent guest speakers—cabinet officers, authors, major players on the U.S. scene—who addressed us in the War College auditorium.

A highlight of the year was an overseas study trip to different parts of the world. Pursuant to my interest in OPEC, I asked to be included on the trip to the Middle East. Instead, however, I was assigned to a trip to France and to the headquarters of NATO (North Atlantic Treaty Organization). NATO headquarters had transferred to Brussels since my initial tour in Brussels, and I had frequently visited France while assigned to Belgium, so the trip held no geographic surprises for me. It was quite informative, however, to learn firsthand about how NATO was operating in Belgium and how it was maintaining meaningful relations with France, which had abandoned NATO several years earlier. Our French military hosts in Strasbourg with the First Army were most hospitable and made a very favorable impression on the military members of our group, some of whom, at least before the trip, had expressed dissatisfaction with the French approach to European security.

Another treat for a female civilian was the traditional end of term "dining-in ceremony," a festive, highly structured military formal dinner. All of the military officers wore their impressive dress uniforms; I believe civilians wore at a minimum dress suits, if not formal tuxedos. Several dining-in traditions were observed: fines were levied for imaginary protocol violations, and recitations were called for. Our guest speaker, the conservative Republican Congressman Dornan from California, tossed ample red meat of support for the military to his most receptive, and well-lubricated, audience. Again, it was an experience not frequently enjoyed by civilians.

In addition to our diplomas at year's end, we were all given a wall plaque listing the year of our graduation and the names of our class members. A senior State Department friend suggested that this was an item that State officers should display in their embassy offices, as it was an excellent credential easily recognized by the military officers we would have occasion to deal with in our future careers. I did so, and it definitely was noticed and appreciated by my military visitors.

The Human Rights Bureau

War College graduation was in August 1980. Before then, we all had to focus on our next assignment. I made my now almost pro forma effort to be assigned as deputy chief of mission, and again made the short list for a few embassies, but again I was not selected. The hunt for an appropriate onward assignment was initially discouraging. I was approached one afternoon toward the end of the academic year by a friend, Charles Salmon, who was concluding his tour as office director for human rights in the Bureau of Human Rights and Humanitarian Affairs (HA) at State. Charlie encouraged me to apply for his position, and said he would recommend me to his boss, the assistant secretary, for the job.

I was initially reluctant. President Jimmy Carter had made support for human rights a key element in his foreign policy. This policy was controversial, and unpopular, including in the State Department bureaucracy. Geographic bureaus charged with maintaining the best relations possible with their countries disliked criticizing these countries on human rights or taking punitive action against them because of human rights violations. Yet Congress had passed several laws mandating that human rights be factored into U.S. relations with foreign countries, and the human rights bureau had been established to ensure that these laws were implemented. Perhaps the most controversial law was the requirement that the State Department produce an annual report assessing the human rights performance of every country that was a member of the United Nations—virtually every country in the world. Getting agreement on the texts of these reports, I knew from my peripheral experience with the Philippine report in Cebu, was contentious. The human rights bureau was not a popular bureau. Its assistant secretary, the feisty, combative Patricia Derian, had ruffled many feathers in her principled, but sometimes undiplomatic, approach to her work. This bothered her not a whit as she fought vigorously for the victims of human rights violations.

Still, human rights was a key element in U.S. foreign policy, and deserved to be so for a country that professed the highest regard for democracy and the rights of the individual. Also, the United Nations Declaration on Human Rights, to which the United States and every member of the United Nations (UN) professed support, was drafted largely by Americans—Eleanor Roosevelt was a major contributor. Service in HA would place me in the forefront of an important policy initiative.

Also, the position of director of the human rights office within the bureau was a good one from a career standpoint, in that the director supervised five FSOs and a secretary. It was a meaty job from both policy and management standpoints. Its principal downside was that the policy, and the office that pressed it, was unpopular. The job would be difficult, and the incumbent ran the risk of alienating senior officers throughout the department in the conduct of the bureau's work, with a possible negative impact on one's future assignments.

Not without qualms, I agreed to be interviewed by Patt Derian, who offered me the job. I was impressed by her spirit and obvious intelligence, and decided to accept.

A Difficult Time

I reported to HA in September 1980. Patt Derian was on an extended vacation on Cape Cod when I arrived, and the bureau was in the quiet, capable hands of Stephen Palmer, the senior deputy assistant secretary in the bureau. Steve was a senior FSO whose quiet manner belied a fierce commitment to improving human rights. We worked well together.

The Aquino Case

I had been in the bureau for a short time when Patt Derian achieved a goal she had long sought—the release from prison of Philippine oppositionist Benigno Aquino. On a highly publicized visit to Manila, Patt had demanded to visit the popular Aquino in prison, where he had been held for several years, and pressed for his release. The incensed Marcos had reluctantly acquiesced, on the grounds that Aquino needed medical treatment, which the United States would provide. In addition, Patt worked to obtain a fellowship for Aquino at Harvard to delay his return to the Philippines.

Shortly after his departure from the Philippines, Aquino spoke in New York at the Asia Society. Patt, on vacation, asked me to go to New York and welcome Aquino to the United States on her behalf. I did so, and was impressed by this vital man, whose years in prison had not dimmed his intelligence, articulateness, and charisma. It was popular belief that Aquino would have been elected president, had Marcos not declared martial law; instead, he was punished for his opposition to that move by being imprisoned.

Meeting this leading political figure, who had languished in prison for years but had been freed as a result of U.S. human rights policy pressure, impressed on me the benefits that could be derived from a well-applied human rights policy. Patt Derian may not have been diplomatic, but she sometimes got results. A blend of her fire with the traditional tact of diplomats could be a fruitful combination, I thought.

Kim Dae-jung

In the summer of 1980, antigovernment rioting broke out in Kwangju, Korea. The military government blamed this activity on a leading oppositionist, Kim Dae-jung. Kim was a democrat, but in contrast to the generals who ran South Korea as dictators, he believed in seeking a modest rapprochement with North Korea. These views labeled him as a traitor in the eyes of the military dictatorship. The rioting in Kwangju was used as an excuse to arrest Kim and accuse him of treason; a death sentence seemed the likely outcome of the rigged trial.

Patt was on Cape Cod as the trial approached. She was in frequent telephone contact with Steve Palmer on how to proceed with the effort to save Kim. Steve and I met with Deputy Secretary of State Warren Christopher to present our concerns and recommend strong U.S. action. Our ambassador in Seoul issued strong démarches, and Christopher agreed to dispatch a high-ranking official in State's legal bureau to attend Kim's trial. In addition, an embassy officer skilled in the Korean language would attend every session, making the point by his presence that the United States was concerned and watching events closely.

The U.S. position in this case, and in our dealings with South Korea, a long-time ally, had been weakened early in the Carter administration when the president announced his intention to withdraw from South Korea, in a phased manner, the approximately 30,000 U.S. troops that had been a buffer against North Korean aggression since the end of the Korean War. This possibility had outraged the military dictators of South Korea, who even with the U.S. trip-wire felt very exposed to North Korean invasion, given the close proximity of Seoul to North Korea. The perceived weakening of U.S. support for South Korea meant that U.S. representations on behalf of human rights issues fell on deaf ears. The prognosis for Kim Dae-jung was not good.

The trial ran its predicted course; Kim was found guilty and sentenced to death. Through our embassy, we urged that clemency be granted and that the death sentence be revoked. Our appeals were received with indifference.

At about the same time, the 1980 U.S. election saw President Carter defeated and a conservative Republican, Ronald Reagan, elected. Sources informed us that the South Korean generals celebrated the Reagan victory joyfully, in (and with) great spirits. Early indications from the Reagan administration were that human rights would be downgraded, if not completely abandoned, as an element in U.S. foreign policy. For example, the incoming secretary of state, Alexander Haig, was quoted as saying that "Terrorism will take the place of human rights in our concerns."

In the time leading up to the new president's inauguration, Reagan's transition team settled themselves into various executive branch departments, including State, to brief themselves and to prepare the new appointees for their positions. The human rights bureau was marginalized during this period; it lacked an assistant secretary until December 1981, and had next to no input as the new administration grappled with the issue. President Reagan's national security adviser, Richard Allen, was briefed on the Kim Dae-jung case by the Korean office director and by other high-ranking officials. Ironically, the incoming administration, whose secretary of state had seemed so hostile to the idea of human rights in foreign policy, saved Kim Dae-jung's life.

The military dictator of South Korea, General Chun Doo Hwan, wished to visit Washington and meet with President Reagan. Richard Allen reportedly told the South Koreans that President Reagan would be pleased to meet with the general—but he could not do so if Kim Dae-jung remained under sentence of death. If the sentence were commuted, President Reagan would meet with the South Korean leader very shortly after the inauguration. Kim's sentence was commuted to life in prison, and the South Korean leader enjoyed a state visit to Washington in February 1981. The incoming administration apparently felt it important to restore an amicable relationship between the United States and South Korea. At the time, I felt that the South Korean leader did not deserve a White House meeting, but I was relieved that Kim's life had been spared, although he remained imprisoned. (For a detailed account of these events, see *Massive Entanglement, Marginal Influence: Carter and Korea in Crisis*, by William H. Gleysteen, Jr., the U.S. ambassador to Korea during this period.)

I Become an Acting Deputy Assistant Secretary

A few days before the Reagan inauguration, Patt Derian popped into my office and informed me that she had obtained authorization from the outgoing secretary of state, Edmund Muskie, to appoint Steve Palmer acting assistant secretary pending the appointment and confirmation of her replacement, and to appoint me an acting deputy assistant secretary. I was delighted, and told Patt so, noting that even though the appointment would most likely last for only a few weeks after the inauguration, it would be a most interesting experience. Patt laughed, and said that I would probably hold the position for months. She was correct; I held this status until December 1981. As such, I was the second-ranking official in the bureau, under Steve Palmer, during a time of great turmoil and unsettledness.

The Changing Human Rights Policy: A Chaotic Time

Nineteen hundred eighty-one was a time of confusion in the Reagan administration's approach to human rights. In addition to Secretary Haig's dismissal of the policy, other conservatives in the administration were calling for the dismantling of the bureau, an end to the annual human rights reports, an end to representations on behalf of human rights abuse victims—an end, in short, to the inclusion of a human rights element in U.S. foreign policy. Proponents of this approach, however, were ignorant of the law. Over the preceding decade, Congress had passed a body of legislation requiring that human rights performance be factored into U.S. dealings with foreign countries. The human rights bureau was mandated by law. The annual human rights reports were mandated by law. Other laws require, among other things, that a country's human rights performance be weighed in determining whether the United States would export military equipment or sensitive computer equipment to it, or whether the United States would support its loan requests to the World Bank or its development needs in International Monetary Fund (IMF) restructuring efforts.

Thus, while the incoming administration belittled the Carter policy and announced plans to dismantle it, the professionals in the bureau viewed it as our duty to continue to implement the relevant laws. At the same time, we attempted to educate the newcomers about our—and their—duty to enforce those laws unless they were revoked by Congress. Naturally, during this period, elements in the department that had chafed under the Derian human rights approach were much less amenable to suggestions from HA that their countries should be cautioned to improve their human rights behavior. Getting cooperation in some instances became a very difficult task. For example, obtaining agreement from a geographic bureau on a department press statement following a human rights violation by a particular country was frequently trying, with the geographic bureau determined to make a mild statement while HA pressed for tougher language.

John Bolton Scraps a Good Human Rights Initiative

Early in my tenure as acting deputy assistant secretary, a colleague with whom I had worked closely in USAID approached me with bad news. A program had been started during the Carter administration through the Asia Foundation, which worked with the Indonesian government to translate the Indonesian constitution and body of laws into several of the many languages of that vast archipelago. It was progressing satisfactorily, with the support of the Indonesian government. Carter human rights practitioners viewed the strengthening of legal systems as essential to a sound foundation for protecting human rights. But a key Reagan administration USAID official had decided that the agency would no longer fund this program.

After consulting with Steve Palmer, I worked with my USAID contact to arrange a meeting with the dissenting official, John Bolton, to discuss the rationale for the program and to try to get the funding back on track. Bolton, the general counsel, received us coolly. I recounted the history of the program, stressed its noncontroversial character, and reported the Indonesian government's support for the effort. Bolton was unmoved; he continued to refuse to approve funding for the program. I asked him why he opposed the program, and his reply, bluntly delivered in a loud voice, astounded me in its ideological zeal: "Because Ronald Reagan was elected president of the United States! We don't do legal aid!"

I attempted again to explain that the program involved only funding the translations of the constitution and laws, not providing legal aid, per se.

He brushed me off, adding forcefully: "When Ronald Reagan was governor of California, legal aid groups brought class action law suits against the state. We are not going to fund this program."

Since HA was still without a politically appointed assistant secretary, we had no recourse. The program was not funded. A year later, however, when Elliott Abrams assumed the post of assistant secretary, I brought the matter to his attention; the program was renewed.

The Lefever Nomination

Reluctantly persuaded that they could not simply abolish the human rights bureau, the incoming administration finally named a new assistant secretary of state for HA. Ernest Lefever was the founder and director of a conservative think tank in Washington, the Ethics and Public Policy Center. He had written briefly about human rights—he stated that they should not play a role in U.S. foreign policy. In addition, his center was under a cloud because one of its studies had recommended that mothers in Africa use baby-food formula instead of nursing their babies. The recommendation was impractical, given the scarcity of pure water with which to mix the formula; moreover, Nestlé, a Swiss company that marketed its baby-food formula to developing countries, was one of the center's funders, raising conflict-of-interest issues. It was clear that Lefever would face a difficult road to confirmation.

It was the job of the bureau to prepare this unlikely would-be HA leader for his confirmation. We prepared briefing books on top of briefing books, informing him of the various laws governing the bureau and prepping him on recent and current human rights cases. As the confirmation hearing approached in midsummer, we held mock hearings, with various officers throwing difficult questions of the kind we anticipated the senators would ask, without mercy. He cooperated and struggled through it all, recognizing that we were working hard to prepare him for confirmation. I believe he came to understand through the many weeks we worked together on this (I was the lead HA officer in this process) that we were honest servants of the president, committed to supporting his nominee. I thought he was a disastrous choice for the job and that his confirmation would make it very difficult in the bureau for a while, but I believed that eventually he would have to recognize that the laws of the land had to be upheld.

The Senate would not confirm Ernest Lefever. The confirmation hearing was brutal. The senators were relentless in their criticism of his past statements concerning the role of human rights in foreign policy, of the Nestlé conflict-of-interest case, of his obvious reluctance to pursue a vigorous human rights policy. They brought leading human rights activists to the hearing to testify against his confirmation, including a brave Argentinean editor, Jacobo Timerman, on whose behalf Patt Derian had intervened when he was imprisoned. The senators were inconsiderate of an older man's need for bathroom breaks and kept the nominee in his chair for hours without one. At the end of the nearly daylong hearing, the Senate Foreign Relations Committee voted against sending the Lefever nomination to the floor of the Senate for a vote. We learned later that President Reagan had been willing to resubmit his nomination, but Lefever declined. And HA remained without an assistant secretary for several more months. Steve and I, and our officers, soldiered on in the nasty limbo created by the Senate's wholehearted rejection of President Reagan's first choice, wondering who would ultimately take the helm of the bureau.

Elliott Abrams Becomes Assistant Secretary

As the year drew near to a close, the bureau received a new, though different, lease on life. Elliott Abrams, a brilliant young neoconservative who had begun his political activities as an aide to Washington State's Senator Henry Jackson, was growing restive as assistant secretary for international organizations. In his early thirties, Abrams was overshadowed and possibly ignored by the high-profile Reagan ambassador to the United Nations, Jeane Kirkpatrick. In theory, the UN ambassador took instructions from the assistant secretary for international organizations. In practice, Jeane Kirkpatrick apparently took instructions from Jeane Kirkpatrick.

Elliott Abrams apparently watched with pain as the Lefever nomination unraveled. In late fall, he reportedly approached the White House and offered his services as assistant secretary for human rights. The offer was accepted. Having already been recently confirmed by the Senate, Abrams was quickly confirmed for the new post and took over in early December, in time for the December 10 commemoration of the adoption of the Universal Declaration of Human Rights. The true Reagan era in human rights, launched by the commutation of the death sentence on Kim Dae-jung, would now begin.

Quiet Diplomacy

Elliott Abrams established himself quickly and competently as the new head of HA. After the chaotic year we had endured, it was a relief to have a chief once more, and one that we knew had the confidence of the White House. Elliott brought in his own political appointees to fill two deputy assistant secretary slots, and recruited a capable FSO, Mel Levitsky, to replace Steve Palmer when Palmer's tour came to an end as summer approached. My tenure as acting deputy assistant secretary was ended, but Abrams did not attempt to replace me as office director for human rights. We quickly established rapport and mutual respect.

Elliott Abrams deserves much credit for salvaging human rights as an important element in U.S. foreign policy—credit he has seldom received. In place of highly vocal, public criticism of human rights violators, he favored quiet diplomacy—traditional démarches and appeals to erring governments, particularly when these governments were U.S. allies.

In 1981, the Berlin Wall had not yet come down; the Cold War was still a fact of diplomatic life. Adopting the thesis put forth by Jeane Kirkpatrick, the Reagan administration, spearheaded by Abrams, developed different approaches for dealing with authoritarian governments and totalitarian ones. The thought was that under authoritarian governments, not all freedoms were circumscribed, and there was some hope that the countries would evolve in democratic ways; under totalitarian regimes, the state controlled all aspects of citizens' lives, frequently by harsh means. Several key allies of the United States fell into the authoritarian camp, such as the Philippines, South Korea, and Turkey. The totalitarian regimes generally were the hard-line Communist countries, principally the Soviet Union and the People's Republic of China. Authoritarian allies with which the United States had some leverage through, for example, aid or security protection, would generally be approached with quiet diplomacy to urge them to mend their ways. Totalitarian governments, with which the United States had little leverage, would be criticized publicly if they did not respond favorably to traditional representations.

The Reagan administration also publicly touted the efficacy of democratic governments as the best insurance of protection of human rights. Spreading democracy became a key element in U.S. human rights policy. This was not a new development; various programs under the Carter administration had been aimed at strengthening democratic institutions and supporting free elections. But the Reagan administration, as represented by Abrams, highlighted this support for the spread of democracy and the differentiation of the treatment that would be accorded authoritarian and totalitarian regimes. These differences may have been emphasized in order to distinguish the two administrations' approaches to this still controversial foreign policy element.

While the public rhetoric concerning human rights policy changed, the practical application of the policy, in accordance with relevant legislation, continued without significant change. The human rights bureau still pressed reluctant geographic bureaus to seek redress from their respective client governments for victims of human rights violations. Export licenses and international bank loans continued to be rigorously scrutinized, and occasionally denied on human rights grounds. But public criticism of friendly nations became rarer by far than under the leadership of Patricia Derian.

Iranian Asylum Issues

We learned early in Abrams's tenure, however, that he had strong views on certain refugee issues. One of the human rights bureau's key functions was reviewing requests by refugees for political asylum. Each case was considered carefully against the practices of the particular host government. To be granted political asylum, the refugee had to be in danger of persecution if returned to his or her home country. In the case of Iran, all indications were that followers of the Baha'i religion were treated badly in Iran, and would be persecuted if returned to that country. The Baha'i were a breakaway sect of Islam, and Islam does not tolerate defections. The human rights bureau generally approved requests for asylum from followers of Baha'i.

Iran regarded Jews, however, as "people of the book," followers of Moses, a forerunner of the Prophet. Christians, followers of Jesus, were also people of the book. We had no indications that Jews were persecuted because of their religion in Iran, and had denied requests for political asylum from Jews who had fled that country.

Within a few days of his confirmation as assistant secretary, Abrams met with the asylum staff and me and made it clear that Iranian Jews would no longer be denied political asylum in the United States should they seek it. He listened to our explanation for the existing policy, but was unmoved. I suspected that Abrams, a Jew himself, was remembering the Holocaust and the fact that the United States in the 1930s and early 1940s had denied entrance to European Jews. I believe that the bureau's reading of the Iranian situation regarding religious persecution was correct. Iran clearly was a totalitarian, harsh state, however, so Abrams's decision probably had merit. We saluted and carried out the new policy.

United Nations Commission on Human Rights

The United Nations Commission on Human Rights (UNCHR), as it existed at that time, met annually in Geneva to review the state of human rights around the world. Unfortunately, not all of the countries elected yearly to the commission and its successor organization (United Nations Human Rights Council) are respecters of human rights themselves. Frequently, the meetings degenerated into contests between competing countries to get resolutions condemning their favorite enemies. Israel was routinely singled out for criticism. The United States usually tried to get a condemnation of China's wretched human rights performance passed by the body.

Abrams was determined that the human rights bureau would be represented on the U.S. delegation to the 1981 meeting in Geneva. Jeane Kirkpatrick, UN ambassador, reportedly resisted, but he won out and I was assigned to go to Switzerland for the meeting. The U.S. delegation had coleaders: the renowned conservative

Catholic theologian, Michael Novak, and Richard Schifter, a noted neoconservative close to the administration.

I was excited at the chance to participate as a delegate at my first international conference. I suspected early on that Novak and Schifter were not excited at the prospect of having an untried bureaucrat, a holdover from the Patt Derian era, on their delegation. On the flight to Geneva, Schifter took the trouble to ask me how much reading I had done about international communism. I don't think he was reassured by my response, even though I had spent almost five years of my career in the effort to attempt to prevent a Communist takeover in Vietnam.

Once in Geneva, however, the two organized the delegation efficiently and quickly set us to work lobbying for the results the United States wanted. I performed capably, in my view, but I still sensed that I was regarded as possibly not enough of a true believer for our delegation leaders' taste.

To my chagrin, a Sunday trip to Chamonix, France, for a look at Mont Blanc with Foreign Service friends assigned to the U.S. mission in Geneva brought an abrupt end to my service on the delegation. Returning to our car at the end of a pleasant afternoon in that charming town, I slipped on ice and broke my right wrist. As I am right-handed, this put an end to any possible note taking at commission sessions, or typing of cables and other reports. After just two weeks in Geneva, I headed back to the United States for medical care and recuperation.

In retrospect, this might have proven to be a lucky break (so to speak). I do not think that longer exposure to my work would have sufficiently reassured Novak and Schifter that I was ideologically suited to be a member of the U.S. delegation to the UNCHR. I felt that I had failed Abrams by my accident, but he never indicated in any way that he was displeased about it. I resumed my usual work in the bureau after a brief respite and read the cable traffic from Geneva with detached interest.

More Effort on Behalf of Kim Dae-jung

The imprisonment of South Korea's Kim Dae-jung continued to be a nagging issue in the improving U.S.–Korean relationship. Once a new ambassador was assigned to Korea (a capable Southern academic), he began quiet dialogue with that government on Kim's behalf. Kim was known to have a heart problem, and the conditions of his detention were not pleasant.

Eventually, the ambassador persuaded the Korean government to allow Kim to go to the United States for treatment of his heart condition. Abrams pressed this matter, along with our ambassador, and helped to arrange a Harvard fellowship for Kim at the conclusion of his medical treatment. Once at Harvard, Kim visited the bureau and met with Abrams. I was privileged to meet with him briefly. He thanked us profusely for our assistance. Some months later, I received a note from Kim, thanking me personally (and undeservedly) for my help.

After an extended stay in the United States (an academic year, or perhaps longer), Kim returned to Korea, perhaps concluding that his political prospects would suffer if he enjoyed U.S. hospitality indefinitely. At the airport, the ham-handed Korean government roughed up Kim and members of his entourage, which included Patt Derian (who had accompanied him in an effort to focus attention on his return, and thus protect him). Kim was imprisoned again, but was quickly released to house arrest.

The political situation in Korea eventually evolved to the point that free elections became the norm. In 1997, Kim was elected president. He reached out to North Korea, attempting to establish family visitations for long-separated people, as well as to help to develop the North Korean economy in very modest ways. For these efforts, he received the Nobel Peace Prize.

Human Rights Cases

Although the Reagan administration's human rights bureau generally publicly criticized only its totalitarian adversaries, much quiet attention was paid to attempting to alleviate abuses perpetrated by America's authoritarian allies. Perhaps the most significant success was the freeing of Kim Dae-jung, but there were many other successful interventions. Benazir Bhutto, politician daughter of the former dictator of Pakistan, was freed from house arrest and traveled to the United States as a result, at least in part, of pressure from the

U.S. government, which HA had a prominent role in generating. She visited the bureau after her release to thank the United States for our help and to discuss ongoing developments in Pakistan. She later was elected to the Pakistani parliament and served as prime minister. Regrettably, her tenure was clouded by allegations of corruption, stemming in part from her husband's actions. (Tragically, she was assassinated in 2008 while campaigning in the national elections in Pakistan.)

A delegation from the Mothers of the Plaza de Mayo visited HA from Argentina to press for help in getting that country's military government to account for the thousands of "disappeared" people who had been rounded up on suspicion of subversive activities and never seen again. HA's doors were open to a vast array of nongovernmental organizations (NGOs) pressing human rights agendas in support of victims around the world. Our African American secretaries were thrilled one afternoon when the charismatic Reverend Jesse Jackson came to call; he charmed them all. Before Abrams came on board, I had spent an interesting hour with the noted folk singer Joan Baez, who wished to inquire about human rights in Vietnam now that it was under Communist control. She had been a committed opponent of the war in Vietnam, but had grown troubled at the Communists' imposition of severe controls in the South.

Meanwhile, HA was encouraging our embassy in Moscow to seek freedom of emigration from the USSR for large numbers of peaceful dissidents, many of whom were Jewish, whose opposition to the Communist regime had resulted in loss of their jobs or, in many cases, imprisonment in Siberia and elsewhere. Under this quiet pressure, the Kremlin gradually opened the doors to many of these individuals. Most of them emigrated to Israel; a leading figure in this group, Natan Sharansky, emerged as a leading archconservative politician in Israel, where he eventually earned a cabinet post. In Africa, quiet U.S. efforts resulted in the emigration of several hundred Ethiopian Jews to Israel.

Export License Disputes

With a strong assistant secretary again on board, HA could play a stronger role in reviewing export licenses of military equipment and sensitive electronic devices (computers that could serve both military and civilian purposes, for example). Manufacturers in the United States who had orders to sell military equipment to human rights abusers had to get Department of Commerce clearance for the sale, and then Commerce had to obtain State Department clearance for the export of the goods—rifles, cattle prods, tear gas and other crowd control items, and big-ticket items such as aircraft and tanks. Several bureaus in State had to review the proposed sale. HA frequently was the dissenter in sales to authoritarian allies. With a conservative Republican administration in power, exporters probably suspected that HA's role would diminish. During the period when Ernest Lefever was sitting in the HA front office prior to his confirmation hearing, for example, he agreed to approve the sale of some crowd control equipment to China. In my view, he had been snookered by a bureaucrat more committed to the sale of U.S. goods than to the human rights' implications of the sale. I reviewed the law with him, and to my knowledge he did not make any additional unstaffed commitments on sales.

Abrams, however, despite his totalitarian-authoritarian thesis, sincerely believed that the United States had an obligation to encourage or, if necessary, pressure its friends as well as its enemies to improve their human rights behavior. For example, unknown to the public, Abrams held the line on military sales to Argentina and Chile, two particularly abusive Latin American dictatorships. In their effort to combat or forestall Communist insurgencies in their countries, the military leaders of these two countries dubbed any opposition as Communist or Communist-inspired, and cracked down ruthlessly. Thousands of young men and women were rounded up and never heard from again. It subsequently became known that these "disappeared" people had been brutally tortured and, in many cases, taken out over the ocean in helicopters and dropped into the sea.

HA faced frequent pressure from the Latin American bureau to approve sales of controversial equipment to these dictatorships. I had many a bitter battle with my colleagues in ARA (Office of American Republics Affairs, the bureau that looked after Latin America). When I would not agree to approve a license, the battle was taken to Abrams by his counterpart in the other bureau. To my knowledge, he refused to approve any significant arms sales to these two countries during his tenure. Again, this was not publicized; our "friends" were entitled to quiet diplomacy, but they were not entitled to U.S. military equipment with which to abuse their unarmed civilians.

El Salvador Certification

The struggle in the little Central American country of El Salvador by the military dictatorship to defeat a Communist insurgency became a particularly difficult human rights issue. The insurgency was aided by Cuba and other Communist countries. The United States firmly supported the incumbent military dictatorship in its efforts to keep a Communist government out of power. Thus, significant quantities of U.S. aid, economic and military, went to the admittedly brutal dictatorship. The regime's egregious abuses included not only terrorizing random Indian villages suspected of harboring Communist guerrillas (thus quite likely inspiring village recruits for the insurgency) but also blatantly assassinating critics of the regime. The Catholic archbishop of El Salvador was murdered on the altar of his church during Sunday mass; he had been outspoken in his denunciation of the regime's human rights abuses. Three American Maryknoll nuns who had been working among the poor were slaughtered. Despite these abuses, the United States believed that the military regime was the lesser of two evils, there being no stomach to watch another Cuba become ensconced in the hemisphere. So aid continued, while remonstrations were made about the necessity of restoring a freely elected government.

Elements in Congress, outraged by the abuses in El Salvador, enacted legislation that they hoped would hamstring the Reagan administration in administering assistance to the military government there. For aid to continue, the State Department was required to submit to Congress an annual detailed report of human rights abuses in El Salvador (in addition to the annual report already mandated) with the "certification" that progess was being made in ameliorating human rights abuses. Before this legislation was enacted, the administration had been intensely engaged with the government in El Salvador in a series of efforts aimed at improving the situation. An ongoing major effort was directed toward strengthening the Salvadoran legal and judicial system, and a new constitution was being drafted, with U.S. input, with a view to reinstating free and fair elections. Our embassy was interacting daily with the Salvadoran government to press for accountability when abuses surfaced. Still, the U.S. administration did not wish to cut off aid to El Salvador, which, first, might well have led to greatly intensified fighting and even more ruthless tactics on the part of the military; and, second, could eventually have led to a Communist takeover, which would preclude free and fair elections. Thus, drafting and obtaining interdepartmental clearance for the certification report on El Salvador was a difficult task. Abrams was insistent that the report be full and honest, but there was no desire to stop aid and have the likely grim scenario mentioned above ensue. The report therefore had to state the facts, but it also had to conclude that progress was being made. Participating in the drafting of this report and the vetting of the final draft, in meetings with sometimes fifteen to twenty others, was the most difficult task I encountered during my time in HA. I was ultimately comfortable that we had made a fair case for continuing aid to El Salvador; progress, however slowly, was being made. At the same time, we knew that the report would be excoriated by some members of Congress and by human rights NGOs.

Over time, our policy succeeded. Prodded by the U.S. government, the Salvadoran military agreed to elections, and a respected civilian was elected president. Reforms were introduced, and the insurgency faded significantly in intensity. El Salvador did not fall into communism, and its human rights situation continued to improve, albeit gradually.

Bringing Our Children Home from Vietnam

From the beginning of my association with Elliott Abrams, I was greatly impressed by his quick intelligence and can-do, let's-get-it-done approach to issues. His contacts with senior administration officials gave him an inside track to the ultimate decisionmakers, and he knew when to use this asset. I sensed that he also wanted to put a caring face on the Reagan administration human rights policy. Therefore, I did not hesitate to seek his assistance when I was presented with a proposal to enact legislation that would allow the illegitimate children of Americans who had served in Vietnam to emigrate to the United States.

One morning in 1982, my work was interrupted by a visit from two old Foreign Service acquaintances from Saigon days. One man was working in the consular affairs bureau in a position roughly equivalent to mine in rank. The other held a similar position in the bureau of refugee affairs. They informed me that they and a few other Vietnam veterans like myself were attempting to put together legislation that would allow the offspring of Americans in Vietnam (overwhelmingly children of our military personnel, but most likely also including some sired by civilians) to emigrate to the United States. He asked if I could enlist Abrams's assistance in getting support from the department and other elements of the U.S. government for this effort, so that Congress could be persuaded to pass this humanitarian legislation.

My friends and I both knew from personal experience that mixed-race children were ostracized in Vietnam and in most other Asian countries. Under the best of circumstances, they faced a difficult life as victims of prejudice. As the probable offspring of a defeated enemy, their situation was much worse. They resorted to begging on the streets and had little opportunity to obtain any kind of education.

We also knew that the French, Vietnam's colonial occupier, had granted citizenship to the offspring of French citizens, and had relocated them in France after the French defeat in the early 1950s. Yet the United States had not faced up to what those of us who had served in Vietnam regarded as a moral obligation to rescue these children from a fate over which they had had no say.

I told my consular affairs and refugee bureau friends that I enthusiastically supported the idea. They gave me a draft of the proposed legislation. It was a short provision to be included in a major overhaul of our immigration legislation, which was expected to be debated in Congress during the current session. I told them I would speak to the assistant secretary, and was reasonably confident that he would endorse the idea.

I went to see Abrams as soon as my friends left and briefed him on the issue. In his typical let's-get-it-done-now manner, he bought into the idea immediately. He said he would call a White House official and raise the matter. He did so as soon as I left his office. He then called and asked me to give him a one-page briefing on the issue immediately, because he planned to take it with him to a luncheon meeting with the White House official. I attacked the typewriter keys, and, in the ten or fifteen minutes available, pounded out a one-page explanation of the issue, which Abrans grabbed as he left the office for his meeting.

Abrams informed me later that the initial meeting had gone well, and he was confident that the White House official had been convinced of the rightness of the cause. Elliott was also confident that the president would agree to the legislation.

The legislation had a rocky ride through Congress, however. The entire bill was debated at length and delayed for well over a year. My fellow protagonists kept me informed of its progress, and I alerted Abrams when a phone call or memo from him could help nudge the process forward. Eventually, the provision to bring the Amerasian children of Vietnam to the United States became the law of the land. The law also provided that the mothers and siblings of these children could also be resettled in the United States, because it would make no sense to bring the children without their mothers. In virtually all cases, the fathers of these children were only casually known by the mothers, or had made it clear they wished no contact.

So the much-maligned U.S. government, funded by Mr. and Mrs. Joe Citizen's taxes, did the right thing and rescued these innocent human mementos of our failed effort to save Vietnam from a Communist takeover.

I am proud to have had even a small role in realizing this legislation. All I did was persuade a strong political insider, Elliott Abrams, to lend his energy, enthusiasm, and political connections toward advocating and tracking the legislation. But I am confident that his role contributed substantially toward gaining White House support for the measure, and that support, I am equally confident, helped garner the necessary support in Congress to pass the measure. Several thousand Vietnamese-Americans were successfully resettled in the United States, where they at least had a chance to achieve a reasonable life, in freedom.

Extension in HA; Next Assignment

As my two-year tour neared its end, the list of available positions coming open in my time frame did not excite me. I was, however, enjoying my work in HA and being back in my own Washington co-op apartment. I was pleased when Abrams said that he would welcome an extension of my tour for a year.

The year passed quickly, and it was again time to seek an onward assignment. I was approached by a counselor in personnel, who urged me to apply to be chargé d'affaires in Laos. I initially was reluctant. I was still scarred from my Vietnam experience, and I hesitated to return to Indochina, to a Communist country that was still hostile to the United States. Once again, however, my quest for a DCM assignment elsewhere failed. I made the final cut on a few good posts, but again, others of the male persuasion were selected. Another call from the personnel counselor, urging me to put in a bid for the Laos chargéship before it was assigned to another of the many FSOs seeking the post, tipped the scales for me. I decided that it was a long shot, because this would be a chief of mission slot, something to which I aspired, but which I did not think was in the cards for at least another assignment or two. I entered my bid.

Abrams keenly wanted FSOs who were assigned to HA to get decent onward assignments. When I told him about my bid to be chargé in Laos, he spoke personally with his fellow political appointee, Assistant Secretary Paul Wolfowitz, who was heading the East Asian and Pacific bureau. I met with Wolfowitz. He did not seem overwhelmed by me, and he was being pressed by several other people to choose their candidate. But he selected me for the position. Since it was a chief of mission slot, though at the chargé level, his word got me the job. Never having served as a DCM, I was now eliminating that step and would soon have my own small embassy to run.

Preparing for my overseas departure, I learned from my physical examination that HA had taken a toll (though minor, I hoped) on my health. I had high blood pressure for the first time in my life, and heart arrhythmia was noticeable. I explained to my doctor that I attributed the high blood pressure to the stress of my job, which frequently involved tendentious dealings with colleagues in other bureaus. A daily generator of tensions was the morning effort to craft press guidance for the department spokesman to use at his noon briefing. When an egregious or suspicious event occurred in a foreign country overnight, the spokesman had to be prepared to respond to questions from the press corps at noon. This press guidance formed the initial basis of U.S. policy regarding the event and the country concerned, and it was thus important to strike the right note of concern. HA usually wanted to go further in the language than the geographic bureaus did, and if agreement could not readily be achieved, the matter escalated to the assistant-secretary level, and sometimes to the deputy secretary or to the secretary himself. This debate took place against the racing clock— the briefing started promptly at noon. Although I accepted the doctor's recommendations concerning certain diet changes to control my blood pressure, I was reasonably confident that when I left the human rights policy struggles behind me, my blood pressure would revert to normal. And it did.

9

Chargé d'Affaires in Laos

In the fall of 1983, I was on my way to the Lao People's Democratic Republic to be chargé d'affaires. I was given a letter of credence from the secretary of state, which I presented to the Lao foreign minister. Had I been an ambassador, I would have had a letter of credence from the president of the United States, which I would have presented to the chief of state of the host country.

The United States had been able to retain a small presence in Laos at the end of the Indochina war principally because of the intervention of Prince Souvanna Phouma. He was one of three key figures in the Lao government during the Indochina war. He represented the neutralist faction in what became a three-party coalition government. One of his brothers, Prince Souvannaphong, was known as the Red Prince—he was a Communist. There was a third faction in the government, a rightist group. Souvanna Phouma was the balancing figure among these three. During the Vietnam War, the United States maintained a substantial presence in Laos.

Laos was an active theater of the Indochina war. Both the United States and Vietnam carried on extensive military operations there. U.S. aircraft regularly bombed the so-called Ho Chi Minh Trail in eastern Laos, a major supply route southward from North Vietnam.

When the Vietnamese succeeded in chasing the United States out of Vietnam in 1975, the Communist faction in Laos, the Pathet Lao (a client of the Viet Minh, its North Vietnamese counterpart), took over power; the coalition government collapsed. That was the end of the large U.S. presence in Laos. Souvanna Phouma, whose status kept him from imprisonment and gave him an initial advisory role with the new government, decided that it would benefit Laos if some U.S. presence remained in the country. He reportedly prevailed upon the leadership of Laos to allow a very small American embassy to remain in country. He could not have done this without the approval of the Vietnamese government, which was the Big Brother of the Lao Communists and very likely called many of the shots. The Vietnamese probably saw benefit to retaining some contact with the Americans. From the American point of view, it was useful to have a window into Indochina. Vietnamese demands for war reparations from the United States made establishing diplomatic relations with that country impossible at that time. Pol Pot's atrocities in Cambodia blocked diplomatic relations with that country. With no U.S. diplomatic presence in either Cambodia or Vietnam, maintaining a small embassy in Laos served the interests of the United States, and most likely of Vietnam as well.

When I arrived in 1983, Vientiane was a quiet little Indochinese town on the banks of the Mekong River. Automobile traffic was scarce; bicycles, imported from China, were a common means of transport, but even these were not many. Traffic of any kind was sparse. Trees were not as abundant as in many Indochinese towns; the government had removed many large trees that had once lined the main thoroughfare, creating a barren look and intensifying the impact of the heat. Communist-style billboards abounded, exhorting the citizenry to strive to achieve government goals. Still, with the river vista and the numerous pagodas and temples that graced the town, Vientiane possessed a sleepy charm.

In 1983, eight Americans were at the post. There was a small Lao staff, some fifteen to twenty people. We still occupied the embassy and a complex across the street, which included our GSO (General Services Office) warehouse and some other buildings in which we rattled around. The administrative and GSO staff had their offices in that complex, and we refurbished some space to provide an apartment for temporary visitors, as the hotels in Vientiane at that time left much to be desired. But compared with what the United States presence had been in the country during our heaviest involvement in Laos, this was a minuscule operation.

I had occasion to visit Laos when I was in Da Nang in early 1974. A good friend of mine from Saigon days, Betty Price, was with USAID in Vientiane. She invited me to visit, and I did so for a few days, during which I got the full picture of the U.S. presence at its peak: the huge housing compounds, the residential hotels, the recreational facilities, the PX (Post Exchange), and so on. It was a far cry from that situation when I returned to Laos not even ten years later to be chief of mission. It was strange to pass compounds that had been U.S. property—and which technically were still U.S. property—but had been confiscated by the Lao and put to their own uses (an issue we were working on with the Lao at that time, and probably still are). I had no illusions that I would be successful in getting the Lao to return the property or to compensate us for it.

We were small and constrained in Vientiane, but it was a very interesting tour.

Souvanna Phouma had been pretty much marginalized in the Lao government when I arrived in 1983. He was respected, but he had nonetheless been sidelined. Although he was aging and ill, he was the individual who had been instrumental in keeping a window open for Laos to the United States and the West. Within the Lao government, there was a lot of conflict about how to deal with the West, and particularly with the United States. This conflict was particularly apparent in the attitudes of the interior and foreign ministries. The foreign ministry was staffed largely by more or less experienced diplomats, foreign educated, who had in some cases served abroad and were aware of the world outside Laos. Some Communist hardliners, of course, were also sprinkled through the ministry to keep the troops in line.

The diplomats in the foreign ministry saw the benefit to Laos of keeping the window open to the United States, rather than continuing to be cut off from and hostile toward the West. The interior ministry people were the die-hard Pathet Lao Communists. They had lived in the mountains for many years, sometimes in the caves in Xieng Khouang Province, where they had endured heavy U.S. bombing. They were not inclined toward friendship with their former enemy, and they did not see the benefits of strengthening a relationship with the United States. Reconciling the conflicting attitudes of the interior and foreign ministries was a challenge for the Lao government.

Accounting for U.S. Prisoners of War and Missing in Action

My primary charge in Laos was to try to further the cause of locating and identifying U.S. prisoners of war and those missing in action. Under the administration of President Jimmy Carter, the impression was conveyed that the POW/MIA issue was not a matter of high priority to the U.S. government. Perhaps President Carter and his people thought it was best to move on and not expend energy and political capital with the host country to try to make progress on these issues. But President Ronald Reagan and his Republican administration made resolving this issue to the extent possible a very high-priority issue. I was directed to give my highest attention to trying to improve the bilateral relationship, with a view to gaining Lao approval for the United States to conduct joint excavations where U.S. planes had crashed during the Vietnam War, and where it was hoped that the remains of American service personnel could be recovered and returned to their families. The White House was deeply engaged in this issue. A private group of family members of the missing in action, the League of Families, exerted a lot of constructive pressure on the White House, Congress, and the State Department to work on this issue. I was completely in tune with this matter. I could envision how agonizing it was for families of servicemen not to know where their husband, father, or brother rested, and how reassuring it would be to recover and properly inter their remains.

Making progress toward this goal, however, was not an easy matter. In addition to overcoming the reluctance of the interior ministry, we had to deal with the negative effects of some private initiatives by American groups that complicated our efforts. A retired U.S. Army lieutenant colonel, Bo Gritz, was active in Thailand, rallying Hmong refugees to conduct raids into Laos across the Mekong River, ostensibly to search for POWs. (The Hmong are a hill tribe, opposed to the Lao coalition government, that had worked with the United States in Laos against the Communists in the Vietnam War.) Gritz claimed that there were camps hidden in the jungles of Laos where U.S. POWs were still being held captive. This is not a view that I shared, although I could not state this view publicly. The official U.S. view was deliberately vague on this issue, as we could not categorically rule out the possibility that some prisoners were being held somewhere. But, basically, those of us who dealt most closely with this issue were persuaded that there were no POWs being held in Indochina against their will. There might have been a few "stay behinds" who had remained after the war for their own reasons, but I strongly doubted that there were any such individuals in Laos. Gritz, however, apparently of a different mind, sporadically conducted raids across the Mekong River from Thailand, allegedly to search for POWs.

Everyday Life

Life in Laos was very constrained for the American community and for Westerners in general. Americans were confined to the city limits of Vientiane. We could go from the city limits on the south side of the city to the airport, a distance of perhaps four or five miles. Going east from the Mekong River, we could drive about a mile or two. That was the extent of the movement we were allowed. This was a very claustrophobic operating environment. One of the saving graces for the embassy staff was that there was a fairly sizable Western community in Vientiane—Australians, Swedes, a few Germans, and a small British presence, which made up in spirit and activities what they lacked in numbers. The Australians and Swedes had fairly substantial aid programs. The Australians had a very nice club next to the Mekong River with a restaurant, bar, and swimming pool; they allowed our staff access to that club, which gave our staff an outlet, a recreation site. I went there occasionally, but I decided that I would not go there too often, because I did not want to constrain my staff's enjoyment of the facilities. I thought they would be a little more comfortable in their off hours if the chargé was not at the next table.

At my lovely ambassador's residence, I had a very nice swimming pool, which I had opened to my entire staff, some of whom would occasionally come and use it. But the jewel in the residence crown was an excellent tennis court, which got very frequent use. My staff and members of the Western community were free to use the tennis court and did so regularly.

To help the staff cope with the isolation and claustrophobic living conditions, we had regular diplomatic pouch runs to Bangkok.

The embassy in Bangkok provided our small embassy with many support services, including the handling of our diplomatic pouches. Once a week, one of our American staffers went down to Bangkok carrying our pouch; the pouch bearer's airfare and hotel tab were paid for two days, and an additional day or so on the messenger's own tab could be added. The basic trips were considered work related, so there was no charge to annual leave.

Usually, the courier left on Thursday and returned to Vientiane on Sunday or Monday, which offered a good respite from the tedium of confinement to the city limits of Vientiane. This helped the couriers a lot. It helped me, too. I went down perhaps every two months. Certain matters, such as administrative support, required consultation with the embassy in Bangkok, and I had to review certain classified materials there from time to time, so I was a willing candidate for the occasional trip to Bangkok.

My Bangkok Friend

I was fortunate to establish an excellent relationship with the American ambassador to Thailand at that time, John Gunther Dean. His reputation was that he was perhaps overly persnickety, perhaps overly convinced of his own brilliance, and perhaps sometimes difficult to work with. But I found him to be a wonderful colleague. He was very helpful to me. He wanted me to meet with him to compare notes whenever I visited Bangkok. He had also served in Da Nang as the senior officer during the CORDS period, so we had something in common. In fact, it turned out that we had had the same maid, a competent Vietnamese woman who, because she was a member of a large family, remained in Vietnam.

In addition to his stellar service in Laos, Ambassador Dean had helped settle some Vietnamese refugees in the United States, as I had done with my children. I think what he enjoyed was that even though my staff was quite small, I was still a chief of mission and we had certain things in common. He could talk to me about common issues or personnel issues—nothing specific, just general concerns. He could speak freely to me, and I could share my similar experiences with him. Neither of us could have done that with a member of our staffs. To that extent, we met as equals.

He could not have been kinder to me. He invited me to stay at his residence, with his lovely wife. I did stay with them a couple of times, but I did not want to outstay my welcome. And there was something relaxing about going to a nice hotel and getting away from the entire official environment once the workday was over. But Ambassador Dean and his wife went out of their way to show me a gracious time.

For me, the confinement in Vientiane was not as trying as it was for the other members of the staff. I always had work to do—reports, analyses, and books to read, for example—that more than filled my time. And I was chief of mission, building a career. For my American staff members, this was a difficult situation. When they went home at night, they were by and large on their own time. They did not have the same outlets of career or work pressures that I did, nor the requisite diplomatic social life that I had to participate in, to occupy their free hours. So the trips to Bangkok served an excellent purpose.

Ambassador Dean always knew when I was coming to Bangkok—diplomatic courtesy required that he be informed in advance of my trips—and often included me in interesting Thai-based activities. On one occasion when I had informed him of my planned visit, the ambassador's wife insisted that I stay with them because there was a particularly interesting event to which she had been invited, and she wanted me to go with her. The event was planned for early morning, so it would be more efficient if I stayed at their residence and left with her for the event. On this occasion, the event was the Royal Plowing Ceremony, at which the revered king of Thailand presided over the symbolic first plowing of the season. The king and his retinue, elaborately dressed, actually led a spotless white ox in breaking the soil and planting some seeds to officially launch the plowing season. Buddhist monks in colorful saffron robes blessed the proceedings. The Thai excel at beautiful, elaborate traditional ceremonies, and it was a unique experience to share in this one and to see the king of Thailand up close from the seats reserved for the diplomatic corps.

I Meet Pope John Paul II

It was thanks to Ambassador Dean that I got to meet Pope John Paul II. The pope had planned his first visit to Thailand, and the ambassador suggested that I make sure my next Bangkok consultations coincided with the pope's trip. He said that the pope would preside over a mass, and other interesting events were planned.

The pope's visit was to occur in two months, about the time that I would have normally had to go to Bangkok for consultations, so the timing worked quite well. Upon arriving at the embassy, I paid my usual courtesy call on the ambassador. After our chat, he told me that the following evening the pope was going to say mass at a downtown stadium, and if I wished, he could get me into the diplomatic corps section for the mass. I of course did so wish, and he arranged the seating for me.

I then went about other business at the embassy. A little while later, the ambassador's secretary tracked me down and said that the ambassador wanted to see me right away—I was to go to his office immediately. I hurried back, and the ambassador told me that he had just had a good idea: He had been invited to a reception being given by the prime minister for the pope, at 5:30 p.m., and he thought he could get me into the reception. He would be taking his wife, and if I were willing to take a chance, I could ride with them and he would see if he could talk me in. The reception was only for the diplomatic corps in Thailand, he said, but he thought he could gain my admittance.

I accepted immediately. I returned quickly to my hotel to change into something more appropriate for meeting the pope than the dress I had worn to the embassy. Since I had not known about the possible meeting, I did not have a perfect outfit, but I was comfortable that the dress I chose would pass muster. I returned quickly to the embassy, and we took off in his car and picked up his wife. He placed me in the back seat next to him, and placed his wife in the front seat. From the standpoint of protocol, the senior people sit in the rear, so this was a signal he would be sending to the Thai reception committee that I was a person of some significance (at least in the ambassador's view).

We pulled up to a beautiful palace, where we were greeted at the car door by a senior aide to the prime minister, dressed in a sparkling white military-type uniform. Ambassador Dean carried off the plan easily. He was tall and handsome, with an imposing presence, a man who looked as though he had been selected from birth to be a significant ambassador. He emerged from the car to be greeted warmly by the palace aide. I followed, and Dean took my arm and said to the aide: "And this is our ambassador to Laos. I thought I would bring her along, too." The aide briefly had a slightly perplexed look on his face, but he nodded and smiled and up I went into the reception.

It was a memorable occasion. The pope arrived, and after being welcomed by the prime minister, he made some remarks, after which he came around and met all of the ambassadors individually. Ambassador Dean introduced me to John Paul II as the ambassador to Laos—the second time that evening he had promoted me. I was absolutely thrilled to meet the pope. I kissed his ring, banishing any thoughts of separation of church and state from my Catholic mind.

The occasion was made even more memorable for me when a few weeks later I received from the apostolic delegate to Thailand, Monsignor Renato Martino, a picture taken at the moment I was introduced to the pope. I knew Martino, a fine man, from his occasional visits to Laos, and he very kindly sent me this memento. I must confess that in the photograph I do not display the cool aplomb of a diplomat—I look positively starry-eyed, about which I make no apology. The pope had an aura of goodness that to me seemed to radiate from his person. It was a rare privilege to meet him.

Religion in Laos

Under the Communist government in Laos, religion was severely constricted. The predominant religion in Laos was, and is, Buddhism, of the type practiced by Buddhists in Thailand. Thai and Lao Buddhists are generally not oriented toward political activism, as was the case in pre-Communist Vietnam, where South Vietnamese Buddhists actively campaigned against the non-Communist governments there. After the Communist takeover in Laos, the government initially attempted to crack down on the practice of religion by all citizens, who, as noted before, were overwhelmingly

Buddhists. The government discouraged the people from practicing Buddhism, and constrained the activities of the many saffron-clad Buddhist monks. But the people quietly resisted these efforts, and by the time I arrived in Laos in 1983, the pressure had eased. In the early mornings, you could see groups of monks leaving their temples with their begging bowls, seeking food and alms from willing Lao, continuing a centuries-old tradition. I believe that the government came to realize that the monks and the temples performed valid, helpful social services for the people. Among other things, the monks were a source of care for the mentally ill. If a family member was mentally disturbed, the family would take the individual to a temple, where he or she would be cared for. Some modest medical care would also sometimes be provided at the temples. Thus, Buddhism managed to survive.

There was a small Roman Catholic presence in Laos, probably originating with the French colonial presence in that country. When I arrived in Laos, there was a rather young bishop in Vientiane, and an elderly bishop who was ill and who did not have very long to live. I believe there was also one priest in Pakse, in the south of Laos. The small Catholic community was striving to hold on to and practice their religion, despite government suspicions and constraints.

When I first arrived in Vientiane, I wondered whether it would be helpful, or harmful, to the status of the Roman Catholic Church in Laos if I attended mass. Would my presence, as the senior American official in Laos, at church be a source of suspicion for the Lao government? Would my attendance help in a sense to protect the church, and the important human right of freedom of religion, by demonstrating to the government that the U.S. government was, in effect, keeping an eye on the fate of practitioners of religion? Before I attended mass, I had one of my staff approach the young bishop and ask his opinion. The bishop was delighted at the prospect at having the senior American official attend his church; he thought it would be helpful. So I regularly attended services and made financial contributions to the church to aid the bishop's various charitable efforts.

On one occasion, early in my tour, I was not as discreet as I should have been. The bishop was in the church courtyard after mass, chatting with parishioners, and I approached him. When the others left, I handed him a sum of money that I had earmarked for his charities (in addition to the usual offering during mass). He looked stricken and asked me not to give him contributions in public. He pointed to an ice cream vendor at the edge of the property, selling his wares to departing churchgoers: "He's with the interior ministry." I got the message, and found less public ways to provide funds.

How did such a young priest become a bishop? The story speaks well of the clever diplomatic skills of the apostolic delegate to Thailand and Laos, Monsignor Martino. Martino, despite Lao government constraints, was determined to maintain basic contact with the church in Laos. He was able to do this because he would periodically seek permission to visit Laos to make a charitable contribution to the government on behalf of the Vatican, such as foodstuffs or medicines. The Lao government did not want to turn down needed supplies, so Martino was granted permission to visit. In the course of his visits, in addition to meeting with government officials (and, during my tour, with me and probably other diplomats), he met with the Catholic priests in Vientiane.

Several months before I arrived in Laos, the monsignor got word in Bangkok that the elderly bishop was very ill and probably did not have long to live; should he die, Laos would be without a bishop. The apostolic delegate arranged a visit to Laos to make another Vatican contribution of humanitarian assistance. During the Sunday mass, at which he presided, he consecrated the young priest to be a bishop. The young cleric took over the duties of the elderly bishop.

Not long after I arrived in Laos, the elderly bishop died. The question of attending his funeral mass arose among the Western ambassadors. We—the British, French, Australians, and I—discussed the matter and decided that we would all attend, in our official cars, flags flying, as a gesture of respect not only to the bishop but to the principle of freedom of religion. We did so, and I am sure it was duly noted. I was interested to see that there was also a large contingent of monks at the funeral as well, showing respect to this man who was highly regarded in the country. But the Lao government was mean-spirited toward the young bishop and demonstrated its pettiness in the context of the pope's visit to Thailand. Priests and bishops from all over Southeast Asia were invited to meet with the pope in Bangkok. But when the young bishop sought permission from his government to leave for the meeting in Thailand, the government denied his request. I spoke with the bishop about it, who said he was very disappointed to have missed this rare opportunity to meet the pontiff. But Laos was not a free country; it was Communist, and the government decided who could leave the country, and when.

The Pakse Operation

In late 1983, the Lao government agreed to let us begin preparations to conduct the first crash-site excavation in Indochina. Achieving agreement for this undertaking was not without challenges. Efforts had been under way between the two governments for some time before I got into the picture, but I added my efforts to those of the National Security Council's dedicated Lieutenant Colonel Richard Childress and the League of Families' articulate, intelligent, determined, pleasant leader in this effort, Ann Griffiths. She had established good rapport with the Lao in Washington and during her occasional visits to Vientiane.

A site in Pakse Province, one of the southernmost provinces in Laos, was chosen for the initial excavation. The first phase of this operation, which took place in December 1983, involved bringing a survey team from the Joint Casualty Resolution Center in Honolulu to Laos to explore the site to determine what would be needed in terms of personnel and equipment to conduct the actual excavation. The survey team, all of whom were U.S. Army personnel, was headed by a very capable and personable army colonel, Joseph B. Harvey. His staff brought a variety of expertise from other recovery efforts in other parts of the world. Their work in some respects mirrored that of archeologists: they had to sift sand and distinguish pieces of bones and useful debris (dog tags, identifying bits of aircraft) from other crash debris. The team impressed me as competent, dedicated professionals, eager to begin the long-sought search for the remains of their missing colleagues.

My principal contact with the foreign ministry was the

director of the ministry's Western capitalist division, Pheuiphanh Ngosivathanh. He was a very capable, intelligent diplomat. He had been educated in France. I had developed a good relationship with him. Working with him, I made arrangements for the team and me to go to Pakse and conduct the initial site survey. Pheuiphanh's deputy, a very capable young woman, accompanied us. She was much more in the Communist mode than her boss. Whereas he was more of a European-trained intellectual, she was much more ideological. This may have assisted our efforts when we ran into difficulty with the senior Communist official in Pakse Province. Regardless of what her personal views may have been about the budding rapprochement between our two countries suggested by the agreement to proceed with the crash-site excavation, she was a disciplined cadre who would do her best to accomplish the mission, I thought.

The day dawned, and we boarded an aging Russian helicopter. It was not constructed for comfort; seats consisted of bare-bones canvas seats arrayed down the sides of the interior of the chopper. The noise level was deafening, eliminating any possibility of conversation. The trip took a few hours, interrupted for a fuel stop about halfway down in Savannakhet.

As we were waiting to reboard the helicopter after refueling, the Lao air force helicopter pilot sidled past me and said surreptitiously, out of the corner of his mouth, "I trained in Texas with the U.S. Air Force," and gave me a quick smile. He apparently had pleasant memories of his past association with the U.S. military. Although I remained somewhat doubtful about the capacity of the old helicopter, I felt reassured about the qualifications of the pilot.

We arrived in Pakse without incident and were met by the senior provincial officials, who were clearly die-hard Pathet Lao who did not seem to have been out of the caves for very long. (The Pathet Lao had lived in caves in remote Lao provinces before seizing power in 1975.) They seemed suspicious of us, but led us out to the proposed crash site. It was a somewhat isolated spot, heavily forested with a lot of underbrush. We tiptoed carefully around the site, avoiding some apparent unexploded ordnance.

Our team went to work. But they had been at the job for hardly more than a half hour when the province chief informed our foreign ministry escort that the team had had sufficient time, and they would now have to leave. She conveyed this to me. I told her, no, no, they are not finished. I verified this with the colonel, who was shocked. He and his team had come all the way from Hawaii, and they had been promised adequate time to do the survey — and they clearly required more time. He correctly insisted that his team needed at least another couple of hours on the site at that time (before night fell), and they might have to return in the morning to finish the job.

I made a spirited representation to this effect to the foreign ministry representative and to the province chief (with the foreign ministry official interpreting for me). I insisted that we had obtained authorization from the deputy foreign minister to come to the site and survey it in the late afternoon and, if necessary, to continue the work the following morning. There was no way we were going to pack up and leave after only a half hour on the site. He was not happy with this, and the foreign ministry official spoke to him at length in Lao. I told the colonel to have his team go back to work and to proceed as quickly as they could, but to be thorough, while I continued arguing with the local official for adequate time for the team to complete its work. He and his team did so.

This unpleasant discussion continued for some time as the team continued its work. I urged the province chief to call the deputy foreign minister to verify my contentions (easier said than done, given the tenuous state of communications in Laos at that time). Eventually, the province chief very grudgingly gave in and agreed that the team could remain on the site a while longer.

Out of earshot of the reluctant province chief, I urged the foreign ministry representative as well to call the deputy foreign minister as soon as we returned to the provincial guesthouse where we were to be accommodated. I stressed that this survey had to be done right. We were moving ahead as a result of a good gesture on the part of the Lao government, but this would blow up in everyone's faces if the province chief's attitude prevailed. It would be a setback if the team, which had come thousands of miles to Laos from Hawaii, was prevented from conducting an operation that the central government at the highest levels had approved. To appease me, the foreign ministry official agreed that she would make the effort to contact the deputy foreign minister that evening. In the meantime, she asked if I would have the team work fast.

We remained on the site for another hour to an hour and a half, to the annoyance of the province chief. The colonel came to me and said that it was getting a little dark, so we packed up and returned to the government guesthouse in a state of some agitation and uncertainty as a result of the province chief's effort to short-circuit the survey. The Lao provided dinner for us at the guesthouse and ate at the same time as we did, but not with us, in the sense that the atmosphere was strained; there was next to no camaraderie. On our side, the team ate quickly and retired to our very basic accommodations. Before going to his room, however, the colonel told me quietly that while they hoped to be able to return to the site in the morning, if this were not possible, he thought that his team had managed to get enough information at the site to make their trip worthwhile. I cautioned him not to say this to anyone, as I had pressed very hard for additional access, which we had been promised when the survey trip had been arranged.

That evening, apparently, our escort got through to the foreign ministry. I also suspect that there may have been a phone call or radio message to the province chief from Vientiane, because in the morning there was a marked attitude change on the part of the province chief and his officials. Do you want to go out to the site again? No problem. We all did so. The province chief was all smiles and graciousness. Because most of the work had been accomplished the previous afternoon, we did not have to remain at the site very long.

We returned to the guesthouse for lunch, and the contrast in tone between the grim meal of the previous evening and this luncheon was marked. The word apparently had come from a top official in Vientiane that official policy was now to cooperate with the Americans on this operation, and the local official complied.

I suspect that the province chief had been persuaded by fellow Pathet Lao officials in the interior ministry to get with the program. I doubt that the word of the foreign ministry meant much to this official in a province a considerable distance from the capital. The incident also demonstrated, I believe, that the writ of the central government did not always extend very forcefully to distant provinces, where the local Communist officials held sway in their own hard-won fiefdoms.

The luncheon offered us became a most enjoyable celebration of cooperation at last achieved. Our Lao counterparts interacted with me and the U.S. military personnel freely and with evident pleasure. The meal was a near feast, with many courses. After the tension of the previous day, it was a relief to relax in the now-friendly atmosphere. The province chief and other lesser officials made frequent toasts with the potent local liquor, *lao lao*, a clear beverage made from rice—a killer of an alcoholic concoction. A tiny glassful could set you back on your heels. When the luncheon began, the province chief invited me to join him in such a toast. I felt I had to acquiesce, so I raised a glass of *lao lao* in a toast to our newfound cooperation. Delighted, he wanted me to have another drink with him, but I insisted that one was more than enough for me. Meanwhile, at the other end of the table, the Lao military personnel were engaging the U.S. military personnel in similar *lao lao* toasts.

The province chief continued to urge me to join him in additional toasts. Finally, I told him that I would designate one of our group to take my place in this ritual. I asked a tall, husky sergeant (who seemed likely to me to be able to handle a few more shots of *lao lao*) if he would be kind enough to do me the honor of handling toasts with the province chief. He complied, drinking more shots with the province chief with no visible ill effects.

So our preliminary venture into crash-site cooperation with the Lao government ended on a good note. We returned to Vientiane, with the Hawaii team satisfied with the results of their survey visit. I knew that when the team passed through Bangkok, they would probably be met by journalists seeking details of their trip, which most likely was the first visit a U.S. military team had made to Indochina since the end of the Vietnam War. I cautioned the colonel not to mention that unpleasant glitch that had concerned us on the first afternoon of our visit, but to instead speak positively and with appreciation of the overall cooperation we had received, stating that we looked forward to conducting the actual crash site excavation in the next dry season, in the spring of 1984. (Excavations could not be conducted in the rainy season, which was approaching.)

One of the issues related to the excavation effort that I worked on with the U.S. military, who were very willing to cooperate with me, was to find means to sweeten the effort with the Lao government, to find a way to make it worth their while to cooperate with us. Laos was a very poor country, but because of the state of our relations, it was not U.S. policy to provide direct economic or development assistance to the country. I talked with our military to get their ideas on what could be done in this regard. The colonel told me that when the actual excavation team came, it would be much larger than the survey team had been, and would include at least a well-trained medic (possibly a doctor), because the work would be dangerous. It would involve digging around unexploded ordnance and living approximately two weeks in the jungle, with the possibility of illness and insect and snake bites; adequate medical care had to be provided for the team. Colonel Harvey told me that the team would bring in very large quantities of simple medications, which they would be happy to leave behind with the province chief for use in villages near where the excavation would be taking place. He also said that the medical team would be willing to treat the villagers' simple ailments, if the Lao wanted it.

Planning Disrupted

The team returned to Hawaii, buoyed by the thought of returning to Laos in a few months to conduct the actual excavation. But plans were disrupted. In early 1984, Lieutenant Colonel Gritz and his friends made another foray into Laos. It was detected. The raiders made it back across the river to Thailand, but they had outraged the Lao. I would estimate that Gritz's operation set back our efforts for about a year. The Lao government did not believe my protestations that these were private efforts that had nothing to do with the U.S. government. From their point of view, these were people obviously funded by Americans, a retired lieutenant colonel was leading them, so how could the Lao be expected to believe that this was not an effort of the U.S. government to push forward access to the presumed prisoners of war, or worse, attempting to foment rebellion in Laos?

I did my best to persuade the Lao that this was clearly a private effort, while noting that it was indicative of how high feelings ran in the United States on this issue, and stressing how beneficial it could be for the Lao if they were to agree to allow us to proceed with the actual joint crash-site excavation. But all plans for scheduling the actual excavation came to a standstill.

Another Setback for Our POW and MIA Efforts

Meanwhile, I encountered another difficult situation that did not help our efforts to get cooperation from the Lao government to allow a joint crash-site excavation. Technically, Vientiane had a curfew; all foreigners were supposed to be off the streets by 11:00 p.m. I did not enforce the curfew with my staff because none of the other diplomats adhered to it. I thought it was difficult enough for my staff to be so constrained, without insisting that they be in their homes by 11:00 p.m., particularly when all of their friends— the Australians, the British, the Swedes—were out enjoying themselves.

But this one evening, my very able deputy, a political officer, was at a party with some of his diplomatic friends. The party broke up about 1:00 a.m., and he headed to his home. As he passed a guesthouse where the Lao government happened to be housing a high-ranking Vietnamese visitor, interior ministry people spotted him. He was stopped and chastised for being out after curfew. The next day, I was summoned to the foreign ministry and was told by Pheuiphanh that this young man had been declared persona non grata for "activities inconsistent with his diplomatic status" (diplomatic code meaning "We think he is a spy").

I was shocked to think that the Lao government was declaring my valuable deputy persona non grata. The explanation I was given was that he was out after curfew—to which I immediately responded that every diplomat in town was regularly out after curfew, and I did not see why my staff was treated differently from the staffs of every other embassy. Pheuiphanh went on to say that my officer's conduct had been suspicious, because he had been driving past the guesthouse where high-ranking officials were staying, so obviously he was there for spying purposes.

I pointed out that my deputy's house was two blocks away from the guesthouse and that he was following the normal route to his own residence, which to my knowledge he took frequently, and that the Lao government's action was absurd. I pointed out that the action would be a serious setback to U.S.–Lao relations and to our efforts to get agreement for a joint crash-site excavation. This would be quite disappointing

I understood that the foreign ministry was simply following the bidding of the interior ministry on this issue. Pheuiphanh was obviously discomfited by the chore he had been directed to carry out in this instance.

It became clear to me that there was nothing he could do for me about this issue. I said that I wished to speak with a higher official in the ministry about the matter. He assured me that it would not make any difference, that this was a final decision. I told him that I certainly hoped he would make it clear to his superiors that if they took the action they contemplated, my government would reciprocate by expelling one of the Lao diplomats from their embassy in Washington—this was standard diplomatic practice. I noted that the Lao embassy was also a small one, as was mine, and that these actions would strain the work of our respective missions.

Pheuiphanh looked distressed at the prospect of losing a Lao diplomat from their Washington embassy. He said somewhat sadly, "But we are a small country, and your country is a big one," implying that the United States should not retaliate for the expulsion of my deputy.

But that is what happened, in keeping with standard diplomatic practice. The Lao insisted that my deputy leave the country within forty-eight hours. When I reported this action, the U.S. government reciprocated, as I had predicted, and demanded the departure of a Lao diplomat of equivalent rank from Washington.

I was saddened, and disappointed, by this turn of events. My officer had done nothing wrong. The Lao internal justification for getting rid of him was that he was a political officer; I knew that. To the Lao government, and probably to most Communist governments, any diplomat whose job it was to find out what was happening in the country to which he or she was assigned was a CIA agent. But this was not the case with my deputy. His job as an overt political officer, like the role of political officers in embassies and consulates worldwide, was to observe and report on developments in their assigned country. These reports are used by various branches of the U.S. government, including the CIA, to assess developments and perhaps influence U.S. policy, if appropriate.

In any event, my deputy was not a secret CIA agent—he was a capable political officer doing his job, which did not include, that fateful evening, casing the guesthouse to spy on the Vietnamese visitors. He was simply returning from a party by his usual route and fell afoul of interior ministry personnel eager to toss a stumbling block in the path of the visibly improving U.S.–Lao relations.

The young man was personally devastated to have to depart in the midst of his tour under a cloud. I was determined that this development would not have an adverse impact on his career, and I made it clear to the department that he had done nothing wrong. I made a point of personally accompanying him to the airport upon his departure. I did not want any Lao observers to have any doubt about my personal support for the officer.

The most serious impact of this episode was felt by the rest of my staff. I decided that U.S. personnel were going to be held accountable to the Lao curfew by the interior ministry, and I concluded that my staff would have to abide by that curfew if we were to make progress on the important bilateral issue of gaining authorization for the joint crash-site excavation. Had we not been working on this issue, I would have been willing to take more chances and allow my staff to continue operating as their colleagues at the other embassies did. I made the decision that we had to give our policy priority over their nightlife entertainment in Vientiane—which was limited mostly to parties at each other's homes, nightclubs being nonexistent at that time in Vientiane. I therefore instructed my staff to adhere to the curfew—this decision did not endear me to my people, but I felt it was necessary. I encouraged my staff to entertain their friends in their own homes. I urged them to extend their stay in Bangkok when they had courier duty, to take a day's annual leave in addition to the usual three-day weekend there to ease the constraints of their confined life in Vientiane. I stressed how important it was to the families of the missing in action that we gain Lao agreement on conducting crash-site excavations.

The staff was not happy, but to the best of my knowledge they complied with my order. Meanwhile, bereft of my only political officer, I attempted to do his job as well as my own and to otherwise hold the fort, while attempting to get the U.S.–Lao relationship back on track and prodding the Lao government for movement on the crash-site issue. After a few months, a replacement political officer was assigned and arrived, easing my burden somewhat.

Go-Ahead for the Pakse Excavation

The year 1984 was disappointing in terms of the overall relationship, with the Gritz raid, my deputy's persona non grata label, and the stagnation of our crash-site efforts. We continued to press for forward movement, and at long last we received the consent of the Lao government to conduct the Pakse excavation. In early March 1985, a dedicated team of U.S. military personnel returned to Laos and began work.

I was delighted that we were finally able to undertake this operation. I am confident that we would not have gotten the go-ahead if the Vietnamese, who were very much the éminence grises calling the shots in Laos, had not agreed to this. I believe that the Vietnamese were viewing this initiative as a test case, a trial balloon, to determine whether the Vietnamese themselves should agree to cooperate with the United States in similar efforts to recover the remains of U.S. military personnel whose aircraft had been shot down in their territory.

At this point, there were approximately 2,500 U.S. military personnel listed as missing in action in Indochina. The bulk of the missing were in Vietnam, but the aircraft of a substantial number had been brought down in Laos. In most cases, but not all, the general locations of the crash sites were known. In some cases, villagers had long since located and scavenged the sites for usable materials, such as aluminum from the aircraft. Locating sites and recovering remains would be a painstaking, site-by-site effort, but a very worthwhile one that might bring closure to the families of these people who had given so much to their country—their very lives.

Getting Press Coverage

I was impressed with the Lao willingness to cooperate with us in this effort. I think it was remarkable that they were willing to open up their countryside to the U.S. military and to have their soldiers assist in the effort to recover the remains of fallen U.S. personnel—and this only ten years after the war's end, when memories of U.S. bombings doubtless remained fresh for some Laotians. I felt it was important to get positive publicity regarding Lao cooperation so that the Lao government could see that there was a benefit to them in working with us. I felt that this operation could influence attitudes in the United States, including congressional attitudes, and perhaps even eventually open the way to providing modest economic assistance to Laos. Economic assistance would in turn increase Lao willingness to cooperate with us on crash sites, which was my principal priority, and on other issues of interest to the United States. Further, improving relations for Laos with the United States could ultimately open that landlocked country to better relations with its non-Communist neighbor, Thailand, and with the world at large.

Accordingly, I encouraged the Lao government to admit journalists to cover the Pakse excavation. When word got out that the excavation would take place, large numbers of journalists from the United States and other nations wanted to come to Laos to cover it.

The initial Lao government reaction was a resounding no. I think the suspicious Lao government may have viewed journalists as spies. I continued to press the government on this question, aided by my Washington counterparts who pushed the Lao embassy to persuade their government to reconsider. Ultimately, the Lao agreed to allow representatives of NBC television and the *National Geographic* magazine to come in. *National Geographic* produced an excellent article, accompanied by the magazine's usual highly regarded photographs. Two or three other media representatives were admitted, including reporters from *Time* and *Newsweek*.

The resultant press coverage was highly positive, as it deserved to be. The operation was a splendid demonstration of cooperation between former enemies on an issue of major importance to the side seeking to properly honor its war dead.

Not all press representatives were seeking positive news,

however. I recall being interviewed by an NBC television reporter in my office shortly before the operation. I concluded early in the interview that it would never be aired in the United States, because the interviewer only wanted to hear me say negative things about the Lao government and the overall situation in the country, and to denigrate Lao cooperation on the excavation efforts. For me, this was not the purpose of this interview. I was perfectly willing to discuss the details of the operation and to express my genuine appreciation for the Lao cooperation on the excavation effort, but I was not going to use the occasion to attack the Lao government on other issues. The television interviewer clearly was trying to play "gotcha" with me, but I did not bite, so from the standpoint of someone seeking sensational news, my comments were a disappointment. When the interview was over and the cameras were turned off, the NBC reporter looked at me and said, "So everything is just fine here in Laos." I said, "You've got it. We are getting this crash-site excavation, and discussing it was the purpose of this interview."

To my knowledge, NBC did not use my interview. But there was substantial press coverage, all positive, from *Time, Newsweek,* some wire services, and the *National Geographic.*

Operation Successful

When the excavation was launched, I accompanied our military team to Pakse to witness the formal beginning of the project. It was moving to see U.S. soldiers digging for remains side by side with Pathet Lao soldiers. It was a positive demonstration to me of what persistent diplomacy can achieve when teamed with intelligent, caring military personnel. I stayed overnight, but returned to Vientiane in the morning. I had my temporary deputy, Terry Breese, a capable young officer sent over to help out in the absence of a permanent replacement for my persona non grata officer, stay at the site for the two-week duration of the excavation, to serve, if necessary, as a liaison between the U.S. and Lao military and provincial officials should difficulties arise. None did. The Americans and Lao worked very smoothly together. The tone throughout the excavation was very positive, according to my deputy, as well as the head of the U.S. military team, Colonel Harvey, the very capable officer who had headed the survey team.

The excavation was successful. The team did recover some remains, which they took back to their facility in Hawaii, where experts were able to make positive identifications. The remains were then turned over to their families for proper interment. Equally important, the Pakse operation started a process. The following year, we were able to do another excavation, this time in Savannakhet Province. Not long after that excavation, the Vietnamese government moved toward similar cooperation, and excavations were undertaken in Vietnam as well.

The Solarz Visit

In December 1985, the embassy received a visit from Representatives Steve Solarz and Robert Torricelli, their wives, and a few staffers. At that time, Congressman Solarz was a very respected legislator, keenly interested in foreign affairs. He was an expert on Asia and was very sympathetic to our efforts to obtain access to crash sites in Indochina in order to recover the remains of our missing in action. I had had contacts with him in some of my previous incarnations at State, and was pleased that he wished to come to Laos. I was confident that he would have a positive influence not only on the U.S.–Lao relationship but also on members of Congress who did not yet see the wisdom of pursuing improved relations with a former enemy. I believe in retrospect that his visit helped move the process forward.

The timing of the visit was awkward, as well as a little inconsiderate. The delegation planned to arrive in Vientiane on Christmas Day and stay overnight with us. Solarz is Jewish, so Christmas had no significance to him. All meetings would have to be scheduled for Christmas Day. This would not pose a problem for the Lao government, a Communist regime in a Buddhist country, but it meant that my entire staff, American and Lao, would have to attend to the delegation at full throttle on Christmas and the day after. My staff was already functioning under tight, almost claustrophobic, constraints in Laos, and to interfere with their enjoyment of Christmas was a significant hardship.

By and large, the staff cooperated well. I tried to arrange to close the embassy one day the following week—possibly on New Year's

Eve — to make up for the loss of Christmas. The department shot this down — there was no flexibility about the days embassies could be closed, but we were apparently free to remain open on Christmas. The department worked with me to find a way to compensate the staff, however. I don't recall the details, but we may have arranged staggered days off for individual staffers or additional financial compensation.

I encouraged the staff to work ungrudgingly to make the visit a success. I stressed anew the importance of obtaining Lao cooperation on issues of importance to the United States. If the United States were able to provide some type of modest economic assistance to Laos, the government might be more disposed to work with us. I reminded them of Congress's role in approving assistance, and told them that a successful visit would have a positive impact on Congressman Solarz's perceptions of the state of the relationship and could perhaps enable him to favorably influence the views of other key congressional players. I told them that we should all work to make the visit a success. We did, and it was.

Accommodations were the first logistical question to address. Only one hotel in Vientiane at that time offered facilities and services that most Western visitors would find acceptable, and even that one was extremely basic. I decided to have the congressmen and their wives stay at my residence, and other staff members accommodated the staffers who accompanied the congressmen.

Arranging appointments with the Lao was not a problem. I had briefed my foreign ministry contact on Solarz's importance, and I suspect the Lao embassy in Washington had also encouraged its government to be accessible to him. We set up a full day's program of appointments, which went well. I accompanied the delegation to all of their meetings. That evening, I hosted Christmas dinner for my entire staff and the entire delegation at the residence. This gave behind-the-scenes staffers (my communicators, for example) an opportunity for face time with the visitors.

Congressman Solarz told me that he had been quite satisfied with the visit. The meetings had gone well. He assured me that he would work from his end to attempt to encourage cooperation between the two countries.

I was impressed by Solarz, as I had been in the past. I was also favorably impressed by Congressman Torricelli, a young New Jersey congressman to whom Solarz, I had heard, was a mentor. Ironically for the career aspirations of both men, they subsequently ran afoul of congressional and campaign finance regulations. A few years later, Solarz was caught up in the so-called House banking scandal, whereby many members of Congress routinely overdrew their House checking accounts without penalization by the bank; his career stumbled, and he was not reelected to Congress. He had been regarded as a likely candidate for secretary of state when the next Democrat was elected president. Torricelli's career thrived for a time. He eventually was elected to the Senate. He resigned from the Senate under an ethical cloud involving campaign finances, but he was not charged with a crime.

An Upsetting Development

When I was seeing the Solarz delegation off at the airport the day after Christmas, I was standing next to my foreign ministry contact, Pheuiphanh, while other more senior Lao government officials stood nearby. As the plane's engines roared, Pheuiphanh whispered in my ear while he looked forward: "Look straight ahead. I have to tell you something." He said that I had to control my staff, because one of them was frequently out after curfew and was "behaving badly." He said that my staff member was going out with Lao women. He said that I had to find out what was happening and get it stopped, as it was interfering with Lao cooperation.

I was flabbergasted. I assured him that I would take care of this. The next day at our staff meeting, I reiterated to the staff the ban on going out after curfew. I also reminded them of the State Department's nonfraternization rule, to which we were all subject. This rule, which applied at the time to all American embassy personnel assigned to Communist countries, flatly prohibited fraternization, such as dating, between American embassy staff and local nationals. The staff listened politely, accepting that they were well aware of these prohibitions. I was still in the dark concerning who, if anyone, had violated these restrictions.

A few days later, Jean Claude Vincent, a French citizen married to a Lao—a gentleman with whom I played bridge at the British Embassy's modest club and with whom I had managed to cultivate a cautious friendship—approached me. Vincent had been a successful businessman before the Communist takeover, and he was attempting to salvage some business activities in the hostile environment. His wife, a lovely Lao, ran a small restaurant featuring French cuisine. They were managing to stay afloat, but were careful in their contacts with Westerners. But Jean Claude enjoyed bridge, and we managed to play relatively frequently at the British Club. He occasionally let me know what was happening on the business scene in Laos—what new obstacles had been placed in his path, or prospects for easing economic barriers. It was useful for me to have this contact with someone outside the government who was friendly to the West and hoped for improved relations between Laos and Western countries.

On this day, Jean Claude invited me to join him for lunch, a rare event. Over lunch, he told me that one of my communicators was having an affair with the wife of a Lao official. I was stunned. He knew the name of my communicator and also told me the name of the Lao official and his wife. He assured me that the information he was giving me was correct; his wife had learned of it from Lao friends in government. Jean Claude warned me that I had to get it stopped, that it was a dangerous situation.

I was disheartened to learn that an embassy staffer had so greatly abused the trust placed in him—particularly a communicator, who has first access to all sensitive cable traffic coming into an embassy. But I was not shocked that the miscreant was this particular individual; although he had never openly defied me, he projected an air of cocky indifference to authority. Fortunately, this man was scheduled to make the pouch run to Bangkok that week. As soon as he departed for Bangkok, I contacted the security officer in Bangkok, informed him of the allegations, and instructed him to make contact with the communicator as soon as he arrived at the embassy. I made it clear that the communicator was not to return to Laos; I would not allow it.

And the communicator did not return to Laos. When questioned by the Bangkok security officer, he confirmed the whole sorry affair. In his view, nonfraternization was just a silly rule. Why couldn't he date Communists, and married ones at that? The likelihood that he was probably being deliberately set up by the Communist authorities apparently never entered his head. He never came back to the post. Our administrative staff packed up his belongings and shipped them to Washington, where I hoped he would face appropriate disciplinary action.

I learned later, to my dismay, that the department had placed a reprimand in his file, and had docked him a couple of days' pay. I thought this a very mild slap on the wrist. Much later, I learned that when this individual was serving at an embassy in Africa several years later, he was approached by a Russian diplomat who attempted to blackmail him over the Lao incident into passing communications to the Russians. To his credit, he reported this attempt to the State Department. I had long suspected that the episode in Laos had been a carefully set trap for a naive man who should have known better.

This affair apparently was the matter to which Pheuiphanh had alerted me. To my disbelief, much later in my tour in Laos, another communicator also decided that he was not bound by the no-fraternization rule, despite knowing that his predecessor had been summarily dismissed from the embassy. Fortunately, I learned about this behavior before it became an issue with the Lao government, and promptly dispatched this man from the post.

I was grateful to Pheuiphanh for letting me know about the problem. At the time, and in retrospect, my conversation with him at the airport struck me as a scene from a James Bond movie— covering his voice, and mine, with the roar of the plane engines, carefully staring straight ahead as we spoke to prevent other Lao officials from detecting our conversation. He clearly feared that the interior ministry, which earlier in my tour had demanded, and gotten, the removal of my political officer for alleged spying, would make an issue of this case before I could take action, further setting back our efforts to improve relations.

The Death of Souvanna Phouma

Approximately midpoint in my tour, the former Lao prime minister, Souvanna Phouma, died. Unfortunately, I had not been able to meet him because of his illness. He occasionally played bridge with a couple of Western diplomats, who had inquired whether I could be included in a game, but his declining health did not permit this.

I had the honor of representing the United States at his funeral, at which I presented a wreath, a gesture recognizing his efforts on behalf of a non-Communist outcome in Laos. I watched respectfully as his flower-covered coffin was set ablaze, with the late afternoon sun intensifying the golden hues of the That Luang pagoda that seemed to preside in the background of the flaming pyre.

John McCain Briefing

My assignment in Laos offered me a surprising opportunity to brief a man who some twenty-odd years later became the Republican Party's candidate for president in 2008.

John McCain, as a naval aviator, was shot down over North Vietnam and spent five and a half years in brutal imprisonment in Hanoi. In the mid-1980s, as a congressman from Arizona and interested in rapprochement with his former captors, McCain accepted an invitation to meet with the Vietnamese government in Hanoi. He asked the State Department to brief him en route on the status of our efforts to get Lao agreement to conduct a crash-site investigation. I was instructed to meet McCain in Bangkok and bring him up to date on the issue.

We met at the Hilton International Hotel in their lobby coffee shop. I briefed him in detail and took his questions for about an hour. I was favorably impressed with his overall manner—he was attentive, interested, and easy to deal with. Particularly striking was that he met with me alone, without aides, a rarity for traveling congressmen. In later years, McCain strongly advocated rapprochement with Vietnam and helped gain bipartisan support for President Clinton's decision in the 1990s to establish diplomatic relations.

Wolfowitz Visit

Also helpful to improving the bilateral relationship was Paul Wolfowitz's visit to Laos in 1986. The Lao were happy to have Wolfowitz, the assistant secretary of state for East Asian and Pacific affairs, come. He was the highest-ranking official visitor from the United States in many years, probably since 1975. I had wanted to house Paul in my lovely residence, but the Lao government, as a gesture of friendship, insisted that he be their guest. Accordingly, he was housed in the one downtown hotel that offered passable accommodations, but the hotel left a lot to be desired in the comfort department. There was nothing we could do about it, short of gravely insulting the Lao when they were extending a friendly hand. He was a good sport about it. I do remember him being less than thrilled when I picked him up at the hotel in the morning after a night in which he had gotten very little sleep because the air conditioning had failed and he had been visited by many varieties of hungry insects. He growled something like, "I don't know about this," and I replied with a breezy, "Oh, come on, we all have to make sacrifices for our country sometimes." But his visit was a success in terms of bilateral discussions and helped moved the overall process forward another pace or two.

I mention this episode because when I knew Paul, he was a serious diplomat. He had helped me get the chargéship in Laos, responding to the recommendation of his friend, Elliott Abrams. He supported me in the job. I found him very easy to deal with, very intelligent, and very pleasant. I had heard from his staff in the department that he was not the most organized assistant secretary in the building; his desk was always cluttered, and papers needing attention could be buried. But he was generally well liked and respected.

I note these impressions because I was frankly surprised when, under the presidency of George W. Bush, Paul became a principal neoconservative war hawk, as deputy secretary of defense leading the effort to launch the war on Iraq. I was stunned by some of his public pronouncements about the war and by how wrong he was on most of his assessments, including refuting dismissively the statement of the chairman of the joint chiefs of staff, General Eric Shinseki, that several hundred thousands of troops would be needed to pacify Iraq. In my opinion, he and his fellow neoconservatives did not serve this country well by pressing for this war, although the ultimate responsibility for the war rested squarely with the commander in chief, President Bush.

When Bush began his second term in office in 2005, he appointed Paul to head the World Bank. Despite initial skepticism by some bank members, initial indications were that he was doing a capable job in that important institution, insisting on greater accountability from recipient governments, attempting to curb corruption, and so on. In April 2007, however, he came under serious criticism for arranging a major promotion and huge salary increase for his girlfriend, who was transferred from the bank to the State Department, where she was earning more—still on the World Bank tab—than the secretary of state. Not long thereafter, Wolfowitz left the World Bank.

Face Time with the Secretary

The East Asia bureau was sensitive to my isolation while I was in Laos. On a few special occasions, they invited me to join in regional conferences, where I had an opportunity to meet briefly with Secretary of State George Shultz. The Association of Southeast Asian Nations (ASEAN) annually hosted meetings with the foreign ministers of the association and several dialogue partner countries, including the United States. In 1984, these ministerials were held in Jakarta, Indonesia. The U.S. ambassadors to ASEAN countries were invited to attend, and to my pleasant surprise, I was also invited to participate. Although Laos was not at that time a member of ASEAN, I believe the department wished me to have an escape from Vientiane, share experiences with my colleagues in neighboring countries, and brief the secretary on developments in Laos.

At the evening meeting with the secretary, all of the ambassadors, their spouses, and I gathered in a small hotel conference room, together with the department officials accompanying the secretary, including Assistant Secretary Wolfowitz. The secretary asked Paul to introduce each chief of mission, which he did (except for me), whereupon each man gave a brief presentation on current developments in his respective country. At the conclusion of these ambassadorial briefs, the "invisible woman" syndrome kicked in. I was inadvertently ignored, as Paul and the secretary acted as if the session was over. I spoke up quickly but politely, saying something like, "Mr. Secretary, I am Theresa Tull, chargé d'affaires in Laos. Would you like to hear something about recent developments in the U.S.–Lao relationship?" The secretary recovered quickly and listened attentively to my brief presentation. I suspect that he had assumed I was somebody's wife, and Paul had simply overlooked my presence.

The following year, I was again invited to the ASEAN ministerials, held in Kuala Lumpur, Malaysia. I attended a reception with the secretary and spoke with him briefly, but to my knowledge none of the ambassadors had briefing sessions with him as we had in Jakarta. But on this occasion I did get to attend, as an observer, a couple of the meetings themselves.

The bureau also scheduled an East Asian and Pacific Chiefs of Mission Conference in Honolulu during my tenure as chargé. I arranged to arrive in Hawaii a couple of days before the conference, where I spent a most enjoyable time with my brother Bob and his wife, who had flown over from Whidbey Island to meet with me. We had a memorable visit to the battleship *Arizona* memorial, escorted by a young navy lieutenant who had been assigned to me for the duration of my visit. We went to the memorial by launch after visiting a most interesting museum depicting and recounting the historic events of December 7, 1941.

Further Openings

As time went on, I was pleased with the progress we were making with the U.S.–Lao relationship, particularly with regard to crash-site excavations. In April 1986, a second crash-site excavation was conducted successfully in Savannakhet.

Meanwhile, I seized any opportunity I could find to build on the momentum created by the successful cooperation on these two excavations. When Laos suffered severe flood damage to its rice crop, I was able to get the U.S. government to make a contribution of rice to the World Food Program for distribution to Laos. I made it clear to the Lao government that when the delivery of glutinous rice (known also as "sticky" rice, a Lao staple) arrived in the country, I wanted to be afforded the same opportunity that other aid donors were given to witness the distribution of the goods in the provinces. The Lao agreed.

When the rice arrived, I made a trip with Lao officials and an embassy staffer to a province that I had not visited before and met with villagers who were delighted to receive the bags of rice, clearly marked as a gift from the United States. Subsequently, I gave my economic officer the opportunity to accompany a rice delivery to

Xieng Khouang Province, which had been the headquarters of the Pathet Lao for many years during the war and was off-limits to Americans. I envied her, but I felt it was important that she get the opportunity for this rare travel. I believe she was taken for a brief look at the mysterious Plain of Jars, a site where huge jars had been found many years ago, and still remained. The purpose of these giant containers—up to nine feet tall—has not been definitively determined, but some sources believe they were prehistoric burial urns.

Meanwhile, I continued to press the Lao government to open up their country to Americans: first, to my staff, so that we would not be so claustrophobically confined to Vientiane; and second, to American business opportunities. With regard to the former, finally the foreign ministry agreed that they would arrange a trip for the embassy personnel to Luang Prabang, the former royal capital. Because of some continuing bandit activity along the mountain road leading from Vientiane to Luang Prabang, it was deemed necessary for security reasons to go there by air. The ministry offered a weekend trip, from Friday to Sunday afternoon. I was very pleased with the offer. Yet when I presented the news to my staff, who had been complaining about being confined to Vientiane, to my chagrin about half of them had no interest in making the trip. I told these folks that they were missing a great opportunity, but it was their call.

Those of us who made the trip found it delightful. Not unexpectedly, we were accompanied by foreign ministry minders, but this actually smoothed the way for us. The foreign ministry made all of the arrangements—transportation, sightseeing trips, and lodging (very basic accommodations in what had probably once been a charming hostelry, but had fallen on hard times under the Communist regime). Luang Prabang was a lovely, quiet town with beautiful temples and the former royal palace. The last king of Laos had been sent to a so-called reeducation camp after the Communist takeover in 1975. The government would not say whether he was alive or dead. The consensus among Western intelligence analysts was that he had probably died in captivity. He was known to have severe diabetes, and most likely was not given his necessary medications while in the camp. The government had maintained the royal palace in reasonable condition, and it was interesting to visit this historic site.

A highlight of the visit was a boat ride up the river to visit a cave in which, over the centuries, hundreds of statues of the Buddha had been placed in little niches. The cave remained a site of pilgrimage for devout Lao Buddhists. In all, the three-day visit was most enjoyable and interesting.

In addition, I was able to persuade the Lao government to approve the issuance of a visitor's visa for my niece, Patricia Tull Cohick. Patty and I had planned a trip to China, for which I had obtained authorization from the department and from our ambassador to China. Following the China trip, I wanted Patty to stay with me in Laos for a few days. At this time, Laos was not allowing tourists in the country, most decidedly not American ones. The only Americans in the country were the embassy staff and a Quaker couple and their young daughter, who oversaw modest aid programs funded by Quakers in the United States. The pacificism of the Quakers, and the religion's opposition to the Indochina War in particular, made this little American family welcome in Laos.

I met Patty in Hong Kong, and we flew to Beijing and spent a fascinating two weeks touring China under the close watch of our Chinese government guides and drivers. When we arrived in Bangkok on our return trip, the Lao government had approved Patty's visa. Issuing this visa was a welcome gesture of goodwill on their part; Americans simply did not get visas to visit Laos for pleasure at that time.

With regard to business opportunities, I frequently encouraged the Lao to open their doors to American businessmen seeking investment opportunities. I felt that the more contact the Lao had with Americans, the more they would be exposed to our positive ideas, to give them an alternative to the doctrinaire views of their Vietnamese Communist mentors. I was approached by people from the Hunt Oil Company in Texas, who were investigating the possibility of exploring for oil in Laos. I was able to arrange a meeting for some Hunt executives with appropriate Lao officials—I believe this was the first American business delegation to visit Laos since the war had ended. The talks went well. Ultimately, after I had left the post, Hunt did get permission to send in an exploration team.

Unfortunately for both Hunt and the Lao, no oil was discovered. But what had been a firmly closed door was opened a crack with this initiative.

About the time that I was getting ready to leave Laos, in 1986, the Lao moved toward the introduction of a modified economic policy, which made room for some limited private enterprise and less state control, along the lines of the economic reforms that other Communist countries, including China and Vietnam, were beginning to initiate. I saw no fruits of this announced new policy while I was in Laos. In subsequent years, however, Laos did open up some to foreign investment and to tourism. I witnessed the results of this new policy several years later when I visited Laos between conferences in Bangkok. The results were striking, as I will describe later.

As I look back on my three years in Laos—from 1983 to1986—I am very proud that I was able to play a role in getting agreement from the Lao government to begin joint crash-site excavations. In retrospect, this was one of the highlights of my Foreign Service career.

On the Move Again: The Next Assignment

By the summer of 1986, I had completed nearly three years in Laos and was ready to move on to my next assignment. Having been chief of mission in a most difficult place—successfully, in my view—I thought I was a good candidate for an ambassadorship. I returned to Washington and began making the rounds of people who would be in a position to further my ambition, that is, people who had some say in the assignment process.

As one rises in the Foreign Service, and I suppose in any hierarchical system, it is necessary to do some self-promoting, to introduce yourself to decisionmakers, to acquaint them with who you are, and to let them know that you are available for further assignment. I disliked this process, but I managed to do enough of it to help me along in my career.

The first person I called on in Washington was Elliott Abrams, who at this point was assistant secretary for American republic affairs. I was flabbergasted when he told me that I had been his first choice to be ambassador to Haiti. He said that he had put my name up, but that I had lost out to another candidate. The White House had its candidate, and it just did not work out for me. He said he was disappointed, but would definitely keep me in mind for other opportunities. I told him that I was pleased and flattered at his confidence in me.

The process by which ambassadors are selected involves both the State Department and the White House. Ultimately, any choice must have the president's approval, but there are some procedures that are followed before the presidential stamp is placed on an appointment. In the State Department, when I was being considered for an ambassadorship, the list of upcoming ambassadorial vacancies was compiled for each geographic bureau. The assistant secretaries and other senior officials submitted their recommendations for each post to a group called the Deputies Committee, which is chaired by the deputy secretary of state. The assistant secretaries from the geographic bureaus have a lot of influence in this process, but other assistant secretaries, from the economic bureau, for instance, may also have candidates for whom they lobby hard.

As I understand it, at the same time, the department coordinates with the White House to determine whether any particular nominees are White House favorites for certain posts. When the Deputies Committee meets, the case for particular candidates is made by their advocates. Frequently, more than one career diplomat is being pushed for an ambassadorship by one or more assistant secretaries or other officials. And the White House might press hard for a candidate favored by a White House official. If the president himself wants to name an ambassador, that post is not even considered by the Deputies Committee. But there are other posts for which a career officer competes with a White House favorite, and sometimes the State Department's choice prevails.

In this case, apparently, Elliott Abrams had put my name forward for Haiti without my knowledge, which is unusual. I might have been the department's choice, because as I recall it, Elliott said that the White House had its own candidate, who had gotten the nod. At any rate, I did not get Haiti. Actually, I was ultimately relieved, because "Baby Doc" Duvalier was overthrown not long after this conversation, and our ambassador had a difficult time of it. Still,

Elliott thought that I deserved and could handle a good assignment. But he had no other embassies open at that point; he had staked his effort for me on Haiti. I expressed my sincere appreciation, and accepted his offer to keep in touch about my assignment.

I then called on the director general of the Foreign Service, the principal personnel officer at the State Department. At this time, this position was filled by a classic old-boy, Ivy League–type diplomat, Ambassador George S. Vest. He was highly respected and had a fine reputation. Our paths had crossed once or twice in the past, but he did not really know me. I gave him a brief recap of my service in Laos and said that I would welcome consideration for an ambassadorship, having successfully served as chargé in a difficult, hostile post.

I was taken back by Vest's performance. He was patronizing, at best, and dismissive, at worst. He said that I had already had a fine career, and had already been a chief of mission, in Laos—most officers never get to be a chief of mission. Perhaps I should think about retiring, he opined. I told him that I was not ready to consider retiring just yet, I had proven my ability to run an embassy, and I would like a shot at another embassy, but this time as ambassador rather than as permanent chargé d'affaires. Failing that, perhaps I could serve as deputy chief of mission at a substantial embassy (although this is not what I wanted at that time). Having been chief of mission for three years, I said, it would be difficult for me to accept anything less than a chief of mission position.

Vest demurred, then said that he recalled that the Latin American bureau had proposed me to be DCM in Haiti. I told him that my understanding was that I had been Elliott Abrams's choice to be ambassador there. No, no, Vest insisted—it was for DCM. I then told him that if I could not be considered for an ambassadorship during this assignment cycle, I would like to be assigned to the Senior Seminar. (This academic-year-length seminar was the senior-most long-term training offered by the State Department. It was designed to further prepare candidates for higher-ranking positions—ambassadorships, in the case of State Department officers, and for flag rank positions in the case of military officers.) Not only would the course be a most interesting one academically, but also it would allow me to stay in the game for consideration for an ambassadorship in the next assignment cycle. (A few years ago, the department abolished this excellent program, citing a desire to provide shorter training programs to a broader range of officers.)

Vest rejected this idea out of hand. He pointed out that I had already attended the National War College and had that year of advanced training; he did not think it would be possible to have both courses. I told him that I was very grateful for the opportunity to attend the War College, but that I knew of some instances in which an officer had attended both courses. I said that the year of study would be most welcome after a very difficult three years in Laos, and would give me an opportunity to compete in the next assignment cycle. Vest said that this would not be possible.

I thanked him for his time and left his office thoroughly puzzled. Elliott had told me that I had been his choice for ambassador to Haiti, yet the director general said I had been put up for deputy chief of mission. I wanted to clarify this. I went back to see Elliott. He assured me that he had pressed for me to be ambassador, not DCM. I recounted the unsatisfactory meeting to him, complete with Vest's patronizing suggestion that I consider retiring and his rejection of my request to be assigned to the Senior Seminar.

At this point, the benefits that accrue to a political appointee with solid White House contacts were made clear. Elliott immediately telephoned Vest. He told him that he had wanted me to be ambassador to Haiti, but that this had not worked out. Since nothing else suitable seemed to be available at this point, he would like to have me assigned to the Senior Seminar: "Could you arrange that?... Oh, thanks a lot." And I was assigned to the Senior Seminar.

The Senior Seminar: Summer 1986 to Summer 1987

This proved to be a very interesting year. It was an opportunity for diplomats like myself who had lived for years abroad to become immersed in the United States once more, to be better prepared to represent the country when next assigned abroad. It also served as a most respectable "parking lot" for those of us awaiting the next significant assignment. As part of the curriculum, the class traveled widely throughout the United States, meeting with a wide variety of local officials and businessmen to learn in depth about the varied issues facing different parts of the country. We went to Miami and met with the Cuban and Haitian exile communities, as well as with the Coast Guard to learn about their drug and refugee interdiction efforts. On a visit to Detroit, we accompanied the Detroit police in squad cars as they made their nightly runs in that crime-ridden city. We also visited the Ford Motor Company for useful talks with its executives, and we met with union leaders of the United Auto Workers. We spent a day and night on small family farms and learned the farmers' perspective on rural issues.

The Detroit trip also awakened me to the presence of a large settlement of Middle Eastern immigrants who were changing the face of nearby Dearborn. Largely from Yemen, these men were lured to the area by jobs in the auto industry. They and their families welcomed the American jobs, but they seemed to me (fifteen years before the terrorist attacks of 9/11) to be replicating the Arab and Muslim lifestyle they had experienced in their home countries. Some of the women wore long gray or black robes that covered everything but their faces. Mosques were in evidence. Street signs were in Arabic as well as English. Businesses seemed to be designed to cater exclusively to Muslim tastes. We had an interesting discussion and meal with leaders of this community, who acknowledged that it was proving difficult to keep their children from adopting American ways.

Other trips included an in-depth tour of the financial sector in New York and a stay in San Francisco, where I managed to have lunch with an old friend from the Brussels embassy, Elaine Olsen, who had since retired to the area. At home in the seminar, we studied the growing drug problem in the United States and arranged frequent presentations by experts in various fields. I had the task of arranging a session with leading journalists to get their perspectives on current events. I managed to get acceptances from Cokie Roberts; Don Oberdorfer, whom I had known in Vietnam; and Hodding Carter, who had been the State Department press spokesman during the Carter administration. Hodding Carter, who came from a highly respected Mississippi journalist family, was married to Patt Derian, former assistant secretary of state for human rights. All of them gave excellent presentations and fielded our questions well.

On to Georgetown

The Senior Seminar year came to an end. As it was winding down, Elliott Abrams asked me if I would be willing to be ambassador to Guyana. I knew this would be a difficult assignment because of the extremely run-down condition of the Guyanese economy and the less than warm relations that had marked most of the period since Guyana had achieved its independence from Britain, but I accepted immediately. Elliott's recommendation won the day, and I was formally nominated by President Ronald Reagan to be his ambassador to Guyana.

10

To South America

After all of the preliminary steps toward my nomination were completed—security checks, tax clearance, and so on—I returned one morning to my Senior Seminar room at the Foreign Service Institute after a lecture and found a telephone message on my desk: call President Reagan at the White House. The president had reinstituted the practice of personally contacting nominees and offering them the position firsthand. It was with a rapidly beating heart that I called the White House and was put through to the president. He asked if I would be willing to serve as his ambassador to Guyana; I accepted, and pledged to do my best to do a good job. He said something about my good record, and wished me well. The whole conversation could not have taken more than a few minutes, but it remains a vivid, satisfying memory for me.

I spent some weeks reading into my assignment in the Latin American bureau, waiting for my Senate confirmation hearing to be scheduled. A senator had placed a hold on one nominee, and the hearing process came to a halt. It did not look like I would get my hearing before the Senate adjourned for the summer. President Reagan decamped for his California ranch, and I waited to hear from the Senate. Unexpectedly, with very little notice, the word came that my hearing would be held within a few days. I scrambled to finalize my formal statement, and brushed up quickly on issues that might prompt questions from the senators. Senator Christopher Dodd, a Connecticut Democrat, chaired my hearing, which also included the nominee for ambassador to Belize, Bob Rich. The hearing went smoothly, the committee reported us to the full Senate favorably, and we were confirmed.

I left for Georgetown, Guyana, in late August 1987, without the customary photo-op meeting with the president, as he was still in California. (Most presidents meet personally with their ambassadors and pose for pictures with them. These pictures, placed in the ambassador's office and residence abroad, demonstrate to the host country that the envoy has had personal contact with the U.S. president. I had to leave for Guyana without this evidence of proximity to power, but it was important to get to post, which had been without an ambassador for a few months.)

Challenges in Georgetown

I arrived in Guyana on Guyana Airlines, the only carrier operating in that economically challenged country. I was very excited to be beginning my service as a U.S. ambassador. I was met at the airport by the deputy chief of mission and Guyana's chief of protocol. The several-mile drive into the city passed by sugar plantations, and I spotted the occasional Dutch *koker* (a sluice) over streams. The houses we passed were generally down at the heels.

Georgetown, the capital, had a certain charm. It was a small city of many striking Victorian-style wooden houses, and boasted a lovely wooden Episcopal church, reported to be the tallest wooden structure in the region. Virtually all of the buildings cried out for a coat of white paint. Still, the abundant tropical greenery softened the somewhat shabby impression.

I served as ambassador to Guyana for three years, from 1987 to 1990. The country was an economic basket case. It was a difficult assignment, but interesting and quite challenging. The country was attempting to emerge from a very dark period of intense socialism that had ruined the economy, and from a constricted near-dictatorship situation. My priorities were to press for economic as well as political reform.

I inherited an embassy with very low morale, attributed in large part to the difficult economic situation in the country, which made living there stressful. Maintaining houses was very difficult. Any repair work that needed to be done usually meant sending to Miami for basic hardware items. The stores in Georgetown were empty, because the country lacked hard currency with which to purchase needed imports. Electric power—or the frequent lack of it—also made for a very difficult situation. There were periodic extended power outages, which tended to damage electrical equipment, make frozen foods thaw, and shut down air conditioners in a climate of stifling heat and humidity. There were very few entertainment options. Although Georgetown was situated on the Atlantic Ocean, there were no usable beaches—the beachfront was mud, not sand. The ocean was dark brown from the mud of some of South America's largest rivers that emptied into the Atlantic near Georgetown. Life was not easy for the American staffers.

Our consular staff was particularly affected by the economic situation. A large percentage of the population of Guyana was seeking to emigrate to the United States by way of legitimate immigration visas, or to get visitors' visas however possible; many applicants for visitors' visas had no intention of ever returning to Guyana. Attempts at fraud were frequent, and the visa refusal rate was very high. Our five consular officers were worked hard and were hard-pressed to tolerate the pressure from people determined to find a better life for themselves and their families in the United States.

All of these factors combined to contribute to demoralization. In addition, my predecessor reportedly was very unhappy in Guyana, and I think that this attitude permeates the post and influences the staff's outlook.

Housing the Ambassador

A further complication for me was that the U.S. government had undertaken to build a new embassy. The embassy was to be built on the grounds immediately adjacent to the ambassador's residence, on land that had held two staff residences and a swimming pool and tennis court. About the time that I arrived, construction was about to begin. A major problem from my perspective was that the new embassy would closely abut the existing ambassador's residence— only eighteen inches or two feet away, at one point. Thus it would not be possible to retain the existing structure as the ambassador's residence. During the embassy construction, this building would be used as the contractors' office. At the conclusion of construction, the plan was to tear down the building. The government of Guyana regarded the residence as a historic building because of its age and design, and was posing some objection to destroying it. I believe the residence was eventually spared from demolition.

This building was an old-style, traditional Georgetown house. It was made of wood, including some decorative Victorian-style wooden touches and wooden shutters on all windows, opening outward and above the windows. It was a roomy building, suitable for ambassadorial entertaining, but it was clearly high maintenance and had been neglected in recent years in anticipation of its ultimate demise.

But my predecessor had been unable to find a suitable residence to house his replacement. Appropriate dwellings were scarce in Georgetown, and the State Department's increasingly stringent security requirements governing ambassadorial residences made the job more difficult. I began my tour living in a few rooms of the ambassador's residence, while the contractors set up their office on the floor below my rooms. This took place while the residence of the deputy chief of mission, which my predecessor had decided would become my home, was prepared for me. This residence proved unacceptable.

Ultimately, I lived in five separate places as ambassador to Guyana. I settled into a modest two-bedroom wooden dwelling and lived there for more than two years. The administrative staff pursued the question tenaciously and eventually located a suitable residence. Unfortunately, the department's diplomatic security bureau refused to approve the purchase on security grounds, over my strong assurance that the house and its location met the requirements. When my successor also faced a search for a suitable residence, he found my interim residence unacceptable, but had to live there while the search continued. He concluded that the residence my staff had located would have worked well, but the owner declined to sell.

Dealing with Morale Problems

Tackling the morale situation at the embassy was difficult, and I probably did not manage this as well as I should have. I tried. Early in my tour, I inaugurated a series of individual luncheons with heads of sections so I could get to know them better and learn the problems they were dealing with in their work.

My first guest was the head of the consular section. She was pleased to be invited, and told me that she had never had a similar get-together with my predecessor. It developed that she was personally miserable in Georgetown—her marriage had broken up recently, and she did not like Guyana or want to be there. I sensed that her negative attitude had percolated downward to her staff of young officers. She and they had the thankless task of screening visa applicants and issuing both immigration and visitors' visas; consequently, they had to deal with heavy workloads, fraudulent documents, demands from members of Congress to reverse visa refusals, as well as provide occasional services for visiting Americans in distress. Their lot was not an enviable one. There was not much I could do to ease their work situation, but I hoped that my recognition of their efforts would help improve their outlook. I do not think it did.

I continued to meet individually with section heads. I visited our USIS section and the excellent USIS library located across the street from the embassy. The USIS officer was an excellent, seasoned professional. His library was well attended, as were the frequent programs he was able to arrange with USIS-sponsored Americans touring the area, among them musical groups, political scientists, and the like. We worked very well together.

I knew before getting to Georgetown that the administrative section would require attention. Before I arrived, the incumbent administrative officer had called the department in distress to announce that he was resigning, that he could not stand it in Georgetown any longer. The senior administrative officer in the Latin American bureau talked him into staying, assuring him that a new ambassador would soon be arriving and would need his help. He reluctantly agreed, but he remained very unhappy. His general services officer did her best, but she was somewhat overwhelmed by her job (however, she was light years better than the man who replaced her not long after I arrived).

But all of the administrative staff had difficult jobs because of the economic situation. American staffers look to the administrative section and the GSO to keep their houses—approximately twenty-five of them in Georgetown—in functioning condition. When problems arose, frequently the replacement part needed to fix whatever was not working had to be ordered from Miami. Frequent power outages were very hard on electrical appliances. With the best will in the world, the administrative staff would have been hard-pressed to meet all of the demands on them. Further complicating their work, the embassy warehouse was full of second-hand furniture and equipment left over from when the United States had a much larger presence in Guyana. This material should have long ago been sold, but arranging such sales was time-consuming and, to my knowledge, no sales had been held in some years.

The gentleman who was the administrative officer was well intentioned and very hard working. As a midcareer entrant to the Foreign Service, he had very little Foreign Service experience. He was a retired major, or possibly lieutenant colonel, in either the air force or the army. His lack of experience made it difficult for me, because the ultimate responsibility for properly handling the embassy's funds lies with the ambassador. I had to make certain that the information I was being given was correct and that appropriate procedures were being followed.

The administrative officer often sent cables or other documents for my authorization that did not on the surface make sense to me. I called him to my office, trying to be gentle as I probed to determine why he had taken a particular approach. When he was not able to persuade me that he was correct, I asked if he had checked the *Foreign Affairs Manual* (the bible for the State Department, a compilation of laws and regulations governing virtually all State Department functions). Yes, he had checked it. I then said that I had not seen this particular reference in a long time. Would he be kind enough to send me a copy of the manual citation with the cable, so that I could familiarize myself with it? As he knew, I was responsible for everything that was transmitted from the embassy, and I needed to understand what I was signing. Well, he was not happy when I did this, but in a day or so, back would come a cable with a completely different approach, together with a copy of the manual's regulation, demonstrating that he had not initially researched the matter. In response to federal law, the State Department holds the ambassador responsible for the accuracy and correctness of all matters involving embassy expenditures. At least once a year I had to certify personally that I had reviewed and concurred in the correctness of all of these figures. I did not want my first ambassadorship to result in my departure from Georgetown for a federal penitentiary, so I took these certifications very seriously. (I had had identical responsibilities as chargé in Laos, but there our budget was much smaller than that for the embassy in Georgetown, and I had had more confidence in the administrative officer in Vientiane.)

I should note that I was confident of the integrity of my administrative officer—I am certain he was an honest man, and I know that he worked very hard. His problem was lack of experience. Nor was his level of competence sufficient to reassure me that I could sign off on his efforts without verifying their accuracy. For example, even knowing that I was likely to ask for the *Foreign Service Manual's* reference in many cases, he did not undertake to provide this backup material until he was asked for it. This placed an additional burden on me. I did not feel at this point that the deputy chief of mission was sufficiently engaged in these matters for me to channel some of this work to him, as would have been the case at embassies staffed with a more efficient DCM. (This DCM had been passed over for promotion and was nearing the end of his career.)

The Currency Exchange Problem

While preparing for my assignment in Washington, I came upon a recent directive from the department instructing ambassadors to curb currency exchange abuses at posts. This was a problem that could arise in countries that did not have a convertible currency, such as Guyana. In some cases, American staffers had profited at the end of their tours of duty by exchanging local currency for U.S. dollars at the embassy at totally unrealistic rates of exchange. I learned from my research, which included consultation with my predecessor, that this was the case at the embassy in Georgetown.

Guyana's currency, which everyone in the country was required to use, had very little value at that time. The Guyanese government established the official exchange rate for converting U.S. dollars into Guyanese dollars at ten Guyanese dollars to one U.S. dollar. This was an absurdly low figure in a country where the black market exchange rate was at least one hundred to one and sometimes as high as two hundred to one. Under pressure from foreign embassies, the Guyanese government had established a rate of twenty-one to one for exchanges involving diplomatic personnel, thus our staffers could exchange their U.S. dollars for Guyanese currency at that rate. This also was not a realistic figure and imposed some hardship on staffers. On the other hand, however, there was not a great deal in Guyana on which to spend money. For the staff, their housing and furniture and all utilities were provided by the embassy. The embassy ran a small commissary where most food needs could be purchased with U.S. dollars. At the beginning of one's tour, the department paid shipping costs for a supply of foodstuffs from the United States for each employee. These measures reduced the hardship imposed by the unrealistic exchange rate.

I learned from the records, and from my conversation with my predecessor, that at the end of their tours, personnel were being allowed to convert any Guyanese currency in their possession at the embassy cashier at the unrealistic ten-to-one rate. Most personnel sold their personal automobiles and household and personal belongings to Guyanese, and brought in large quantities of Guyanese currency to the embassy for conversion into dollars at the ten-to-one rate. (Goods of most sorts were so hard to come by in Guyana that secondhand clothes, linens, and miscellaneous kitchen and other household items up for purchase from Americans were highly valued by the Guyanese.) According to the recent State directive, which was simply echoing directives and warnings of previous years, this conversion of currency at improper rates was against department regulations, if not against U.S. law.

My predecessor argued strenuously that his practice of converting end-of-tour transactions at the ten-to-one rate should continue. He contended that it was partial compensation to personnel for the difficulties of living in Guyana. In some cases, he said, personal electrical appliances might have been damaged by

Guyana's frequent power outages. I remained concerned that the practice was in violation of the department's directive. I also felt (and later learned that I was correct) that the prices the Guyanese were willing to pay for used American goods was sufficient to give the employee a comfortable sum even if exchanged at the rate of twenty-one to one, at which employees had received their own Guyanese currency.

Shortly after I arrived at the post, I moved to change the conversion policy to using the rate of twenty-one to one. I was not only concerned about this violation of department policy but also felt that the possibility of converting currency at the ten-to-one rate could tempt some people to fraudulently accumulate the currency for conversion to their profit. The embassy had little use for the local currency. The dollars employees got for it came straight from the U.S. treasury.

I recognize in retrospect that I did not handle this well. I discussed the problem with the administrative officer and my DCM, but I made the decision rather abruptly. Staff reaction was extremely negative—I had hit them all in their pocketbooks. State Department regulations be damned; I, not the department, had done this to them. My decision was extremely unpopular and did not endear me to the staff, coming as it did when I was attempting to instill more professionalism throughout the embassy's operations. I may have fared better had I established a committee of section heads, with participation by one or more junior officers, to study the problem and give me a solution consistent with the department's requirements. Then my ultimate decision—to abandon the ten-to-one conversion rate—might have been better received. But this necessary change was definitely not a morale booster in an already dispirited embassy.

The Post Inspection

Almost immediately after my arrival, we were scheduled for an official State Department inspection of the post. From one point of view, this was good timing for me as a new ambassador because the problems that might be uncovered could not be blamed entirely on me: I had not been there long enough to be fully responsible for possible long-standing deficiencies. My decision to revise the rate at which end-of-tour currency conversions were made, however, had negatively affected morale, and when the inspectors arrived they found the American staff very unhappy with me.

In preparing for the inspection and in researching the exchange rate issue, I asked the administrative officer to give me the records of all of the cash-out records covering the end-of-tour sale of automobiles and personal effects for the previous year. This proved quite revealing, and confirmed my concern about this dubious practice. I discovered that two former employees, who were husband and wife, had, in effect, illegally converted Guyanese currency at the ten-to-one rate, for which they had received about $80,000 in U.S. dollars from the embassy.

I noticed, for example, that one transaction covered funds received from the sale of a car, which they had sold to an incoming junior officer, for which they had gotten, according to the records, a massive amount of Guyanese dollars. I was suspicious: where would a brand-new arrival get that quantity of Guyanese dollars? I called the young man to my office and asked him how he had paid for the car. He immediately replied that he had given the couple a U.S. dollar check; he had gotten a loan for the car's purchase from the State Department credit union. So this couple, having received U.S. dollars for the car, had fraudulently claimed to have received Guyanese currency, for which they received U.S. dollars at the rate of ten to one. I learned later that apparently this couple had made occasional trips to Manaus, Brazil, which was notorious as a site for obtaining Guyanese currency for U.S. dollars at a very high rate, sometimes approaching four hundred to one.

I reported this matter to our security officer, who initiated an investigation through his channels. Just about this time, the inspectors arrived at post. Interestingly, the head of the inspection team was my predecessor. Because he could not inspect his own post, he had remained elsewhere in the region, doing preliminary work for another embassy inspection. But he was the boss of the men who had arrived to inspect me. I called the inspectors into my office and presented them with this information. They swallowed hard, shifted in their seats, and told me that this would be awkward for them, in view of whom they reported to. I said that I realized who their boss was, but I had discovered this problem that had occurred on his watch, and it would have to be reported and investigated. I told them that if they felt that they could not take the problem on, I would simply deal directly with the State Department on it. No, no, that would not be necessary, they said; they would take care of it.

I subsequently learned that when the department concluded its investigation of the couple's fraud, it submitted the case to the Justice Department for possible prosecution. The Justice Department decided that they did not have sufficient personnel to prosecute a case that involved only $80,000. The State Department, however, did take disciplinary action against the pair. I believe that they were both fired and may have had to forfeit any claim to a pension.

To me, uncovering this case demonstrated the kind of problems that arose when an embassy was willing to convert local currency into dollars at an unrealistic rate. It clearly was a temptation for some individuals to take advantage of the laxity and defraud the embassy, and thus the U.S. treasury. I took my responsibility of oversight of U.S. funds and property very seriously, and know I made the right decision in stopping the ten-to-one exchange rate.

I paid a price for my decision, personally. As I had surmised, the staff was very unhappy with me about the exchange rate decision, in particular, and apparently resented my efforts to improve embassy performance across the board. These grievances were fully aired by the staff to the inspectors. When they met with me at the conclusion of their inspection, they informed me that morale was poor and that I should work on improving it. They also pointed out major deficiencies in the administrative operations of the embassy, many of which I had been in the process of uncovering (incomplete inventories and other property management shortcomings).

My DCM at this time was a pleasant man and a capable political reporter, but he had not filled the traditional role of a DCM to be, in effect, the executive officer of the operation. His job was to monitor the overall operation of the embassy, particularly the administrative section, as well as to serve as a protective buffer between the staff and the ambassador. He did not fill either of these roles well, and I had far too many interactions with staffers that he could have handled, sparing me from playing a disciplinary role. I had learned before going to Georgetown that this man's tour would end the summer after I arrived, as would his career. He had not been promoted for several years and was facing time-in-grade separation from the service, which has an "up or out" policy very much like that of the U.S. military. He worked adequately, I would say, but his full attention was not on his job at the embassy, and since he already knew his days in the Foreign Service were growing short, I had no real leverage with which to prod him to better performance. He put in his hours and left promptly at day's end to enjoy other pursuits, including participating in amateur theatricals; he was a good actor.

Fortunately, when the summer of 1988 arrived and the DCM left, he was replaced by an excellent officer who clearly was marked for rapid advancement in the Foreign Service. Dennis Hays was a go-getter, very capable, an excellent people person. He quickly assumed the proper functions of a DCM, which eased my tasks greatly, and he helped improve the morale of the embassy.

Gradually, we got the embassy into shape. It took time. The administrative deficiencies were major, and the personnel assigned to deal with them were not up to the task. Dennis, at my direction, spent time working with the administrative officer and GSO on these problems, which was helpful. As an indication of what we had to deal with, however, it developed that the GSO officer who replaced the woman who had held this position when I first arrived proved to be an incompetent alcoholic. We did not discover this immediately, and when we did, it took time to persuade him to leave voluntarily to get help. I had to threaten to expel him from the post, which would have darkened his personnel record much more than voluntarily leaving to check himself into a substance abuse program. His incompetence and affliction hindered our efforts to straighten out the mess in the administrative section.

Action Priorities

My priority areas of policy emphasis as ambassador to Guyana were economic reform and political liberalization. I encouraged the government of Guyana to make progress in both of these areas.

Guyana had been a British colony (British Guiana) for a century and a half when it achieved independence in the early 1960s. Britain acquired British Guiana in 1815 from the Dutch. Black slaves from Africa cultivated sugar and rice on large plantations. When the British abolished slavery in 1833, instead of converting the black slave labor force into a paid one, the British imported large numbers of indentured laborers from its colony in India to take their place in the field. The blacks gravitated to urban areas. Laborers were imported also from Portugal and China; the bulk of these workers abandoned the fields as soon as their seven-year contracts had been fulfilled and, in many cases, went into business. The Indians generally were content to settle into the agricultural life, where most of them remained as independence neared.

The British established a top-quality education system in their colony. The freed black slaves made excellent use of the education available to them. Over time, the blacks gravitated to the skilled professions (law, medicine) and to the police and military forces. They were not heavily represented in the business world—blacks in Guyana generally did not start their own businesses. Resentment existed among blacks at the gradually large role taken in the small-business sector by the Portuguese and Chinese, and to some extent by the Indians.

For the most part, the Indian agricultural workers did not take much advantage of the British educational system. Possibly because of cultural and religious differences with the British and black communities, they tended to stay on the agricultural plantations. Not many Indians entered politics as independence approached.

The exception to this rule was a U.S.-educated dentist named Cheddi Jagan. As independence neared, Cheddi Jagan was the leading politician in the country, who also happened to be a card-carrying Communist, eagerly supported by the Soviet Union. He drew his support from the Indian sugar and rice workers, whom he helped organize. Neither the United States nor Britain was eager to see a winner-take-all election that would put a Communist in the presidency of Guyana in the early 1960s, not long after Fidel Castro had overturned the government in Cuba and established a Communist dictatorship. Guyana, on the northern coast of South America, was too close to the Panama Canal for either major power to be comfortable with a Communist government in Guyana.

Consultations among the United States, Britain, and local Guyanese factions resulted in an election plan based on proportional representation. Cheddi Jagan's party, composed largely of his Indian agricultural worker followers, competed in the election to choose the government that would launch Guyana into independence. The leading black politician, Forbes Burnham, headed a party made up almost exclusively of black Guyanese. Peter D'Aguiar, a respected Portuguese businessman, formed an eclectic third party drawn from smaller ethnic groups, including the relatively small European-origin citizens. Thanks to the proportional representation arrangement, neither Jagan nor Burnham received enough assembly seats to form a government. Burnham and the Portuguese-headed group joined forces against Jagan to form a coalition government, with Burnham as president.

It did not take long for Burnham to destroy this coalition of convenience and assume full control. For the next nearly twenty years, Burnham, a committed socialist, ruled as a near dictator. He nationalized Guyana's leading industries, including bauxite production, and, by placing unqualified black sycophants in key positions in government and in the nationalized industries, ran the economy into the ground. At the same time, he cozied up to Communist powers and did his best to alienate the United States, which had undertaken a substantial assistance program to the country.

Finally, in the early 1980s, he ordered the United States aid officers and their programs to leave the country. This program affected not only relatively large-scale public works projects but also the importation under extremely concessionary terms of flour under the U.S. P.L. 480 program. With foreign exchange virtually nonexistent, Guyana had nothing with which to import flour, and bread disappeared from the daily diets of Guyanese. Burnham encouraged the Guyanese to substitute crackers made of tapioca for flour-based bread. This was not popular with the black population, but the Indian community, for whom a flour-based bread (roti) is a staple of daily life, were severely affected. Some observers suspected that this negative impact on the Indian community was why Burnham had the P.L. 480 program terminated.

In 1985, Burnham died on the operating table at the hands of a Cuban surgeon; apparently, the president had a heart attack while undergoing surgery. He was replaced by his prime minister, a much

debt-clearing effort and continued our P.L. 480 program (despite continued resistance from a key USAID official who did not think that Guyana had changed sufficiently, if at all, from the bad old Burnham days to merit a P.L. 480 program). The restructuring program also made Guyana more attractive to potential foreign investors.

Gradually, Georgetown's store shelves began to fill up with foreign imports that had largely been unavailable because the foreign exchange necessary to purchase them had been lacking. Initially, there was a hint of optimism in the air. Sustaining such programs in a country whose government remained at heart socialist was difficult. Despite Guyana's natural resources, which included some of the finest quality bauxite in the world and highly regarded sugar and rice, there was no dramatic economic turnaround for the country. But the program did improve the situation somewhat.

Political Liberalization

As I noted before, I also pressed the government throughout my tour for political liberalization. The followers of the Indian politician Cheddi Jagan were convinced (rightly, in the opinion of most observers) that there had not been a free election in the country since the very first nationwide one that resulted in Burnham forming a short-lived coalition with D'Aguiar, the highly regarded Portuguese businessman. Although Indians outnumber blacks in Guyana, election after election had seen Burnham's black-based party win by substantial margins. Cheddi Jagan was the leader of the opposition in the national assembly, where he roundly criticized Burnham's government at will, but he had no power to speak of.

My representations on behalf of political liberalization, respect for human rights, and free elections did not endear me to President Hoyte. Nor did he appreciate my maintaining occasional contact with persons opposed to his government, such as the leader of the opposition, Cheddi Jagan. It is every ambassador's duty to meet with a range of personalities in the host country and to keep open channels to nonviolent oppositionists and nongovernmental groups. I called on Cheddi when I arrived at my post, regularly invited him to my major receptions, such as the July 4th reception, and treated him with the respect due the leader of the opposition.

I also made it a point to have occasional, open contact with a group of British Jesuit priests, who were very opposed to the Guyanese government on human rights' grounds. The Jesuits published a small newspaper and fearlessly recounted human rights abuses as they discovered them. Under Forbes Burnham's rule, some egregious abuses had been carried out against political opponents. Such thuggery was virtually unknown under the Hoyte government, but the Jesuits had long memories, sharpened, perhaps, by the murder of a visiting priest when Burnham led the government. This visitor, who bore a remarkable likeness to the senior elderly Jesuit of the group, went for a walk after dinner one evening and was brutally murdered. The Jesuits were convinced that the murderer had mistaken the visitor for the senior resident Jesuit, whom the government detested.

These priests were knowledgeable about developments in Guyana, and I occasionally met with them to learn their latest concerns. On a few occasions I paid a Sunday night visit to their residence to play a game of Scrabble. I never made any attempt to conceal my activities from the Guyanese government. I was confident that they were keeping a close eye on what the U.S. ambassador was doing, and I made their job easier by traveling to such meetings in my official vehicle and having my driver park in full view of the road. I learned that Hoyte did not like my meetings with the Jesuits. But just as I had in the case of the Catholic bishop in Laos, I thought it was important to let the government know that I, and therefore the U.S. government, was interested in these people. While I had no fear that Hoyte personally would act against them, there remained some thuglike elements in his government who had learned under Burnham how to treat oppositionists; I would not have put anything past a few of them.

A regularly scheduled national election was to be held not long after my tour was to end. I fully supported the U.S. government's position that I press for a truly free election. I warned the department, however, to be prepared that such an election would surely bring to power a card-carrying Communist, Cheddi Jagan. The Soviet Union had helped to finance Cheddi's political party and activities, and annually welcomed him in the Soviet Union, where he frequently vacationed at a Soviet government resort on the Black Sea. By this time, however—1988, 1989—the Soviet Union was beginning to crumble.

By the time I left Guyana in the summer of 1990, the Berlin Wall had fallen and Soviet republics were beginning to pull away from the USSR. I was therefore not concerned that Guyana, under Cheddi Jagan, would become a new Soviet beachhead in the region, as Cuba had in the early 1960s. I was concerned, however, that Cheddi's government would not follow through adequately on the economic reform program instituted under the Hoyte government. Unfortunately, when Cheddi was elected president, my concerns proved correct. He did not openly abandon the program, but his government, I was told later, let it limp along without much encouragement.

As my tour drew to an end, I frequently encouraged Hoyte government officials to allow international observers to come to Guyana to observe the national elections. They were noncommittal. I raised this matter directly to President Hoyte during my farewell call on him in the summer of 1990. I urged him to consider inviting former President Jimmy Carter and representatives from his Carter Center, who have observed many foreign elections, to witness Guyana's election. He dismissed this idea, saying that if he invited any observers, they would be from the regional organization of the Caribbean Community (or CARICOM), his neighbors. When the election was held about a year later, after a postponement, he did agree to allow the Carter Center to observe the election. The election was deemed acceptable, and Cheddi Jagan, now weaned from support from the collapsing Soviet Union, was elected president. President Hoyte graciously accepted the defeat of his party and served in the national assembly as leader of the opposition under Cheddi's presidency.

Maintaining the P.L. 480 Program

The restoration of flour to Guyana, thanks to the efforts of my predecessor after Forbes Burnham's death, was an important development for the foreign exchange–starved Guyanese. The availability of flour allowed the Indians to enjoy their staple roti with their meals again, and the blacks to have bread rather than the crunchy crackers made from the cassava root. The program brought much goodwill for the United States from the people of Guyana.

One of my most annoying challenges as ambassador, however, was maintaining this key program. Since the program had been reinstated, there had been a change of personnel in the midlevels of the USAID bureaucracy in Washington dealing with the Caribbean countries, with which Guyana was included. The key figure, an office director, as I recall, had served in Guyana when Burnham was president, and had been evicted by Burnham when the president abruptly terminated the U.S. aid program. This man did not believe that Desmond Hoyte represented any meaningful change from Forbes Burnham. When this director discovered that the P.L. 480 program had been reinstituted for Guyana, he appeared to me to be determined to find ways to terminate it.

Combating his efforts to end the program took considerable, repeated efforts on my part. I waged many battles with the USAID bureaucracy to maintain the program. I had to line up allies within the State Department to support my position; this was not difficult, as the department understood the value of the program in terms of our other efforts to wean Guyana away from dependence on Cuban and Soviet influence (for example, by increasing military-to-military contacts). But the USAID bureaucracy seemed reluctant to counter my vociferous opponent, who seemed to be simply trying to punish the government for past poor behavior, without recognizing that the situation had changed for the better since his departure from Guyana.

To me, terminating a program that was so meaningful to the Guyanese people, just as we were pressing the Guyanese government for both economic and political reform, was, in that overworked but apropos State Department term, "counter-productive." The constant arguments with him over keeping the program were exhausting and aggravating. One ploy he attempted was to contend that I did not have the staff to handle a USAID program because I had no USAID officers at the embassy. I said that I would welcome receiving a USAID officer to the staff; sorry, he replied, no one was available. Yet when I visited our embassy in Barbados, a USAID official there told me that he would be happy to transfer to Guyana and that he thought the workload in Barbados could be handled with one fewer officer. When I proposed this to USAID in Washington, the proposal was rejected, as I had expected.

Still, I was able to prevail in this ongoing bureaucratic battle. The program was sustained over the disgruntled USAID official's objections, and the flour continued to improve the quality of life of the Guyanese throughout my tour.

Revival of U.S.–Guyana Military Cooperation

I was also able to reinstitute some low-level cooperation between the United States and Guyanese military forces. Such cooperation was virtually nonexistent during the Burnham era, with Burnham's Socialist leanings and close Communist allies. I was alert to all ways to improve the overall U.S.–Guyanese relationship, and military cooperation was one possible route. The U.S. Southern Command (USSOUTHCOM) was interested in establishing contact with the Guyanese military. I had good relations with the commander of the Guyanese military forces (the equivalent of the U.S. chairman of the joint chiefs of staff) and his deputy. I worked with him on the question of how we could increase cooperation between our two militaries.

The result of my discussions with both USSOUTHCOM and the Guyanese military was a visit to Guyana by the then commanding general of USOUTHCOM, Frederick Woerner. The Guyanese were delighted to host his visit and put on an excellent program, complete with visits to Guyanese military establishments, television appearances, and a celebratory dinner. As a result of this visit, we were able to arrange some visits by American forces for training purposes with Guyanese forces. The Guyanese terrain, particularly toward the Rupununi area in the southern part of the country, was rugged and offered wide-open spaces for practicing helicopter landings in unfamiliar terrain and the like. At that point our armed forces were looking for alternatives for military training exercises to replace those in Panama, which we expected to vacate in the next year or so.

Our military, working alongside their Guyanese counterparts, ultimately concentrated on two specific training exercises: medical and dental clinics, and well drilling. On the first such exercise, U.S.

medical and dental technicians flew down to the Rupununi area in helicopters with all of the necessary support staff and set up camp for about ten days. Once the clinics were established, the Guyanese military got the word out to villagers, and the clinics rapidly became inundated with patients. Some native Indians in the area, one U.S. officer told me, had walked as far as twenty miles to get treatment. The missions were a rousing success, much appreciated by the Guyanese and highly valued by the U.S. military for the unique training opportunities the remote, barren terrain provided.

On at least two occasions during my tenure, the U.S. military sent in teams to dig wells in water-deprived villages. These exercises, also, were successful and much appreciated. Our military personnel conducted themselves very well and won many friends where they worked. The joint exercises did much to heal the estrangement that had infected the military-to-military relationship as a result of Burnham's courtship with the Socialist and Communist countries, and helped improve the overall U.S.–Guyana bilateral relationship. While I was in Guyana, the most visible assistance provider to Guyana was Cuba. Castro's government had sent hundreds of health care workers—doctors, nurses, and technicians—who provided greatly needed assistance in the health field. I was anxious to forge whatever links I could between our countries, to remind Guyana that the United States was not their enemy and was more than willing to enjoy a friendly, helpful relationship.

The U.S. relationship also benefited from the many visits by private American groups that offered assistance, particularly in the medical field. Groups of doctors with different specialties came to Georgetown and provided their services free of charge. On one such occasion, for example, a team of ophthalmologists performed cataract surgery on a wide range of patients, well off and poor. One of the persons successfully operated on was the chief of staff to President Hoyte. He was absolutely delighted with the results. This kind of surgery was simply not available in Guyana at that time.

Sisters of Mercy: A Runnemede Connection

The United States also benefited from the excellent service provided to the Guyanese by the Sisters of Mercy at the Mercy Hospital, which was located immediately next door to the embassy. This hospital was the best in Guyana when I was there. The hospital was staffed primarily by American Sisters of Mercy. The head surgeon at the hospital was an elderly American nun who was widely regarded as an excellent surgeon. The nuns were truly doing God's work. They kept the hospital clean and sanitary and functioning under extremely difficult economic conditions, including frequent power outages.

Not long after my arrival at post, my next-door neighbors invited me over to their convent for a get-acquainted lunch. I was eager to meet them, particularly the distinguished surgeon. I had read about her in *Reader's Digest* magazine, which hailed her skills and dedication in her unlikely assignment. The surgeon and I were chatting, exchanging initial personal information as one does in such encounters. When I said to her question that I was from Runnemede, New Jersey, she shocked me by saying that she knew Runnemede well: she had spent her summers there as a child, with her aunt, who lived in a small house on the Black Horse Pike near Fifth Avenue.

I had been born and raised around the corner on Fourth Avenue. I remembered her aunt, whose little house was set back rather far from the street, covered with drooping wisteria vines, on an unkempt lot. To my child's eyes, it was a scary looking place, and the elderly lady who lived there was a frightening sight in her long black and deep purple dresses. I was not afraid of her, as I had gotten to see her on occasion with my father, who was active in politics and community affairs and knew everyone in town, it seemed to me. She was never anything but nice to me on our encounters, but I had playmates who would not venture near her or her house. Naturally, I did not share these recollections with her niece, the renowned Sister of Mercy surgeon. I simply told her that I had known her aunt, and wondered at the startling coincidence, the strange tricks of fate that took the summer vacationer from the Pike and Fifth Avenue and the little girl from Fourth Avenue and sat them down to lunch in Guyana, where one was a renowned surgeon and the other the American ambassador.

Corruption

Unfortunately, another aspect of life in Guyana, as perhaps in many countries in difficult economic straits, was corruption. The temptation to take bribes for performing services, and in the case of a couple of Guyanese members of my consular staff, to take money for issuing visas, was a strong one. When I first arrived in the country, I quickly became aware that there were rumors on the street that U.S. visas could be obtained quickly, for a price. My security people were looking into the matter, but it was difficult to pin anything down, to get beyond the rumors to find hard evidence of malfeasance.

About halfway through my tour, however, we got fairly firm evidence that two Guyanese members of our consular staff apparently had been on the take for some time. I am uncertain how we ascertained the names of the two women; it might have come indirectly from someone who, having been denied a visa, heard that if he been willing to pay a bribe, he could have gotten one. (Preliminary screening of visa applicants typically is performed by a local national employee, who reviews documents and makes a recommendation to the American consular officer about the likelihood that the applicant is bona fide. Ultimate responsibility for the issuance rests on the American officer, but in high-volume visa posts, which Georgetown surely was, the officer relies somewhat on the endorsement of his local staff.)

We learned that the two women were planning a "vacation" trip to New York in a few weeks. My security people worked with their counterparts in New York and arranged to have the women arrested in New York City. The U.S. government had no authority to make arrests in Guyana, and we decided not to involve the Guyanese police in the matter, in part because of concerns about how vigorously the cases would be pursued. The women were arrested and charged. This action sent a clear message to the consular staff that such criminal activities would not be tolerated. Still, in a country where the economic situation was so dire, individuals desperate to improve their lives and those of their children would risk a great deal to obtain the ticket to the promised land, an American visa.

Fortunately, after I was at post about a year, the tour of the unhappy head of the consular section came to an end. She was replaced by an excellent, enthusiastic officer, Nicholas Williams. He had an infectious upbeat attitude that greatly brightened the outlook of the young officers under his charge in the section. I was delighted to find an opportunity toward the end of my tour to allow Nick to serve briefly as chargé d'affaires. The DCM was on leave and I had to leave town unexpectedly for a night or two, and I designated Nick as interim chargé, an indication of the confidence I had in him. This gave him the privilege of having his name, in lieu of mine, as the sending officer on all outgoing cables. I had every confidence that Nick had a fine career ahead of him, with the possibility of becoming an ambassador, and I told him this. I believe he has done very well since Guyana.

Thus, after an extremely difficult first year, I now had an excellent DCM and an excellent consular section chief, both of whom performed very well and helped to lighten my load. Unfortunately, the performance of the administrative section did not improve much, despite DCM Hays's work with them. By the end of my tour, the administrative section was still a work in progress, but a gradually improving one, in my view.

Reflections on the Guyana Experience

My tour came to an end in the summer of 1990. As I looked back on a very difficult three years, I took some satisfaction in the fact that Guyana had undertaken a challenging economic reform program, to which the United States had contributed not only in terms of my verbal encouragement but also with a $5 million contribution to the bridge loan that enabled the country's initial debt restructuring. In addition, despite USAID obstruction, we had retained the P.L. 480 flour import program. The groundwork had been laid for free elections, which were due to be held a few months after my departure. We had strengthened military cooperation between the United States and Guyana. In addition to the army joint exercises in the medical, dental, and well-drilling fields, we had arranged at least one U.S. Navy ship visit, which was very well received. We had increased private business dealings between U.S. companies and Guyana. Reynolds Aluminum had expanded its activities in the bauxite field, and the Hunt Oil people were interested in exploring oil possibilities in Guyana's Rupununi region (this, unfortunately, did not prove fruitful). The climate for American business had definitely improved.

I was satisfied also that I had improved the quality of the political reporting at the embassy, and I was pleased that the young economic officer had handled the complicated economic issues so well with very little oversight. The administrative section had improved slightly during my tenure. But I was disappointed to recognize that I had not greatly improved the morale of the staff, who continued to suffer under the difficult living conditions in Guyana, and many of whom I suspected still regarded me as too demanding. We had been able to persuade the department to provide generators for each of our residences, which eased the difficulties created by the ongoing power shortages. But by and large, most of the American staff did not have the same level of professional satisfaction that I gained from our efforts in Guyana, which helped me tolerate the difficulties of everyday life. I wish I had been able to better convey to the less contented staffers my enthusiasm for what we were accomplishing in terms of improving the relationship with a country that just a few years before had been, in many respects, hostile to the United States.

Presidential Meetings

In my career, I had the honor of three meetings with presidents: two with President Ronald Reagan and one with President George H. W. Bush, who succeeded him. Although President Bill Clinton appointed me ambassador to Brunei, I never met with him. I did witness his inaugural parade and caught a brief glimpse of his gray-white head as he walked past the Treasury Department. My three meetings took place in the context of my Guyana ambassadorship.

Hoyte Visit

In approximately June 1988, Guyana's president, Desmond Hoyte, was invited to Washington for a low-key visit to reward his consideration of economic reforms and the political moderation he was demonstrating. The visit included a meeting with President Reagan, to which I, as ambassador, would accompany him. I asked the department to see if I could perhaps arrive a bit ahead of Hoyte to allow me to have my ambassadorial photo taken with the president. No, I was told, this would not be possible. I could, however, go back to the White House the day after the Hoyte meeting for the protocol meeting and photo op.

The Guyana desk officer at State undertook to arrange the photo meeting. He was told that I could be accompanied only by my spouse, parents, and children. I told him that I had none of the above, but that I would be accompanied by my two sisters; I asked him to work it out with White House protocol people. I then hurried to accompany President Hoyte on his meeting with the secretary of the treasury.

When I returned briefly to the department between appointments, the chagrined desk officer told me that the White House was adamant—only the relatives initially indicated could attend the meeting with the president. I "went ambassadorial" and instructed him to call the White House protocol office again and inform them that I would not go unaccompanied to meet the president, that I was not alone in the world, and that I had a very supportive family, which would be represented by my two sisters, one of whom was my godmother. I told him to insist on speaking directly with the chief of protocol, an army major general whose name escapes me, and if this could not be accomplished, to have the general call me directly to explain why. I then dashed out to take President Hoyte to another appointment, this time with the U.S. trade representative.

Returning to the State Department, the relieved desk officer informed me that my sisters could indeed attend the meeting with the president; he asked for their names, dates of birth, and social security numbers for White House security. He said that my insistence on his asking to speak directly with the general had gotten the message across. As I was preparing to call my oldest sister, Betty (the godmother in the story), I received a most warm, apologetic phone call from the major general, informing me that of course my sisters could accompany me, so sorry for the misunderstanding, et cetera. I thanked him for taking care of the matter.

A startled Betty Waldis received a quick phone call from me about 1:00 p.m. on a Monday. I told Betty, who could be quite a talker, that I had no time to talk but wanted to invite her and Hazel to come to Washington the next day for a meeting with President Reagan on Wednesday morning. I asked her to inform Hazel and call my office at State as quickly as possible with the needed security data. Betty snapped to in her usual efficient manner, called Hazel at her office, and within an hour or so the desk officer was giving the White House their needed security data.

Presidential Charm

On Tuesday morning, I accompanied President Hugh Desmond Hoyte of Guyana to the Oval Office for his meeting with the president. I had helped to prepare briefing papers for the president for this meeting, as is standard in such cases. President Reagan was very gracious. The Guyanese officials sat on one bank of comfortable chairs, the Americans, a small group, on the other. I sat next to then national security adviser, General Colin Powell, close to the president.

The meeting proceeded smoothly. The press had already begun to snicker about President Reagan's mental acuity—he had reportedly dozed off at a meeting with the pope, and so on. At this meeting, however, he was fully in command of the situation. He referred to the notes State had prepared for him, conducting a most productive meeting at which he was comfortable with all of the issues. Photos were taken. When I returned to Guyana, I received a letter from Colin Powell enclosing photos of myself with President Reagan, as well as photos of the two presidents together. It was a most professional meeting.

Hazel and Betty came down to Washington late Tuesday afternoon. We had a great dinner at a French restaurant in Washington. Hazel had been slated to conduct a seminar at her place of work, and it was an awkward time for her to take a day off. When she told her supervisor the reason, the woman acceded to her request. Her office workers knew about my position and were willing to accept what must have sounded like a far-fetched reason for absenting oneself from an important, long-scheduled commitment. Hazel determined to show her supervisor and colleagues the photo when it materialized.

We went to the White House as scheduled and were admitted

to the Roosevelt Room, which adjoins the Oval Office. One or two other ambassadors and their families were there, awaiting their meeting with the president. A tall, middle-aged man in civilian dress came over to us and said, "You must be Ambassador Tull.... And which of you is the ambassador's godmother?" Two blank faces greeted the question. "Betty is, general," I said as the girls fought back giggles. (Our special link obviously had made a big impression on her.)

We were then ushered into the Oval Office, where I introduced Hazel and Betty to the president, whom I had met the day before in the official meeting with President Hoyte. Ronald Reagan, even in his midseventies, was a handsome man, strikingly so. Hazel spoke for all of us when she said, "Mr. President, you look wonderful!" He clearly appreciated the remark. There were a few minutes of small talk, and then the president said: "I had a meeting with your sister yesterday, and with the president of Guyana. She is doing a fine job there, and I wanted you two to know that." The photographer arranged us for the photos, which turned out very well. The president then gave each of us a little souvenir of the White House. Mine was a lapel pin; I think the girls received key chains.

Throughout our brief meeting, President Reagan was genuinely charming and gracious. He came across as a thoroughly decent man. It was a memorable experience for all of us.

President George H. W. Bush

About a year later, in June 1989, I returned to Washington for another meeting between the U.S. and Guyanese presidents—again, in recognition of Hoyte's reform efforts. Our new president was George Herbert Walker Bush, who had been elected the previous November. As required, all serving ambassadors had to submit their resignations upon the election of a new president, as we serve at the pleasure of the president. In my case, apparently, no political appointee was eager to go to Guyana, so President Bush declined to accept my resignation and I remained in place.

The Oval Office meetings were quite a contrast. I had expected President Bush, a most experienced government official, to insist upon a certain decorum being maintained in his office. But this was not the case. When our party entered the Oval Office, I introduced President Hoyte to President Bush, and prepared to take my appropriate seat with senior American officials. But a large group of senior U.S. officials, including the national security adviser, the White House chief of staff, the deputy director of the CIA, and assorted hangers-on, plopped themselves down on the available U.S. places, leaving me, the ambassador, standing. Bush did nothing to correct the embarrassment, but gracious President Hoyte invited me to sit next to him. This was incorrect protocol, but I of course accepted and the meeting proceeded.

I was struck throughout the meeting at the improper behavior of some of the senior American officials present. They whispered to each other, laughed, and fidgeted (from my perception) while the two presidents were discussing the issues with each other. Their behavior was reminiscent of unruly schoolboys, and I was surprised and embarrassed at their conduct. President Bush seemed oblivious to their conduct—including their acing me out of my appropriate seat.

At the meeting's conclusion, we were suddenly startled when the president gave a sign and the French doors of the Oval Office opened and a crowd of newsmen and photographers rushed into the office. A wild scene of shouted questions and snapped photos ensued. It was, it seemed to me, highly unpresidential.

A few weeks later, photos of Bush and Hoyte arrived in Guyana for me to deliver to the Guyanese president. Although I had also been photographed with President Bush, I never received a copy of the photo. When I asked the national security adviser about the photo, I was assured one would be sent, but it never materialized. Clearly Colin Powell, who had sent me photos of the two presidents for President Hoyte, and a photo of me with President Reagan, had left the White House.

Diplomat in Residence

When I left Guyana, I had thought that my next logical assignment in the continuation of my hopefully upward career mobility would be to become a deputy assistant secretary, preferably in the East Asia bureau. This did not materialize. Having checked out available positions, and finding no good possibilities, I ended up spending an academic year as a diplomat in residence at Lincoln University in Chester County, Pennsylvania, not far from Philadelphia and my home turf of New Jersey.

Lincoln University was the oldest historically black college in the United States. It was established by Presbyterians in the 1850s to educate free blacks. It acquired an excellent reputation. In the early twentieth century, it was called the "Black Princeton." It had high standards. Thurgood Marshall, the first African American Supreme Court justice, obtained his bachelor's degree there. A couple of future African heads of state were educated there. By 1990, the academic caliber of the university had ebbed slightly. The university was admitting students with lower high-school averages than previously, as were many universities at that time. But it still was a respectable college, providing a valuable education to its overwhelmingly black student body.

Lincoln was situated in a beautiful part of Pennsylvania, in a rich and attractive agricultural area. The farm fields in the surrounding area were lovely. The university's campus was traditional in appearance, with attractive, deep red brick buildings placed with taste around ample greenswards. A statue of Frederick Douglass occupied a prominent place on the campus. The overall effect was quite pleasant.

As diplomat-in-residence, my job included teaching a couple of courses, and in general being a resource for the university and the students, providing insights into the work of American diplomats and encouraging Lincoln's students to consider careers in the State Department. The year I was dispatched to Lincoln, the State Department's diplomat-in-residence program focused almost exclusively on sending ambassadors to minority universities, as part of an outreach effort specifically designed to encourage minority students to consider Foreign Service careers.

I taught a course in human rights as an element in U.S. foreign policy. This was a political science course for upper classmen. Drawing on my three years of experience in the human rights bureau, I put together a lot of information and developed the course from scratch. I enjoyed teaching the course; I think it came together rather well, although I may have asked a little too much from the students in terms of course reading. But I believe that our discussion of the origins of the Universal Declaration of Human Rights proved informative for the students, as did our discussion of specific examples of the United States pressing human rights concerns in certain foreign policy initiatives.

I also initiated a series of brown-bag lunches, open to all. Students and faculty could bring their lunches and eat while a speaker made a presentation on a particular subject; questions followed. I made the first presentation and lined up other speakers from the faculty for subsequent get-togethers. I also presented a series of speeches on foreign policy challenges of the 1990s for the United States. These were given in a large auditorium and were open to the entire student body. Attendance was optional, and these speeches were not very well attended.

To stimulate students to think about Foreign Service careers, I organized sessions in the evening for anyone who wanted to discuss such careers. I obtained guidebooks on typical Foreign Service examination questions and reviewed them with students at these sessions. I made a point of bringing maps of the world and reviewing country locations with them, as I was aware that the teaching of geography had been rather neglected in the U.S. educational system in recent years.

I enjoyed my time at Lincoln. I was struck from the very beginning by the politeness with which I was treated by all of the students I encountered. Walking across the campus, I was routinely greeted by the students, who did not know me, with a "hello" or "good morning." In the classroom, the students were uniformly courteous and attentive. They did not hesitate to ask challenging questions. One young lady asked why the United States was pressing for respect for human rights when many of the Founding Fathers owned slaves, and the Constitution did not acknowledge black slaves as full persons. I acknowledged that it had taken the United States a long time to redress these weaknesses, but I asked that the students consider our history in the context of the times. When the American experiment was launched in 1776, governments worldwide were headed by absolute monarchs who ruled by fiat, as a result of the accident of their birth. Establishing a government of white male landowners was a considerable improvement over the divine right of kings. And over time, the United States had expanded the rights enjoyed by its citizens.

I was asked to remain beyond the completion of the regular academic year to teach in the summer program. I was pleased to do this, and the department agreed. I put together a seminar on Asian politics and governments. This required a fair amount of research, which I enjoyed.

Life as a diplomat-in-residence provided a welcome change of pace for me. The academic year was a respite from the hectic, stress-filled three years as ambassador to Guyana. I rented an apartment in a pleasant complex in Kennett Square, Pennsylvania, about a fifteen-minute drive down a good road through the lovely farm fields to the university. Kennett Square claimed to be the "mushroom capital of the world," and structures with plastic sheeting roofs and sides dotted the fields, harboring mushrooms. I would occasionally spot a trotting horse being put through its paces on a private track. The drive was a relaxing way to start a workday—no hectic commutes, as most people must endure.

A major benefit of being at Lincoln was the proximity of several members of my family. Two of my brothers and my two sisters lived no more than an hour's drive away. We had many enjoyable get-togethers in Kennett Square and in their homes. After so much time abroad, it was wonderful to be "at home" again, able to take part in the family celebrations of first communions, birthdays, and holidays.

In sum, I enjoyed my year at Lincoln, and believe I made a reasonable contribution there as diplomat-in-residence. I was proud of the courses I taught and the ancillary lectures I gave. If nothing else, my presence among the students, as a woman ambassador, was tangible proof that there was room at the top levels of the State Department for women, and, by extension, minorities.

11

Back to the East Asia Bureau

Finding the next assignment is always an issue in the Foreign Service, particularly when one's current assignment was only a one-year stint, as mine was. Being away from Washington did not help me in my search, and initially, the hunt did not go well. Again, I felt that I was a competitive candidate for a deputy assistant secretaryship, particularly in the East Asia and Pacific bureau. This proved to be a nonstarter. I then lowered my sights to explore a position as office director. As a former ambassador, this was not the kind of position I would have preferred, but I did know of other competent ambassadors who had subsequently been assigned as office directors.

There were three such positions coming up for assignment in the East Asia bureau in the summer of 1991. The position I felt best qualified for was office director for Philippine affairs. I had served in the Philippines, in Cebu, for two years. The Indonesia–Malaysia–Singapore directorship was also opening up, as was the directorship for the Office of Regional Affairs.

The assistant secretary at that time was Richard Solomon, who was a political appointee. I met with him, but it became quite clear that he was not interested in me for the Philippine desk position. He had already selected the man he wanted for that job, an officer who had served as his staff assistant in the bureau; this man was below the grade level designated for the position. He also had another officer in mind for the Indonesia desk. I could understand my problem: I had been out of the East Asia bureau for four years. There were new people at the top who did not know me. I could imagine the powers that be in the bureau wondering, "Who is this Terry Tull who wants an office directorship? She had her ambassadorship—why doesn't she retire?"

At any rate, I persevered. I was not yet ready to retire. The regional affairs directorship remained unfilled, but I learned through the grapevine that the assistant secretary had someone else in mind for that slot, too. At this point, I spoke with State personnel about the problem. I told them that I felt that I should have gotten the Philippine job, and also felt that I was fully qualified for the Indonesia position. But I understood that the assistant secretary was pressing for his choices for these jobs, one of whom was an officer who was below grade level for the job. On what grounds, I asked, was I not qualified for the regional affairs position? My personnel counselor agreed that I had a point. I later came to learn informally that personnel had told the assistant secretary that I was too qualified an officer to be rejected out of hand, and that he would indeed have me as an office director. While I preferred the Philippine position, I was willing to take the regional affairs job. If he concurred in this, personnel would allow the assignment of the below-grade officer to the Philippine position.

So, on this awkward note, I became office director for regional affairs in the East Asia and Pacific bureau. Initially, the job was less than satisfying professionally. Once I was on board, I learned that some of the functions that in my view should have been handled by the regional affairs office had been handed over, long before I was a candidate for the job, to a special assistant who was a political appointee. In addition, dealings with ASEAN, with which I had considerable familiarity and which were clearly of regional interest, were being handled by the Indonesia–Malaysia–Singapore desk.

What was left for my office? Security issues were, including approval of licenses for the sale of military equipment to countries in our region; I had an army lieutenant colonel working these issues. The United Nations and international organization affairs was still in the regional affairs purview; a career civil service officer handled these matters. Still, the regional affairs portfolio was thinner than I would have preferred.

I was discouraged. I wondered whether it was time, after all, to retire. I was eligible to retire; I would have an adequate pension. With no children in college, I did not have to hang on in an unrewarding position just for the salary. I remember sitting in my office one beautiful fall morning and looking out the window, thinking, "I don't have to be here. I have been an ambassador, so that ambition has been achieved. I could be out enjoying a nice walk, looking at the gorgeous autumn leaves. I don't want to be here where I'm not required to use my brain to the fullest."

I was debating this situation and seriously contemplating retirement when Congress made changes to the Foreign Service Act, which resulted in a substantial salary increase for the senior levels of the Foreign Service. At the same time, the State Department adjusted the time-in-class requirements for officers. Before this change, I would have had only about another two or three years before my time in class would have expired. I knew I would not be promoted again. I had already reached a high level, and relatively few of my peers would be promoted to the next level, which was career minister. Thanks to this legislation, I would not only receive a substantial salary increase, which would increase my pension upon retirement, but I would also have several additional years in grade before I would have to retire.

Retirement now, I quickly concluded, would be foolish. I determined to do the best I could in the job, despite the assistant secretary's lack of enthusiasm for me and my office. I quashed any thought of retirement. I would stick it out and hope that, being physically in the department once more, I would be able to lobby successfully at the end of this assignment for a more interesting one.

At the United Nations

I did receive one interesting assignment while Richard Solomon was the assistant secretary. I was dispatched to New York in the fall of 1991 and again in 1992, for about two months on each occasion, to serve as the so-called East Asian expert on the U.S. delegation to the United Nations during the General Assembly session. During these General Assembly sessions. several additional officers augmented the U.S. mission to the United Nations. Each geographic bureau sent a high-ranking officer, usually someone who had served as an ambassador, to New York to help with the heavy workload during these sessions, which included a lot of lobbying of other delegations to gain support for U.S. positions on the wide range of resolutions and issues that came before the General Assembly.

When I arrived in New York in 1991, the first thing I did was to pay calls on the heads of delegation for all of the countries in the East Asia and Pacific region. The fact that I had been an ambassador, and retained that title, gave me entrée. Having made this initial contact paved the way for me to approach these ambassadors later when it was necessary to ask for their support for U.S. positions on various issues and to learn their countries' positions on issues of concern to the United States. Making these calls broadened my knowledge of the city of New York. Some of the diplomatic missions were housed in exquisite old townhouses; others were in high-rise buildings, where the ambassador's office afforded panoramic views of the city and the river.

At the United Nations, the work pace was very brisk during the week, and we had to attend occasional evening receptions to continue our contact work. Absent a crisis, however, most ambassadors left town over the weekends, allowing most of us to be generally free to enjoy the limitless attractions of New York. I rented a two-bedroom, two-bath apartment in the Tudor City apartment complex, within walking distance of the United Nations and our mission, which was directly across the street from the United Nations. I invited various family members and friends to visit me over the weekends. I enjoyed both the assignment and the attractions of New York very much.

I had the pleasure of hosting a visit from the former British high commissioner to Guyana, David Small, and his wife, Pat, for several days. Subsequently, the former Canadian high commissioner to Guyana, Bill Sinclair, and his wife, Jean, stayed with me for a few days. We had been very close to each other in Guyana; our three governments had almost identical policies regarding Guyana, and we had become very good friends.

The experience of working in multilateral diplomacy was new to me, and I found it very interesting. The first thing in the morning, all of the officers met in the conference room with the ambassador—Thomas Pickering the first year, and Edward Perkins the second—who reviewed the current issues and sought input from the staff, as appropriate.

In addition to career diplomats, each year the president appointed a few public members to participate in the delegation. One public member when I was on the delegation was the singing star Gloria Estefan. I sat next to her during one General Assembly session, and was struck by how seriously she addressed her duties. She was a Cuban refugee, based in Miami, and was very concerned about Cuban human rights violations. She was very pleasant and down-to-earth and put on no airs whatsoever.

One of the highlights of my UN assignment was the overturning of the detestable "Zionism is racism" resolution that had been passed many years ago, and which the United States had attempted often to have revoked. Heavy lobbying in 1991 brought about the defeat of that unfair resolution against Israel. The U.S. mission also successfully lobbied for limits on certain fishing practices, getting restrictions on the size of drift nets used by fishing boats.

It was also during my tenure under Solomon that I began helping to develop ways to encourage the ASEAN countries of Southeast Asia to undertake discussion, and eventually action, in the area of regional security. These efforts took concrete form in the ASEAN Regional Forum, a discussion platform for ASEAN members that began, with our encouragement, as an add-on to the long-standing annual foreign ministers meeting of ASEAN and its dialogue partners, which included the United States and other major powers with a presence and interest in the Pacific region. These efforts, and my role in them, became more concrete after Winston Lord became assistant secretary following President Clinton's election.

In the fall of 1992, the presidential election brought a change of party to the White House and the departure of the political appointees made by the George H. W. Bush administration. After William Clark's brief service as assistant secretary, Winston Lord was appointed. Lord's perspective differed from Solomon's on the proper role of the regional affairs office in the bureau, and on what my job should be. My job completely turned around under Lord. I was given a much broader role in the work of the bureau. This proved to be a very interesting experience, and ultimately led to my second ambassadorship, to Brunei.

Winston Lord, former ambassador to China, was very intelligent and very pleasant to work with. He did an excellent job as assistant secretary, in my view. He also regarded me as an asset rather than someone who had been foisted off on him. We connected right away. He apparently felt that my former ambassadorship gave him the leeway to use me rather broadly to represent him and the bureau at conferences within the department and in foreign countries, as well. He asked me to attend his daily meetings with his deputy assistant secretaries, apparently taking the view that the regional affairs office should participate as appropriate in all of the activities of the bureau. In many respects, he treated me like a deputy assistant secretary.

Establishing a Precedent: The APEC Summit

A highlight of my time in the regional affairs office was my role in encouraging annual summit meetings of the heads of government of the members of APEC (Asia Pacific Economic Cooperation).

APEC is an organization created to further economic cooperation among Pacific Rim countries. It was initially limited to twelve countries, including ASEAN countries, the United States, Canada, China, Japan, Australia, and New Zealand. Taiwan, although not an independent country per se, was a full member. APEC's membership has since expanded.

APEC began slowly. It reflected U.S. interest in providing Pacific Rim countries a forum for improving economic cooperation concerning trade, tariffs, taxes, access to fair courts, and the like. Unlike the Europeans, who have the European Community for economic and political cooperation, the Pacific countries had little interaction on these increasingly important issues.

Gradually, APEC took shape and acquired focus. At first, economic, finance, and trade ministers gathered together annually for relatively informal discussions. Venues rotated among the countries involved.

In November 1992, Bill Clinton, a former Rhodes Scholar and governor of Arkansas, was elected president. To our knowledge, he had had little exposure to Asia. In the fall of 1993, the United States was scheduled for the first time to host the APEC gathering. Seattle, with its Pacific location and trade focus, was selected as the site. In the East Asia Bureau, we wished to engage our new president in Asian issues.

I recall clearly that early in 1993, shortly after Clinton was inaugurated, the Seattle APEC meeting was discussed at the bureau's senior staff meeting, at which I was present. I suggested that a good way to immerse the president in Asia would be to have him attend the APEC meeting—give a speech to the ministers, host a brief reception. We brainstormed the idea. Sandra Kristoff, then deputy assistant secretary for economic affairs, was keen on the idea. The two of us just about simultaneously came up with the idea of asking Clinton not only to go to Seattle but also to invite all of the other heads of state for the meeting: that is, to have an APEC summit meeting. Our new president could meet the heads of state of a dozen of the leading Asian nations in one fell swoop. Since Clinton was known as a person with excellent people skills, Sandy and I thought he would welcome this opportunity and would run with it in terms of making the strong personal contacts with the leaders that would be important to the United States in pursuing our interests in the region. We felt the likelihood was strong that if the United States hosted such a summit, all subsequent nations hosting APEC would also have a summit. This would ensure that the U.S. president would visit Asia and meet at least once a year with not only the major powers but also with the leaders of the less important small countries that were useful to U.S. interests. U.S. presidents visit the major regional powers, such as Japan and China; for the smaller countries, such as the ASEAN states, an APEC summit would most likely be the only opportunity their heads of state would have to meet with the U.S. president.

The East Asia bureau bought into the idea enthusiastically. The idea was floated in the White House, persuasively, and planning began. Two major issues quickly emerged. China was being stubborn on the issue of Taiwan's attendance. There was no way a Chinese premier would attend a meeting at which Taiwan was represented, some analysts feared, and many thought that the Taiwanese would insist on sending their equivalent head of state. We thrashed this around at a few meetings. I took the view that Taiwan had to be represented, but not at their head-of-state level. As for our China office director's view that the People's Republic of China would not attend if anyone from Taiwan was present, I contended that the Chinese premier would not pass up an opportunity to visit the United States and meet with the new U.S. president. Our director for Taiwan interests was concerned that Taiwan would not attend unless at the head-of-state level, to which I argued that this would be a unique opportunity for a ministerial-level Taiwanese official to meet with a U.S. president—something that had not happened for many years—and that after grousing, Taiwan would indeed attend at the ministerial level.

Malaysia was another potential problem. The ASEAN countries (at that time, six in number—the Philippines, Malaysia, Singapore, Thailand, Indonesia, and Brunei) had an unwritten code of operating by consensus—one for all, and all for one. Malaysia's prime minister, Mahathir Mohamad, was a feisty, egotistical sort who, we felt, might welcome a chance to snub our proposed summit meeting. This prompted concerns among my colleagues who followed ASEAN affairs that none of the ASEAN countries would attend, and that the proposed meeting would fizzle. I insisted that in this case, the other ASEAN countries, offered a rare chance to visit the United States as the guest of the new president and to meet with him for extensive discussions and camaraderie, would not let Mahathir use the usual ASEAN consensus to block their attendance.

In fairness to Mahathir, his resistance to the idea may have stemmed from his concern about the direction in which APEC might be pushed by what he might have regarded as an overly enthusiastic United States. He might have viewed this direction as counter to his support for purely Asian institutions and his resistance to moving away from the ASEAN model toward an institutionalized and bureaucratic regional structure. Meanwhile, before proceeding formally, our embassies in the region were taking soundings in capitals to determine governments' reactions to the proposed summit and the likelihood of acceptance of the idea. In no case would we risk issuing invitations for the president and having them rebuffed.

I argued my views concerning China, Taiwan, and the ASEAN

countries forcefully, and eventually minor in-house reluctance to proceeding was overcome. China sent its premier, Taiwan a trade minister. Mahathir declined—to his chagrin, I would bet—because every other ASEAN head of state accepted the invitation without hesitation.

In late October 1993, President Clinton went to Seattle, and the first APEC summit meeting was a rousing success. As I had expected, the APEC summit became a firm tradition. Every fall since then, the U.S. president has traveled to whatever Asian nation is hosting the summit. (President Clinton missed the event once during a budget crisis, but he did send the vice president.) President George W. Bush attended these summits as well, as has President Obama.

Have I overstated my role in helping to create the APEC summit? Perhaps, but I would like to think not. At the time, Sandy Kristoff thought that the two of us were largely responsible for the idea, and for prodding it through the bureaucracy. I know that my arguments concerning the China–Taiwan issue and the Mahathir question were received positively and helped to overcome qualms in the bureau. Success has many parents, of course. The important thing is that the useful tradition was established.

Regional Affairs: Conferences and Other Travel

While serving as regional affairs office director, I had occasional opportunities for bureau-related travel. On one occasion, the embassy in Bangkok alerted us to a human rights conference (the World Conference on Human Rights) that was to be held in that city and recommended that a high-level representative from the East Asia bureau attend. Given my experience in HA and my title, the bureau suggested that I represent the United States at the conference, held March 29 to April 2, 1993. Embassy Bangkok was enthusiastic about my attending, and asked whether I would be willing to stay for a few days after the conclusion of the human rights conference to attend another related one at which the embassy wanted to have a Washington U.S. presence.

I was willing. I suggested that I use the time between the two conferences to visit Vientiane, Laos, my old stamping ground, and assess the situation now as opposed to when I was chargé. This was agreed. I attended the first conference, and proceeded to Laos for the few days between conferences. An old friend of mine, Charles Salmon, was our ambassador to Laos, the United States having upgraded the level of relations.

I was pleasantly surprised by the changes I found in Vientiane. Sleepy, quiet little Vientiane, where in my time you saw only the occasional car on the streets—and these usually belonging to government officials or diplomats—was teeming with activity. Private automobiles; motorcycles; and colorful, three-wheeled jitneys called *tuc-tucs*, imported from Bangkok to provide inexpensive transportation, were abundant. There were some new hotels to service the tourists who were now permitted to enter Laos.

This flurry of activity apparently stemmed from the new economic policy the Lao had announced in 1986, toward the end of my tour as chargé. While I was chargé, there was very little indication that the policy was moving forward. By the time of my visit, in 1993, however, progress clearly had been made. There had been some economic loosening, as the Lao began reaching out for ways to earn some badly needed hard currency. A few American companies were doing modest business there. The oil exploration effort by Hunt Oil Company, which I had helped initiate, had proven fruitless, but there were a couple of small enterprises run by Americans, including one that hired Lao to weave beautiful fabrics for export to the United States.

Ambassador Salmon had arranged a series of meetings for me with government officials, who received me most warmly. The following morning, the government newspaper (the only newspaper) featured photographs of me and the ministers I had met with, all of us smiling broadly, with the headline noting that the government was welcoming me back.

It was an enjoyable visit. I was pleased to see how much the Lao government was now reaching out to the West and welcoming tourism and foreign investment. It was also a pleasure to stay again in the lovely ambassador's residence, as Charlie's guest, and renew my acquaintance with the charming and most competent Lao residence staff.

Burundi Beckons

While I was in Vientiane, I received an unexpected phone call from George Moose, a very capable officer who was at that time assistant secretary for African affairs. George and I had known each other casually in Vietnam when he was in Hue and I was in Saigon. George asked me if I would be willing to be the African bureau's candidate for ambassador to Burundi.

In the meantime, I had been approached by one of Winston Lord's deputies, and by Winston himself, about the possibility of becoming a candidate for appointment as the next ambassador to Brunei. But nothing had been spelled out concretely, and now I had another bureau asking if I wanted to be considered as an ambassador to one of its countries.

I thanked George for his offer and asked whether I could have a little time to think it over. I reminded him that I had not had any African experience, but he downplayed this, saying that I could learn and that my overall reputation suggested I could do the job. I thanked him again for his confidence, and said I would get back to him in a day or so.

In the back of my mind was the recollection that Burundi was a very difficult place in which to serve. Tribal problems between the Hutu and the Tutsi continued, and relations between Burundi and its neighbor Rwanda were difficult. On the other hand, it was a serious offer, and I resolved to take a serious look at it. I borrowed Charlie Salmon's latest human rights report from the Department and read Burundi's entry. Sure enough, the situation was as I had thought, with ethnic and tribal problems a continuing issue. The embassy was a decent size, however, with a full array of U.S. representation: USIS, USAID, Peace Corps, and so on, in addition to the State Department presence.

I decided that I would not turn down George's offer, and called him to accept it. But I resolved to tell Winston about the offer, and my willingness to be the African Bureau's candidate, when I returned to Washington. Once in Washington, I informed Winston's senior deputy about the development. He immediately said, "But you're our choice for Brunei." I told him that while this had been hinted at, nothing concrete had been put forward, and since I would like to have another embassy before I retired, I had agreed to have my name put forward for Burundi.

He said he would get back to me as soon as possible. Not long afterward, he informed me that Winston had confirmed that I definitely was his choice for Brunei; my name would be put forward as the East Asia bureau's candidate for that post. Within a few weeks, the deputy secretary's meeting to decide the State Department's choices for the ambassadorships opening in the next cycle was held. I learned that I was put forward for both the Burundi and Brunei ambassadorships. I was told subsequently that the White House had a nominee for the Burundi post, a political appointee who possibly had a scholarly interest in the region or country. I understand that this strengthened Winston Lord's argument in favor of my candidacy: if another bureau wanted Tull for one of its embassies, this proves how qualified she is for this post. (This is what I learned indirectly; I do not know what precisely was said to forward my candidacy.) At any rate, I emerged from the meeting as the State Department's choice for Brunei, and the White House accepted it.

Cambodia at the United Nations

In the meantime, I had another interesting stint at the United Nations. In the early spring of 1993, I was sent to New York to head up a small U.S. team to work with representatives of other countries to help refine the UN plan to organize and supervise free elections in Cambodia. Cambodia was going through a major transition from brutal Khmer Rouge domination and Vietnamese occupation to a period in which, it was hoped, free elections would allow the Cambodian people to choose a better system of government for themselves. The United States was strongly supportive of this initiative.

The UN plan involved grass-roots organizing efforts at provincial and village levels, ensuring public safety for the exercise, monitoring human rights conditions, and bringing in large numbers of observers to oversee the election itself. This was a major undertaking, and the resultant budget proved to be a very costly one. The United States was part of a group of concerned nations informally known as the Contact Group, comprising mostly Western nations and a few Southeast Asian ones. All of the countries were concerned about the huge cost of the program. Our respective governments would be funding the program, so it was determined that the Contact Group should thoroughly vet the program and its budget with a view to trimming costs, if possible, and, conversely, to determining whether any aspects of the plan called for additional financing. We especially wanted to thoroughly understand the entire program and its budget, so that we would be able to defend it to our home governments and funding agencies—in the case of the United States, the Congress.

A small staff was assigned to assist me—note takers, primarily. We met daily at the French mission to the United Nations. The French ambassador to the UN chaired the meetings, with me as cochair. We studied the plan and its budget point by point. We found a few areas that we felt needed refining or that could be looked at a bit more carefully. But we found no major problems.

At the conclusion of our study, we met at the United Nations with the UN under secretary for administration, Richard Thornburgh, a former U.S. attorney general, to present our findings. We also heard at that meeting from the Australian general who was to handle the security aspects of this effort. It was a very interesting experience. Our work received positive comment from Washington, which I appreciated. The resultant elections were conducted in accordance with the UN plan, generally safely and fairly.

Off to the Island of Guano

Assistant Secretary Lord occasionally asked me to attend, in his place, international conferences to which he had been invited. In the summer of 1993, my brief vacation with friends at their villa in Italy was disturbed by a phone call from the department. Would I be willing to head the U.S. delegation to a meeting of the South Pacific Forum, in Nauru? Winston Lord had been expected to make the trip, but decided that I could handle the task for him. Of course, I agreed. Almost immediately upon my return to Washington, after a quick briefing on the conference issues, I took off for Nauru, via Honolulu.

The South Pacific Forum is a loosely structured organization composed of the various island countries of the South Pacific, and Australia and New Zealand. The forum meets annually in different island capitals. The meetings consider various economic, security, and assistance issues. The United States and France, countries that have specific interests and concerns in the region, are invited as guests to attend a special meeting incidental to the annual forum meeting.

That year, the meetings were to be held in Nauru, a tiny island in the middle of the South Pacific about 1,500 miles from New Zealand. Nauru's economy was based almost exclusively on foreign firms' extraction of bat and bird guano for conversion into fertilizer. When I had served in INR, in the mid-1970s, the government of Nauru was seriously considering buying another island and moving Nauru's population there when the encroaching extraction industry rendered the island uninhabitable. By 1993, however, this idea had been shelved. The extraction companies apparently had worked out ways to repair some of the ecological damage to the island, which they would undertake at some future date. There was no evidence that any restoration of the soil had been undertaken in 1993. The island looked like an eerie moonscape, for the most part. A narrow outer rim of road and buildings circled the entire island, but the overwhelming majority of the interior of the island was devastated from the guano extraction. The government and people of Nauru earned a sizable income from the sale of their sole resource.

I flew to Honolulu and checked in at a modest motel very close to the airport, because I had an early take-off the next day. The flight was booked on Air Nauru. It would have taken a good part of the day to get to Nauru, with stops at a couple of islands en route for refueling.

I got up very early in the morning, anticipating the early departure. An officer from CINCPAC (commander in chief, Pacific), the U.S. Navy headquarters in Honolulu, had met me at the airport the night before and was planning to pick me up at the motel and see me safely on the plane to Nauru. Shortly before he was due, he telephoned and told me that the flight had been delayed. He asked me to stay at the motel, close to a phone, and told me he would keep me posted. A couple of hours later, he called to say that the flight had been cancelled. The Air Nauru office had told him that they hoped to have the flight running the following morning.

I was very disappointed. The principal function to which the United States was invited was to take place that evening. It was a banquet hosted by the president of Nauru, and the heads of delegation from all of the countries attending were to be there. The South Pacific countries, and Australia and New Zealand, were to be represented by their heads of government. I was going to miss the experience of dining with the prime ministers of Australia and New Zealand and the leaders of the island countries, which would have been memorable. I would have welcomed the opportunity to sound out these gentlemen on their thinking about the best prospects for assistance projects to the island countries. Fortunately, two members of my delegation, including the office director for Pacific Island affairs, had arrived in Nauru a day or so before. The office director could substitute for me at the dinner; this would be a bonus for her, and an unexpected thanks for her work in preparing for the conference.

I passed the day quietly, reading and reviewing briefing papers for the conference. The next morning the plane did indeed arrive, and we took off more or less as planned. A fellow stranded passenger was the French ambassador to the United States, who had flown to Honolulu from Washington; he was not amused to have missed the opening banquet and discussions.

It was a very long flight. We stopped at one island for refueling, which we were told was called Easter Island—clearly not the one with the statues that belong to Chile, but with the same name. This process, for undisclosed reasons, took a couple of hours. We then flew to Tarawa, where another long wait ensued. I persuaded some personnel at the airport to take some of us on a brief ride up the beaches, which had been hallowed, for me, by some of the heaviest fighting of the Second World War. We saw a few gun emplacements as I conjured up images of the horrific fighting that our marines had engaged in with the Japanese. Again, I had never thought I would set foot on Tarawa. In my own private way, I paid my respects to the Americans who had died there.

Off we went yet again en route to Nauru, arriving about dinner time, having spent the entire day wending our way south from Honolulu to this tiny, but rich, little island. We learned that the reason we had been stranded in Hawaii was that Air Nauru has only one airplane, and the president's brother had decided that he wanted to use it to fly to a neighboring island ("neighboring" is used loosely, given the great distances separating Nauru from the rest of the world), and the plane had been rescheduled to suit his pleasure.

I will never forget the approach into Nauru. I recall flying over this vast, endless Pacific Ocean, beautifully blue, under a similarly blue sky. Suddenly I noticed that the plane was descending, but I could not see any land. I kept looking: Where? Where is the land? All of a sudden, this tiny little dot of land appeared, and we landed safely.

That evening, over dinner with the second tier of diplomats (the heads of government having left that day), we had interesting discussions. The next day I had bilateral discussions with the forum representatives and the Nauru delegation. We had no earth-shattering issues to deal with, and the talks went well. For the islanders, meeting on their turf with representatives of the United States, one of whom was an ambassador, was appreciated.

In the afternoon, our hosts took us on a brief drive around the island. There is just one road that circles the island, probably not more than fifteen miles or so in circumference. Seeing up close the stark devastation wrought by the guano mining was chilling, but the Nauruans seemed comfortable with their revenue and with the pledges of restoration they had received from the principally Australian mining interests.

Preparing for Brunei

After I returned from Nauru, my attention was focused on preparing for my Bruneian assignment and making arrangements for the APEC summit to be held in Seattle in the fall. At one point, it was suggested that I might go to Seattle for the summit, because the sultan of Brunei would be there. Traditional protocol intervened, however; we remembered that it is not considered proper for an ambassador to meet his or her host head of government before the formal presentation of credentials. So I remained in Washington, continuing my briefings and reading in preparation for my assignment to Brunei. I attended the two-week Ambassador Seminar and appeared before the Senate foreign relations committee for my confirmation hearing. I was duly confirmed.

12

Ambassador to Brunei

I was sworn in as ambassador to Brunei in November 1993, the Friday before the Veterans Day holiday. I had a beautiful ceremony in the Benjamin Franklin Room of the State Department, attended by some sixty-seven family members and a large array of friends. It was a lovely occasion. Immediately after the ceremony, I hosted a reception for everyone who attended. That evening, I gave a dinner for family and close friends at the DACOR Bacon House, a beautiful early nineteenth-century mansion on F Street, which at one time had been the residence of Supreme Court Chief Justice John Marshall. I had also celebrated my appointment to Guyana there. Although the Guyana reception had been very nice, this dinner has stayed in my mind as particularly enjoyable and memorable.

On Saturday, most of the family spontaneously gathered at my Foggy Bottom apartment for more reminiscences and relaxing. When my brother Jack started recalling his World War II experiences, I tape recorded his recollections, and later, those of my other siblings. Each had a different experience during the war, the gist of which is now on tape as a mini–oral history of the Tulls at war. It was a most happy day for all of us.

Shortly thereafter, I was off to Brunei to begin this next chapter of my life.

First Impressions

Brunei Darussalam (*Darussalam* means "abode of peace") is a very small country on the northern coast of the island of Borneo. Brunei shares that large island with two other countries: Malaysia to the east and west, and Indonesia to the south. At one time in history, the sultans of Brunei ruled the entire island. Over the centuries, however, stronger powers sliced away at the sultan's holdings. By the early twentieth century, only a minuscule part of Borneo remained under the sultan of Brunei. The Dutch had taken the southern half of the island and incorporated it into the Dutch East Indies, which became the country of Indonesia after independence. Britain had chipped away at the northern part of the island, creating the provinces of Sabah and Sarawak, which today are part of Malaysia.

Brunei never was a British colony. The ruling sultan appealed to Great Britain for protection in the nineteenth century, and the remains of the former domain of the sultans became a British protectorate. Fortunately for modern-day Brunei, the tiny territory left to the sultanate proved to be abundantly rich in oil and natural gas. Modern-day Brunei has a very high per capita income as a result of the country's oil wealth. I arrived in Bandar Seri Begawan, the capital, on December 18, 1993. At that time, Hassanal Bolkiah, the ruling sultan who was descended from the same family that had ruled Brunei for 600 years, was believed to be one of the wealthiest men in the world, second only to Microsoft's Bill Gates.

Driving into the city from the airport, I was struck by the quiet beauty of the place: attractive homes, lush tropical foliage, and a clean modern highway. We passed the sultan's palace, a 1,700-room abode by the river. As we approached the city center, the skyline was dominated by the beautiful golden dome of the massive mosque built at the bidding of the sultan in honor of his late father. In the river by the city center was Kampong Ayer, the famous "water village" where hundreds of Bruneians lived in wooden houses on stilts in the river itself, as their ancestors had as far back as (according to Chinese historical records) 600 AD. Chinese traders at that time wrote of doing business with a community living in houses on stilts on the river. The houses were accessible in some instances by long, wooden walkways. Travel between houses was often accomplished by small boats. The current sultan's father lived in the water village as a youth.

The embassy was housed in an office building in the center of town, across the street from the river. I could see the water village from my office. Interestingly, the embassy was the only American embassy in the world that was situated immediately above a Chinese restaurant. The embassy was small, but we had adequate space and, given the high level of security in the peaceful little country, Washington had no reason at that time to build a separate embassy. (In 2011, however, a separate embassy building was constructed.) We had no security at all, nor did we need any. That restaurant came in handy more than once when I chose to work through the lunch period.

When I arrived in Brunei, the sultan was out of country; after attending the APEC summit in Seattle, he had flown to London. I was in limbo until he returned and I could present my credentials to him. I was in full charge of the embassy, but I could not conduct business with the Bruneian government. Any representations that required an embassy presence at any of the ministries had to be handled by my deputy. But the respite gave me an opportunity to read further about embassy operations and to get to know the American and local national staff before I presented credentials and began my formal calls on officials.

Christmas was a quiet affair. I was invited to a New Year's Eve Party at the Sheraton Hotel, at that time the only Bruneian hotel up to international standards. Because a senior government minister was going to be present, I hesitated to accept the invitation, as technically I did not have any status until I had presented my credentials. I was assured by my host, Timothy Ong, that he had cleared this with the minister, who had no problems with the protocol. Timothy Ong was an outstanding Chinese businessman, very well educated in Australia, and well plugged in to the Bruneian government. I accepted the invitation and had a most agreeable time. The minister was one of the perhaps ten celebrants in a private room. He did not blink an eye when wine was poured to those who wanted it, although in Brunei, a Muslim country, alcohol could not be purchased or sold in public places. Diplomats could import what they wished for their needs, and non-Muslims could bring in small amounts for their own consumption when they returned from trips abroad. A well-traveled businessman like Mr. Ong no doubt had a well-equipped cellar. Not only did the evening prove enjoyable, but it was also a good introduction to the type of professional-business-diplomatic socializing that I, as the American ambassador, would find abundant in Brunei.

Presenting Credentials

When the sultan returned, I presented my credentials. It was a very formal ceremony. The chief of protocol visited the embassy and explained in detail how I was to conduct myself during the ceremony. I was instructed to bow my head when presenting the credentials, and then to take several steps backward, reflecting the ancient tradition that one does not turn one's back on the ruler. I rehearsed this procedure carefully. I was determined not to give gratuitous insult; I would follow their rules. I was the first woman resident ambassador to this small Muslim country.

After the formal presentation of credentials, I had an audience with the sultan in his formal receiving room. It was a very large room, lavishly decorated. Every table and chair was thickly gilded, and gold threads were woven into the carpet. The walls were decorated largely with paintings and photographs of the sultan, his two wives, and his children. We had a proper, cordial chat. He welcomed me to Brunei, and I conveyed the good wishes of President Clinton. The sultan had just met the president in Seattle, and he told me how much he had enjoyed the experience and the APEC summit. He told me that the president had invited him to come to Washington, an invitation the sultan took seriously, but the seriousness of which I could not get the State Department to share. I felt afterward that I had established a degree of rapport with the sultan, and that I would be able to conduct business with him comfortably.

I might note here that in contrast to his predecessors, President Clinton did not meet with all of his ambassadors before they left for their posts. Nor did he, as President Reagan had done, call me personally to offer me the post of ambassador to Brunei. Initially, when I inquired of the Bruneian desk officer about setting up an appointment for my photo with the president, I initially distrusted his assertion that Clinton had abandoned this practice. I learned several years later that the desk officer was right. Clinton indeed did not see the point of ambassadorial presidential photos. He was wrong, in my view; displaying such photos in one's embassy and residence demonstrates to the host country visitors that the ambassador has presidential access.

Celebrating the End of Ramadan

Shortly after I presented my credentials, the Muslim fasting month of Ramadan ended, which the sultan marked by inviting all the ambassadors and their spouses, plus his ministers and their spouses, to a formal reception at the palace. This proved to be a very interesting occasion. When I entered the massive reception room, an officious older gentleman approached me and insisted that I should go off to the right where, behind some poles, some tables and chairs had been set up and where the spouses of the ministers and diplomats were gathering. I explained politely to the gentleman that I was the American ambassador, not a spouse, and I moved on to the main area of the room to mingle with ministers and my diplomatic friends. The same gentleman, whom I learned later was not currently a minister but was a retired elder-statesman type, followed me and, pointing to the female enclave, said repeatedly, "Women over there! Women over there!" I said as politely as I could that since I was the American ambassador to Brunei, my place was with the ambassadors and ministers. At that point I spotted the vice minister of foreign affairs and told him that that gentleman was insisting that I stay with the spouses, but this was not my role. Looking a little uncomfortable, the vice minister nevertheless said I should ignore that, and stay where I was. Fortunately, the Philippine chargé d'affaires at that time was also a woman, and she had also resisted the effort of the elderly gentleman to shoo her over to the spouses. She stayed by me—safety in numbers, I suppose—and we greeted various ministers, as our male colleagues were doing.

Before the sultan's arrival, the chief of protocol lined up the ministers and diplomatic corps in protocol order to greet the sultan and his family. For the diplomats, our places in line marked the order in which we had presented credentials. I was not the lowest ranking in terms of protocol; the new Japanese ambassador had presented his credentials a day or so after I had. The Philippine chargé, not being an ambassador, brought up the rear.

The sultan, his wives, and his children moved through the line, greeting all of us cordially. Afterward, most of the ministers and spouses attacked the bounteous array of food that had been prepared for us. I was determined to use the occasion, as most of my diplomatic colleagues were doing, to make contact with the sultan. I managed to have a brief conversation with him—nothing substantive, but an opportunity to further our acquaintance and facilitate future business-related meetings.

The British Role in Brunei

Under the British protectorate, Brunei looked to Great Britain for its security and assistance in conducting most of its affairs. In the late 1950s and early 1960s, Brunei was subjected to incursions by guerrillas from Malaysia and Indonesia, abetted by a small number of Bruneian citizens. These elements, believed to have Communist leanings, attempted to foment a revolution. They managed to take over some buildings in downtown Bandar Seri Begawan briefly, and thoroughly frightened the current sultan's father. The British, aided by the Gurkha battalions they had brought from Nepal, quelled the attempted revolt. The sultan suspended the parliament and subsequently ruled as an absolute dictator. Some observers contend that it was this experience that made him loath to end Brunei's status as a British protectorate. As Britain was granting independence to its former Southeast Asian colonies (Malaya, Singapore, Sabah, and Sarawak), it was more than willing to free Brunei from its protectorate status. Speculation remains that the former sultan's decision in 1967 to abdicate his throne and install his oldest son, Hassanal Bolkiah, as sultan when he was barely twenty-one years old, was an effort to prolong the British role in Brunei. The effort succeeded for a time; the protectorate was not formally abolished until 1984, when the British finally nudged the fledgling little country out of its nest.

The British nonetheless retained a major role in Brunei. They had a large contingent (over 200) of military officers working with the Bruneian military in logistics and training functions. Also, the British-commanded Gurkha battalions were the backbone of Brunei's defense, guarding the palace and the oil enterprises.

There were many British connections to Brunei, both economic and sentimental. British Petroleum is the major oil company in Brunei, for example. The sultan was attending, and reportedly thoroughly enjoying, the British military academy, Sandhurst, when his father pulled him back to Brunei to assume the throne. The sultan is an avid and competent polo player, who has played with Prince Charles. He is regularly invited to British royal weddings and special anniversaries, and has substantial investments in the United Kingdom, including the opulent Dorchester Hotel in London. He bought the firm Asprey, which is the London equivalent of Tiffany in terms of its reputation for high-end jewelry and luxury goods.

U.S. Interests in Brunei

I had a twofold mandate from Washington as ambassador to Brunei: I was to (1) improve the professional functioning of the embassy, and (2) continue to improve relations between the United States and the wealthy sultanate by increasing economic and commercial ties, among other things.

Embassy operations had suffered because the ambassadors had been political appointees in recent years. These individuals were fine people, but they had no experience with the State Department, and the post was not performing at a level the department preferred. Political and economic reporting was very sparse. Further, as a small mission in a Muslim country that offered little in the way of recreational opportunities, it had been difficult to staff the post.

Complicating the situation, my predecessor, Donald Ensenat, had arrived in Brunei in October 1992 as the appointee of President George H. W. Bush; Ensenat had been a roommate at Yale of the president's son George W. Bush. Upon the election of a new president, all serving ambassadors are required to submit their resignations. Those whose resignations were accepted were required to depart post by the time of the incoming president's January inauguration.

Ensenat's resignation was accepted. He asked to remain in Brunei until June, ostensibly so that his daughter's school year in Singapore would not be interrupted. His request was denied. He continued to press for an exception, in concert with the political appointee ambassador to Singapore, Jon Huntsman. Their requests were repeatedly denied until, I have been reliably informed, Senator Orrin Hatch of Utah (Huntsman's senator) weighed in personally with Clinton's secretary of state, Warren Christopher. The desired delay was granted, and Ensenat and Huntsman stayed at their posts until June.

I was not able to arrive at the post until December. During that period, the political officer who served as the deputy chief of mission filled in as chargé d'affaires. His professional reputation in the department was poor, but he held the fort until I arrived. My task was to improve the overall operations of the embassy, particularly to increase the quantity and quality of political and economic reporting.

I Lose My Political Officer/Deputy

The department did not make my job easy. I knew going into the assignment that the political officer/DCM most likely did not have much more time left before his generally mediocre service resulted in his being selected out either for exhausting his time in class allowance or for having been ranked low in the annual performance assessments. Still, I found him knowledgeable about Brunei, and engaging. I had a certain sympathy for his lack of productivity, given that he had not really had a professional ambassador, and he had been, as chargé d'affaires, the sole substantive officer at the post for a long period after the ambassador left .

I was shocked when the day after Christmas—unkind timing— he received a cable from the State Department informing him that he was being selected out for consistent poor performance. He was told he would have to report to Washington no later than February 1.

He was devastated, and so was I. It was the middle of the year; the transfer cycle had been completed. The likelihood that I would get a replacement for him before midsummer, at the earliest, was scant. He was the only substantive officer at the post, after me; the consular officer doubled as the administrative officer and occasionally tried her hand at reporting, but she had a full plate without that. So there I was at post for two weeks, and about to lose my deputy and institutional memory.

I weighed in with the department, asking if his departure could be delayed until the summer transfer cycle, to no avail. The department did grant him an extra month at post. Understandably, the man was not inclined to extend himself to do any extra work during his remaining weeks. He worked the requisite hours, period. This made it very difficult for me. And, of course, no replacement for him reached Brunei until August. From the time of his departure on March 1 until August, I was the sole substantive officer in the embassy.

Policy Emphasis

On the policy front, I was instructed to do what I could to strengthen overall U.S.–Bruneian ties on a variety of issues. Brunei was a member of ASEAN, with which the United States cooperated regularly. We wished to strengthen Brunei's cooperation with the United States in this body, including with regard to the ASEAN Regional Forum. We wanted Brunei's cooperation in regional security issues, in international institutions, and in bilateral military operations, including modest training exercises with U.S. forces.

I was also strongly encouraged to promote trade and investment between the two countries. The modern U.S. ambassador must be a strong advocate and salesman of U.S. products in competitive situations in which other countries' envoys are energetically pressing their countries' goods and services. I took this responsibility very seriously. I met regularly with visiting U.S. businessmen and, with occasional success, personally lobbied the Bruneian government, and the sultan himself, on behalf of major U.S. manufacturers, particularly in the defense field. I lobbied heavily on behalf of the Boeing Company, and for Brunei to purchase Sikorsky's Black Hawk helicopters, a procurement issue that the British and French hotly contested. I succeeded in this case; Brunei selected the Black Hawk to upgrade its military's small helicopter fleet. There were also some pending purchases of small ships under consideration. I doubted that the United States would succeed in this competition over the British, who were clearly the favored foreign supplier and whose military officers were assisting the Bruneians in the award of the contract. Nonetheless, I arranged high-level appointments with appropriate government officials for representatives of U.S. shipbuilders. These contracts ultimately went to the British.

The sultan, whose immediate security was in the hands of British-led Gurkha battalions, was aware that the worldwide reach of the British military establishment had waned. He was favorably disposed toward the United States, and very aware of the strength and reach of the U.S. Pacific Fleet. He welcomed increasing military links, modest in nature, with the United States, and was happy to receive the wide range of high-ranking U.S. military visitors who came to Brunei on my watch. Although our CINCPAC did not visit Brunei while I was there, two or perhaps three of his senior deputies did—the navy and army commanders in the Pacific, at least. In addition, Admiral William Owens, the vice chairman of the joint chiefs of staff and a man well known for his creative thinking about the changing needs of modern warfare, visited us; he made a fine impression on the sultan and his military leaders, and on a group of private businessmen I gathered to meet him at lunch.

These visits were educational for the U.S. visitors as well as for the sultan and his officials. In addition, they were a means of letting the leader of this small ASEAN country know that the United States cared about the region; we were still a Pacific power, and we were showing him the courtesy of acknowledging his place in ASEAN and in Southeast Asia. These visits, including occasional visits by U.S. naval ships, very effectively "showed the flag" and augmented my efforts to strengthen the bilateral relationship. These visits also served to remind other countries in the area, such as the Chinese, that the United States was very much a part of the Pacific and Southeast Asian scene.

Negotiating Concerning the Status of U.S. Forces Visiting Brunei

As the frequency of our ship visits and military exercises increased, it became necessary to consider the legal aspects of our occasional troop presence. In this regard, I had the opportunity to negotiate a memorandum of understanding on defense cooperation with the Bruneian government. This constituted, in effect, a type of status of forces agreement. I worked on this over several months in direct negotiations with the Bruneian minister of justice. The United

States wanted to be sure that if any U.S. troops in Brunei for military exercises committed criminal offenses in their off-duty hours, our personnel would have protection along the lines provided by a status of forces agreement. In general, we wished our personnel to be tried by the U.S. military in courts martial. There are certain categories of lesser offenses, however, for which the U.S. would, under normal circumstances, allow the host government to prosecute the offenders; others are reserved to the U.S. military justice system. One reason for this push was that caning of violators was still permitted in Brunei, a punishment we did not want carried out on any alleged military miscreants.

The caning issue was initially a sticking point for the Bruneian government as well as for the United States. I had to work long and hard on this issue, crafting language with the minister of justice that would satisfy both of our governments, but leaving no doubt that caning was not a punishment option for U.S. troops. Finally, we were able to work out language that exempted our people from caning. I was pleased with this outcome. I enjoyed the one-on-one negotiation process with the minister, and believe the result was a satisfactory document. The minister and I signed the memorandum of understanding on November 29, 1994.

A Difficult U.S. Citizen Protection Case

A very difficult situation arose with regard to an American pilot who worked for Prince Jefri, the sultan's younger brother and finance minister. The pilot was known to abuse his wife. My consular officer, Mary Martinez, a fine young officer, knew the wife. Mary came to me one morning and said that she had just gotten a phone call from this pilot's wife, begging for help. Her husband had been beating her with a golf club. Mary wanted me to know that she knew the woman personally and wondered whether it could be misconstrued if she went to offer help. I told her that this should not be a factor; there was a very small American community in Brunei, and it was understandable that she would be personally acquainted with the woman. We could not deny help simply because she was known to the consular officer. I authorized her to go to the woman's home.

I instructed our capable young general services officer-communicator to take an embassy vehicle and accompany Mary to the home. When the two embassy officers reached the woman's home, she emerged with her young son, a boy approximately five years old, and hurried into the car for the trip to the embassy, where next steps could be contemplated. The American pilot angrily ran to his own car and chased the rescuers, attempting to run them off the road in his effort to get them to stop the car. At one point, he even banged into the rear of the embassy vehicle. According to my staff, this action took place near a ravine, and they were terrified. The enraged husband, I am reasonably sure, was trying to get them to stop the car and not trying to push them into the ravine, but this extremely dangerous situation could have turned tragic.

At this point, my officers were close to the Pakistan embassy. The GSO, who was driving, wisely pulled into the courtyard of the embassy. They told the Pakistani ambassador, a general in the Pakistani army, what had happened. He took them into the embassy and, outside, tried to reason with the furious American pilot who had followed them into the embassy driveway area. Meanwhile, my staff called me to report what had happened, and I got on the phone immediately to the police and to the minister of justice to hasten the dispatch of police to the Pakistani embassy to get the situation under control. The police did respond, and they arrested the pilot—doubtless with some qualms, in view of the young man's favored status as one of Prince Jefri's pilots.

My staff brought the pilot's wife and son to the embassy. She had a black eye and other visible signs of having been nastily beaten. She was extremely grateful to the embassy officers for their help. The police photographed her to document her injuries and took her statement (our consular officer accompanied her to the police headquarters). She pressed charges against her husband.

An issue for our embassy, which we worked with the State Department to decide, was whether to press charges against the pilot for his assault against an embassy vehicle carrying American officials, and for the damage the vehicle incurred. Complicating the issue was the fact that, as I noted above, Brunei caned some violators. A few months before, an international incident had developed when the Singapore government convicted an American teenager and sentenced him to caning for vandalism. Over strenuous U.S. objections, and worldwide publicity, Singapore carried out the sentence, and the young man was caned. Likewise, Brunei, which had modeled many of its laws on those of Singapore, kept caning in its arsenal of punishment.

I had a telephone conference with several high-level State Department officials to discuss the ramifications of filing charges against the American pilot, among them the assistant secretary for consular affairs, a senior official in the department's legal bureau, and a deputy assistant secretary in the East Asian bureau. Everyone was adamant that these deeds had to be punished. Our officers had been put at great risk and embassy property had been flagrantly damaged—such conduct against official diplomats and U.S. property could not be tolerated. I shared this view, but I insisted that these officials focus on the caning issue. I said that I wanted them all to remember that farther down the road the punishment for this man might be caning. I did not want to proceed with charges and then suddenly hear from Washington that, "Oh, dear, we can't have that; we can't have an American caned." I encouraged them to make up their minds now, and that if caning was the sentence, Washington would not attempt to have it overturned. I was assured by all that they agreed with me, that there would be no protests if caning was the punishment.

Accordingly, we pursued charges. I met with the minister of justice on the case. Ultimately, we hired a lawyer to help me understand the Bruneian legal system processes. The lawyer, a capable Chinese woman in her forties, was somewhat brave to take me as her client, I think, given the status of the pilot's protector, Prince Jefri.

As the trial date drew near, I became concerned about the impact of the trial on my two officers. I was worried about putting them through the ordeal of testifying in open court, of reliving the harrowing event and testifying about it against Prince Jefri's man. I decided that I needed legal support from the State Department, and succeeded in getting the department to send over the legal bureau's adviser to the East Asia bureau. He arrived at the same time that Assistant Secretary Winston Lord was visiting to attend an ASEAN Regional Forum security meeting. Our small staff was overtaxed, but we persevered. I had less time with Winston than I would have liked, as I juggled the two disparate visits as best I could.

Our legal adviser did a fine job. About the time that he was arriving, we learned that Prince Jefri's legal team had engaged a high-ranking QC (Queen's Counsel) from London to lead the defense effort. Our man met with the defense team and with my Bruneian lawyer, and succeeded in working out a reasonable, though less than ideal, settlement of the contentious case. There was only one day in court, and my officers did not have to testify. The representative from the legal bureau was under the impression that as part of the terms he had worked out, the American pilot would serve a brief jail sentence, but would not be caned. He also obtained a cash settlement of $30,000 for the abused wife, and $10,000 each for the two embassy officers involved, plus payment for the repair of our damaged embassy vehicle.

When push came to shove and the sentence was announced in court, there was no jail time given to the pilot. Despite this shenanigan, it was a great relief to have the ordeal over with. The abused wife was absolutely astounded that she had received a cash payment and was very grateful to all of us. The embassy officers likewise had not expected to receive any compensation for their ordeal, and were similarly appreciative of the efforts of our State Department lawyer. They were also grateful that the embassy had stood behind them and supported them in the difficult situation.

Celebrating the Sultan's Birthday

Being the official representative of the world's sole superpower to the ruler of a wealthy oil- and gas-producing state—reportedly the second richest man in the world—might understandably have been overwhelming to me, a woman of modest means from the blue-collar town of Runnemede, New Jersey, had I not been something of an actress at heart. I carefully concealed my private reactions to meeting with the sultan and his wives in his office or in their private quarters, surrounded with magnificent French Impressionist paintings and other manifestations of great wealth, such as the gold-threaded carpets or a piano encrusted with malachite. I was, in my view, a professional diplomat representing my country competently and with a degree of warmth that I believe helped to establish cordial working relations with Brunei's leader.

Serving in Brunei presented rare opportunities for me to observe and participate in spectacles not found in New Jersey. The celebrations surrounding the sultan's birthday were unique. The formal events were spaced throughout the day. In the morning, the sultan presided over an outdoor military review. This was followed by a formal awards presentation to deserving officials held in the palace, followed by an informal luncheon, buffet style. In the evening, a formal dinner was held in the palace.

There were strict dress codes for diplomats attending these functions, which particularly affected women. Wives of ambassadors, and I, were required to wear long-sleeved black dresses for the morning and noontime events. For the formal dinner, women wore long white gowns. The men wore business suits to all of the events, except for the British high commissioner, who appeared at the morning activities clad in a crisp white uniform, gold braided, wearing a white pith helmet. This apparently was the official uniform of a British high commissioner or ambassador assigned to a tropical country. He was good-naturedly teased by his diplomatic corps colleagues when he arrived so splendidly attired, à la the days of the Raj.

The military review at the parade began the day's ceremonies. This event was about the only time music could be heard publicly in Brunei. The Bruneian military had an excellent band, which played invigorating marches as the sultan reviewed the troops. Music apparently was not consistent with Islam as practiced in Brunei, and there were no bands, choirs, or school choruses in Bruneian schools. Despite the inevitable heat, it was enjoyable listening to the band music as we tried to identify which high-ranking foreign guests were attending the celebrations. Usually there were a few cabinet ministers from Indonesia and Malaysia and a Middle Eastern official or two.

The main event of the celebrations, however, was the formal dinner in the evening at the palace. For this occasion, I commissioned a lovely two-piece, white silk gown—high neck, long sleeves, appropriate for a woman to wear in a Muslim country. I was pleased with the way I looked as I left the residence for the dinner.

Throughout my tour in Brunei, I took pains to dress modestly (which was my natural bent anyway). I generally wore high-necked dresses or blouses and longish skirts, and I always wore hose. If my blouse was short-sleeved, I made certain I had a light blazer in my office to don should I have to make an unexpected call on the sultan or on a government minister. I did not cover my head, however: This was not necessary for a non-Muslim foreigner in Brunei.

My excitement grew as my official embassy vehicle, flags flying, approached the palace. On Muslim holidays or special occasions such as this one, the trees on the roads approaching the palace, as well as those on the palace grounds, were ablaze with tiny colored lights. As we neared the massive marble palace, I felt as though I had stepped into an ancient tale of the *Arabian Nights.*

Upon arriving, ambassadors and their spouses were escorted to an outdoor reception area adjacent to the formal dining room, where juices and soft drinks were served. We mingled with government ministers and diplomatic colleagues, picking up tidbits of information where possible, as our work required on all such seemingly social occasions.

The diplomatic corps and government officials and ministers were then escorted into the formal dining room. Several hundred other invited guests remained outdoors and were seated and fed more informally. As an ambassador, I was seated in the formal dining room with my ambassadorial colleagues, placed in protocol order, not far from the head table where the sultan and his family sat.

The large formal dining hall was beautifully decorated. The dining tables were inspired by the Taj Mahal—they were white marble, with inlaid semiprecious stones, including lapis lazuli, jade, and malachite, forming patterns similar to those on the Taj. The china—beautiful English bone china encrusted with gold—was exquisite, and the lustrous flatware was most likely gold plated. The food was not remarkable, but the white-gloved footmen—one for every four guests—served it with finesse.

Striking to me, as the meal progressed, was that on this presumably festive occasion—a birthday celebration—you could cut the silence in that large room with a knife. No one stood to offer best wishes to His Majesty, which I would have expected from the senior minister or one of the sultan's brothers. It was as though none of the officials wanted to be heard, lest they say the wrong thing. At the ambassadors' table, we perhaps unconsciously adopted the protocol of the room and spoke to each other in very low voices. In my case, however, I was seated next to the Japanese ambassador, who spoke mostly to his wife in Japanese. We exchanged some words, but not many. To my other side was the Indian high commissioner, the maharajah of Jaipur, a charming man who had once entertained Jacqueline Kennedy in India while her husband was president. We were good friends. He suffered a major stroke while in Brunei, which affected his speech. The second year I attended the birthday dinner, the Indian high commissioner could barely speak. I spent a very quiet evening.

On both of these occasions, I found myself wondering whether the sultan, despite being surrounded with almost surrealistic luxury and opulence, was having a "happy" birthday. The silence in the room and at the head table suggested otherwise, that he was merely complying with a centuries-old tradition.

The evening concluded with a fireworks display, which thousands of Bruneian citizens could enjoy from vantage points along the river near the palace.

The Secretary Visits: The ASEAN Ministerials and Regional Forum

One of the reasons I was pleased to accept the assignment as ambassador to Brunei was that I knew that it would be Brunei's turn, in 1995, to host the annual ASEAN ministerial meetings and ASEAN Regional Forum. This would bring the secretary of state, Warren Christopher, to Brunei. I looked forward to preparing for and being involved in these meetings, and to welcoming the secretary. I was eager to participate, in concert with other concerned ambassadors, in helping to develop the agenda and to draft the relevant joint documents. It was very interesting, professionally, to work on these meetings from the field, having been an ASEAN follower for many years in the department.

The State Department sent a large advance team to work out the logistics of the secretary's complicated visit. My initial reaction was that I should monitor these efforts, but it became clear early on that the group was quite capable, as was my own deputy; thus reassured, I concentrated on the substance of the meetings.

I had encouraged the secretary's staff to keep the size of his delegation and team as small as possible, given the limited availability of hotel space in Brunei. Nevertheless, the U.S. contingent was massive, in my view. We were able, thanks to heavy lobbying with the Bruneian government, to reserve practically the entire Sheraton Hotel for the secretary and his approximately one-hundred-person entourage.

The secretary's entourage included a bomb-sniffing dog and his handler. It took some diplomacy on the part of my staff to get the large dog, a German shepherd, admitted into a Muslim country—the majority of Muslims consider dogs to be ritually unclean. This dog came in handy for me: Early in the visit, I was informed that a caller had phoned in a bomb threat to my residence. The dog and his master were dispatched to my residence and did a thorough search, fortunately finding nothing; they performed the same service at the embassy, with similar results.

I had developed a very high opinion of Secretary of State Warren Christopher from my days in the human rights bureau during the Carter administration, when Christopher, then deputy secretary of state, was deeply involved in the implementation of Carter's human rights policy. On this occasion, however, I was a little disappointed in Secretary Christopher. Perhaps some of the difficulties we encountered in handling his much-welcomed visit were caused exclusively by an overly zealous staff.

In any event, the secretary's performance was not as gracious as I would have liked to have seen. For example, the Bruneians, as hosts of the conference, instituted certain security procedures to handle a gathering that would bring together the foreign ministers of more than a dozen nations, including that of the world's sole remaining superpower as well as China, Russia, Australia, and New Zealand, among others. They installed a metal detector at the entrance to the convention center, where the formal conferences would take place. All persons attending the conferences were required to pass through the metal detector. Secretary Christopher's staff informed my DCM that the secretary did not go through metal detectors; he would have to be exempted from this requirement. My DCM asked whether there was a medical reason for this, but the staff refused to answer, insisting that the secretary would not go through the metal detector. When the DCM informed me of this development, I instructed him to see what he could do about this request in his dealings with the foreign ministry. He did so, but was told that everyone, including the Bruneian foreign minister—the sultan's brother—had to go through the metal detector. The DCM conveyed this to the secretary's staff, who were adamant that the secretary would balk. Given their insistence, he asked bluntly whether the secretary had a pacemaker, which would be an understandable reason for avoiding the metal detector. Again, this sensible question was dismissed without an answer. The secretary's staff insisted to my deputy that I must personally raise this matter with the Bruneian government.

The final exchange on the issue took place on the day before the conference was to begin. I was at the convention center reviewing the arrangements when my DCM conveyed this impasse to me. My principal foreign ministry contact, Permanent Secretary Lim Jock Seng, an extremely capable Bruneian of Chinese ethnicity, was also at the convention center. I approached him and said I had been asked to raise the matter of the metal detector; he groaned and said, "The foreign minister himself is going through the detector." "Fine," I replied, adding, "Thank you very much. I have raised the issue." We sent word back to the secretary's staff, and when the conference convened, the secretary went through the metal detector and lived to tell the tale. Apparently, he did not have a medical condition that would have precluded passing through the metal detector. Perhaps he never even knew about the fuss his staff had raised on this nonissue, or perhaps it was just a little power play on the part of the staff. I don't know. But I do know that it was irritating, unnecessarily so.

Another irritant was the secretary's failure to arrive at key functions at the appointed hour. Bruneians were punctual with regard to their government functions. Although we had given the secretary's staff detailed schedules for all events, including arrival times, and had firmly emphasized that these meetings would start precisely on time, the secretary arrived late at the very first meeting at the opening of the conference on July 29, 1995. We had to parade into the meeting room, where the foreign minister had already called the meeting to order, and disrupt the affair as we wended our way to our assigned places. All of the other foreign ministers and their delegations had managed to arrive on time. It was humiliating for me, and it smacked of arrogance, in my view, on the part of the United States—even though the mighty country had deigned to send its foreign minister, its representatives apparently did not have to follow the same timetable that lesser mortals did.

The formal meetings proved useful, however, and constructive things were accomplished on the fringes of the meeting, as well. For example, we were able to arrange a private meeting between the secretary and his Chinese counterpart, which helped thaw relations that had been virtually frozen for several months, the product of a tense naval encounter between U.S. and Chinese vessels in the South China Sea in late October 1994. The meeting proved constructive, and relations between the United States and China returned to a more even keel.

Getting the secretary to the meetings on time proved to be a continuing challenge. The last instance occurred on the final evening of the conference. Traditionally, on the concluding evening, the host country offers a sumptuous banquet, and each of the participating delegations takes part in a type of floor show, offering songs, dances, or jokes in a lighthearted vein. The affair provides an opportunity for the senior officials to let their hair down after the serious conferences, to unwind and to get to know each other better. Usually, the foreign ministers themselves participate in the skits or musical numbers created by their staffs. Secretary Christopher chose not to participate, which disappointed some other delegations but was not a big issue for me. What did trouble me was his failure to arrive at the evening's festivities at the appointed hour.

The foreign minister had invited the visiting foreign ministers to a predinner reception at the conference center, in a private room near the large room where dinner for the entire delegations, diplomatic corps, and Bruneian government officials would be held. The arrival time for this private get-together was set for 7:30 p.m.; the banquet would begin at 8:00 p.m. I went to the conference center well before 7:30 p.m., as did my DCM. We observed the prompt arrivals of all of the foreign ministers and saw them escorted into the private room for their final opportunity for a few words with their peers and the Bruneian foreign minister before the evening's lighter moments began. But Secretary Christopher did not arrive.

The appointed hour passed, and additional minutes ticked by. Anxious high-level Bruneian officials approached me and asked where the secretary was. My DCM, meanwhile, had been on the phone to the secretary's staff at the hotel.

These phone calls netted nonchalant promises that the secretary would be along shortly. Time passed; the Bruneian hosts became increasingly annoyed at his failure to appear. Finally, well after the scheduled arrival hour, the secretary arrived. There was only time for him to quickly greet the Bruneian foreign minister before the entire cast of foreign ministers had to leave to get to the main dining hall in time for dinner. I learned subsequently that the reason for Secretary Christopher's late arrival was that he had decided to hold a press conference in his suite at the hotel, which was clearly his privilege. But then he reportedly decided to invite his key staffers to join him for cocktails. I was flabbergasted that he would keep more than a dozen foreign ministers waiting while he had cocktails with his staff. From my perspective, noblesse oblige should have prevailed—the superpower should have showed up on time. My staffer, who was in touch with the secretary's staff, was told that he should tell the ambassador to relax: "The secretary will get there when he gets there." Again, how much of this the secretary knew about, I do not know.

I had also hoped to get the secretary over to the embassy. This is standard practice for visiting secretaries of state. I thought it would have been informative for him to see our "above the Chinese restaurant" embassy, totally unprotected; such a visit would also have been a morale boost for the embassy staff. He could not fit an embassy visit into his schedule, but he did agree to block out fifteen minutes to meet with our staff at the hotel. I invited all of our staff, Americans and local hires, and their families to come to the hotel for this opportunity. He was very gracious and posed willingly for photos.

Another surprise awaited me the next morning, the final day of the conference. A press conference featuring all of the foreign ministers was scheduled at the conference center. There was a substantial press presence in Brunei for the conference—several U.S. media outlets were represented, together with reporters from all over the world. Secretary Christopher informed me in the morning that he intended to leave for Malaysia earlier than originally planned, and that I would take his place at the press conference. I asked whether there were any particular points he wished me to make, and he said there were not. So I was left to more or less wing it. I saw him off at the airport, returned to the conference center, and took the place marked "United States of America" on the stage, along with the foreign ministers of Russia, China, France, Australia, and New Zealand, among others, as well as their counterparts from the ASEAN countries. The first two questions were directed to me, and I handled them as best as I could. The other foreign ministers and the press seemed disappointed that the secretary was not present. For me personally, this was an exciting event, to substitute for the secretary of state in such a forum.

Staffing Problems

Unfortunately, my deputy, who had done a splendid job coordinating with the advance team and the secretary's staff to ensure that the visit went smoothly, became ill shortly after the conference. He was excessively tired. I encouraged him to go to Singapore for a medical assessment and for a little R&R break after all of his hard work for the conference. His wife and two young daughters went with him. We were all hoping that his health would improve with a few days rest. He and I both thought that he was simply exhausted (and indeed, we both were). In Singapore, however, our excellent regional medical doctor detected something more serious, and ordered tests. To all of our shock, he was diagnosed with non-Hodgkin's lymphoma, a type of cancer. He never returned to Brunei; he was immediately medically evacuated to the United States. His wife and children came back to Brunei to pack and left shortly thereafter.

Once again, I had lost my deputy. Again I was alone at the post, the only substantive officer juggling the many issues our little post had to deal with. Almost immediately after my deputy's departure, my very capable administrative-consular officer, who had performed at a very high level throughout her time in Brunei, departed after completing her tour of duty. She was replaced by an incompetent malcontent, who negatively affected post morale and, in the absence of a DCM, placed increased supervisory duties on me.

In the case of this officer, I had to micromanage her operation. I lacked confidence in her understanding of visa law, among other things. On one occasion, I knew in advance that the sultan's brother-in-law, a permanent secretary in the ministry of foreign affairs, had accepted a U.S. invitation to attend a regional conference in Honolulu. I was concerned that this official might be issued the wrong visa and denied admission by the U.S. immigration service when he reached Hawaii. I informed my administrative-consular officer about the conference, and stressed the importance of making sure he received the correct visa for his official status at the conference. I instructed her to show me the passport and visa before returning the documents to the foreign ministry.

Time passed, and I did not see the passport. When I asked the officer about the matter, she looked mildly upset and said that she had forgotten to show me his documents. I asked to see his visa application to determine what kind of visa she had given him. As I had feared, she had given him the wrong type of visa—a simple visitor's visa instead of the category of visa given to an official attending an international conference. I instructed her to retrieve the passport from the foreign ministry, void the incorrect visa, and issue the correct one. The ambassador is not expected to serve as a visa officer, but in these circumstances, I had to intervene. As embarrassing as it was to have to tell the foreign ministry that we had issued the wrong visa, it was far better than having the permanent secretary refused admission in Hawaii. It was especially frustrating for me because I had anticipated the possible problem and given careful instructions to avert error, but despite the firewall I had constructed, the error was made nevertheless. This, unfortunately, was not atypical of this woman's performance.

The North Korean Nuclear Flirtation

The prospect of a nuclear-armed North Korea was, and is, a grim one. When it became apparent in the mid-1990s that the North Ko-

reans were attempting to develop nuclear power, concerned countries, led by the United States, considered ways to prevent them
from achieving nuclear capability that could be converted to weap-
ons. At one point, the United States, under the Clinton administration, was seriously considering military action if diplomatic means
did not deter the North Koreans. Fortunately, this scenario did not
transpire. Diplomatic efforts produced an agreement to help North
Korea obtain needed electricity by nonnuclear means. The Korean Energy Development Organization (KEDO), comprising the
United States, China, Japan, Russia, South Korea, and North Korea,
was established. The countries agreed to provide alternate means
to North Korea to meet its immediate energy needs. The five countries promised fuel oil and nonnuclear generating plants to North
Korea, which agreed to curtail its nuclear research and to open its
facilities to outside inspection.

The concerned countries sought international help to fund
KEDO. As ambassador, I was charged with seeking financial
assistance from the sultan of Brunei for this project. He agreed to
help and pledged $5 million for the purchase of fuel oil.

Retirement Beckons

In late 1995, deciding that it had too many senior officers, the
State Department offered a $25,000 buyout to qualified officers. I
considered this offer carefully and decided to take advantage of it. I
opted for retirement as of December 31, 1995, at which time I would
have served a very difficult two years in Brunei, for the most part as
the only substantive officer at post. Frankly, I was tired; there was no
replacement in sight for my departed deputy, and I faced months of
again single-handedly carrying the substantive load of the embassy.
In addition, with the departure of the excellent administrative-
consular officer, I could no longer relax with the knowledge that
these functions were well in hand; her replacement required
minute supervision. I was becoming mentally ready to retire. I
wanted to retire when it was my idea, unlike some senior officers
who, not realizing that their careers had plateaued, remained in the
department filling positions that were beneath their capabilities. In
some cases, financial considerations prompted their overstaying

their careers—children in college, perhaps. I never wanted to be in the position where someone would wonder about me, "Hasn't she retired yet?"

More important to me personally, I felt that I had achieved the maximum that I could have achieved in the Foreign Service. I had been chief of mission three times: in Laos as permanent chargé d'affaires, and as ambassador to Guyana and to Brunei. I had had a great ride. I had no illusions that I would be awarded a bigger embassy at the conclusion of my Brunei tour, nor was an assistant secretaryship a realistic option. I wanted to go out of the service on top—to retire as a serving ambassador, and have retirement be my own idea.

In addition, my extremely supportive family of brothers and sisters was aging: some siblings were ailing. Jack, the husband of my oldest sister, Betty, was struggling with Parkinson's disease. I thought it was time for me to be home and to perhaps take Betty and Jack out for lunch, to have the family stay with me at my Sea Isle City shore condo—in other words, to be there for my family. (Of course, I also intended to have good times myself, perhaps traveling to parts of the world that 1 had not visited on my Asia-centered Foreign Service assignments.)

So I decided to retire, at post, and set the date for December 31, 1995, working on the assumption that the department would have sent a DCM by that time. When I had the department's agreement, I made plans with a friend from the United States to take a long-contemplated extensive tour of Indonesia for the month of January. I would have liked to have been assigned to that fascinating country, but this had not happened. I had visited the country twice, briefly: once from Vietnam for a week, principally on Bali, and once again for an ASEAN conference when I was chargé in Laos. I encouraged my sister Hazel and her son Bob to join us in Indonesia for the trip, which they did for about two weeks.

As the situation developed, the department could not find a replacement for my departed deputy. As December 31 grew close, I informed the department that if I were allowed to take January off for my trip, for which my friend and family and I had already made extensive plans and financial commitments, I would be willing to delay my retirement to the end of April to allow more time for the department to find a replacement ambassador, or at least to assign a DCM. But in the meantime, the department would have to find an interim chargé to replace me for the month of January.

The department agreed and sent a capable man to serve as interim chargé. He arrived a few days before my departure. I introduced him to Bruneian officials and the diplomatic corps, briefed him on pending issues, and happily departed at the end of the year for Singapore, from whence we launched our fascinating tour of Indonesia.

Indonesian Journey

My friend Florence Wrobel, who lives for travel, had arranged a fantastic trip for us, working with a travel agent in California who specialized in Indonesian travel. Meanwhile, we put my nephew in touch with the same travel agent, who arranged that Bob and Hazel would meet us in Sulawesi Province, Indonesia. Florence and I toured Sumatra in some depth in our own private Range Rover, complete with a driver and a very knowledgeable guide. We then went to Java, where we toured at some length. Highlights included the masterful Buddhist temple complex of Borobudor, and the similarly overwhelming Hindu complex, Prambanan. Amazingly, these two complexes, honoring different religions, are within about thirty miles of each other.

We then flew to Sulawesi, where we were met at the airport by a guide and driver. The driver knew that Hazel and Bob were due in a couple of hours, but said that they would have their own vehicle and driver and guide. He suggested that we begin our journey to North Sulawesi Province. We drove up the main road toward the north and stopped alongside the water, where there was a very colorful array of boats unique to the island. Our guide explained that in earlier years these boats had been the kind used by the *Bugis* or *Buganese,* pirates who frequented these waters. He said that the pirates and their behavior had inspired the legend of the "bogeymen"—whether this originated from the Indonesian word for the boats or their sailors, I am not sure.

We were relaxing and taking pictures of the boats when another vehicle pulled up, and out came my sister and nephew. We had quite a reunion, meeting unexpectedly on this almost deserted road en route to northern Sulawesi. From that point on, we were together on that most memorable trip.

One of the places we had planned to visit on this trip was Irian Jaya, the western portion of the island of New Guinea. The Indonesian government exercised tight control over access to the remote province, requiring a special visa for visitors. We had obtained not only these but also, as I was aware of the occasional rebel activity in the province, permission from the American embassy in Jakarta to make the journey (particularly since I was still a serving ambassador). I had invited my secretary's husband, Jack Tuckish, to meet us in Irian Jaya, correctly anticipating that he and my nephew would enjoy each other's company on hikes into the interior, where natives still lived in Stone Age conditions. I had agreed to the trip, but I proclaimed my intention to relax by a hotel pool, if such could be found, and read mystery novels while the intrepid explorers did their hiking.

Unfortunately, shortly before we began our Indonesian journey, there was a massive rebel-initiated kidnapping in Irian Jaya. Several British anthropologists and their Indonesian assistants were captured by rebels and were being held in an unknown location. (Ultimately, two of the Indonesians in the party were killed.) Elements in Irian Jaya resisted Indonesian control of the province and continue to do so to this day. These rebels contend that, in effect, Indonesia acquired their province, by means of a questionable UN plebiscite, for the purpose of exploiting Irian Jaya's mineral riches, which include major gold and massive copper deposits.

Our embassy in Indonesia had initially agreed that I could take the Indonesian journey, but asked that I touch base periodically about the situation in Irian Jaya before proceeding there. This visit was scheduled for the end of our extensive trip, and we hoped that the situation would be settled by that time. Unfortunately, it was not. When I checked with the embassy at the conclusion of our stay in Sulawesi, I was advised that our ambassador in Indonesia did not want us to go to Irian Jaya. The situation there was not resolved; Indonesian troops were planning action against the kidnappers. I was not only an American but also a serving ambassador. I could well be in danger, and the Indonesian government would have to divert troops to guard me. I fully understood this, but asked if my family could proceed with the trip. Again, the answer was no; the Indonesian government did not wish to admit any more potential hostages to the area.

We were all disappointed, but my nephew was particularly so. I recall him saying with good-natured chagrin, "Travels with my aunt—don't!" The embassy in Jakarta tracked down Jack Tuckish in the airport as he was about to board his flight to meet us in Irian Jaya; he too was told he could not make the trip. A couple of years later, Bob and Jack, who hit it off beautifully when they finally met in Brunei at the conclusion of the Indonesian trip, managed to make the trip to Irian Jaya. They hiked into the mountains for several days and spent time with the Stone Age tribes and had a thoroughly satisfying time

My punishment for ruining the Irian Jaya trip for my family and friends was a miserable cold that struck me as we concluded our stay in Sulawesi, where we contacted our California travel agent to make other arrangements to make up for the cancelled Irian Jaya portion of the trip. My cold invaded my ears and gave me a wretched ear infection. The flight from Sulawesi to Bali was pure torture for me—the pain in my ears was excruciating. I could not contemplate another flight until the infection healed. The four of us had planned to visit the island of Lombok, near Bali, but I stayed instead at our comfortable hotel in Bali. I recovered while the others proceeded to Lombok, which they enjoyed very much.

Despite the Irian Jaya disappointment, it was a wonderful trip. I was satisfied that I had gotten a thorough grounding in the varied cultures of Indonesia.

Leaving Brunei

After Indonesia, I returned to Brunei for a final three months as ambassador to that lovely little country. The department still had not found a replacement DCM, so I labored without another substantive officer for the conclusion of my tour. The department decided to send the gentleman who had replaced me in January to serve as interim chargé again after I left the post on April 30. Meanwhile, a career FSO had been selected to replace me; he would not arrive until August. I was pleased that the post would have the continuity that a career officer could provide.

Time flew by, and my departure date drew near. I was touched by the many farewell dinners offered to me by officials and diplomatic colleagues. I did what I could to leave the post in good shape, substantively and otherwise. I embarked on a grueling round of farewell courtesy calls, visiting all of the ministers and the sultan's two wives, leaving the sultan for last, as required by protocol. The sultan always treated me with the utmost courtesy and friendship. I appreciated that. We accomplished some things together. On a few occasions I had to call on him hat in hand, seeking financial assistance for certain good causes—for example, aid to the Palestinians after a successful negotiation fostered by the United States and the funds for KEDO, the Korean Energy Development Organization. I paid my farewell call on the sultan on Thursday. I was scheduled to depart Brunei for Singapore on Monday at 8:00 a.m.

Farewell Gifts

Gift giving is a deep-rooted, and generous, Bruneian tradition. When I paid farewell calls on the sultan's two wives, each of them presented me with wrapped farewell gifts. When I opened the gifts later in private, it was clear that the value of the gifts far exceeded the acceptable limits set by the State Department. The senior wife presented me with a large, gem-encrusted pendant on a chain; the stones were a ruby, an emerald, and a sapphire, circled with small diamonds. The junior wife's gift proved to be a diamond-encrusted, gold Rolex watch—exquisite. I knew I would have to deal with the gift issue before I left the country.

My farewell call on the sultan was most pleasant. We briefly exchanged pleasantries about the progress the bilateral relationship had made during my stay in Brunei and wished each other well. His Majesty then presented me with two wrapped farewell gifts. Once more, these proved to be most generous, and far above the gift acceptance limits. (I believe at this time officials could accept gifts up to a value of $100. Gifts worth more than that amount had to be sent to the State Department for eventual display or auction, or returned to the giver.) The sultan had given me a package from Asprey's in London, which his family had recently purchased. It contained a wafer-thin elegant watch; an ostrich leather wallet; and a bracelet adorned with red, blue, and green gems, highlighted with diamonds. I was confident that the gemstones were real. The large package contained a beautiful photographic depiction of Brunei, which he had autographed for me.

I faced a dilemma—send the gifts to the department, where they would languish in a safe until some uncertain point in the future when they would most likely be auctioned, or risk offense by returning them to the royal family. Earlier in my stay, I had sent the department a wristwatch that Her Majesty had given me, and all of the ambassadorial wives, on the occasion of her birthday; a preliminary appraisal I obtained when visiting the United States over Christmas disclosed a value of at least $5,000. I hated to simply send all of these beautiful, valuable gifts to oblivion in the department. I also felt that I knew the sultan well enough to enable me to return the gifts without offense.

I prepared a letter to the sultan and took it to my principal contact at the foreign ministry, Permanent Secretary Lim Jock Seng. I explained my dilemma to him and my reluctance to simply consign the gifts to the State Department. He was respected by the sultan, I knew, and could explain my situation. He could not understand why I was not at liberty simply to keep the gifts, particularly since I was retiring. I told Lim that if he thought the sultan would be offended, I would simply send the gifts to the State Department, with the exception of the book. Lim was puzzled by the strange ways of the U.S. government, but agreed to raise the matter with the sultan, whom he was scheduled to meet shortly after our meeting. I left the letter and the gifts with him. He called me later and said that the sultan understood my situation, and assured me there would be no hard feelings if the gifts were returned. Thus did I hand back gifts worth, I estimated, at least $75,000.

My gift traumas were not over, however. When I returned home that evening, there were two packages awaiting me from my landlord and his wife. He was the senior mullah, the head of Islam (under the sultan) in Brunei. One package contained a lovely piece of silk fabric suitable for making a lady's dress. This I could accept, I decided. The other box, however, contained a beautiful solid gold necklace and matching gold and diamond earrings. These had to be returned.

This was easier said than done. When I called on the mullah and his wife the next day, they were stunned when I explained that as much as I appreciated their thoughtfulness, my government had rules about officials accepting gifts, and I would have to return the gold necklace and earrings. The mullah's wife was brought to tears as I explained my mission and said, puzzled at my unwillingness to accept their gifts: "All of the other ambassadors accepted them." I quickly explained that as most of my predecessors were political appointees rather than career officers, they may not have been as familiar with the regulations as I was. I enthused about the silk, and said that I could accept that. My hostess immediately said, "I will get you another silk," and promptly did so. In the light of her distress, I accepted it. She also presented me with a lovely English bone china dish commemorating a Muslim ceremony at which the sultan's two daughters had demonstrated proficiency in reading the Koran.

Last-Minute Business with the Sultan

With my farewell calls completed and a Monday departure looming, I concentrated in the office on Friday on finishing up loose ends. To my dismay, a cable arrived with the text of an urgent letter from President Clinton that had to be delivered personally to the sultan, immediately. In Muslim countries, Friday is the day of religious observance, and government offices are closed. There was nothing for me to do but to track down Lim Jock Seng on his day of rest and inform him that I had to see the sultan before I left the country to deliver a letter from President Clinton. Lim and the sultan obliged; I called on the sultan Saturday afternoon at 2:00 p.m. at the palace and conducted my business. I used the occasion to thank the sultan for his understanding about my returning the gifts, explaining that I would have loved to have kept them as reminders of my enjoyable relationship with the royal family, but U.S. law and regulations prohibited that. He was gracious, noting that all governments have laws and regulations that must be obeyed.

I should note that my meeting with the sultan after I had paid my farewell call was a breach of protocol. Technically, after paying a farewell call on the head of state, the ambassador has in effect concluded all official duties. That is why this call is the final one, and why we had arranged it with the foreign ministry for a Thursday afternoon, the last official work day before my planned departure. The lure of a letter from a U.S. president was sufficient, however, for the sultan and his government to forget that I had technically left the country after calling on him earlier.

This unexpected visit gave me a final look at the sultan's private office. Our first couple of meetings had taken place in a huge formal reception room. After that, he received me in his smaller, almost cozy, private office. Arrayed on the walls of this office were exquisite original French Impressionist paintings—at least two Renoir's, a Van Gogh, a Monet, and others. I learned after my first visit to this private office that the sultan is one of the major private collectors of Impressionist art. I saw several such paintings when visiting the sultan's two wives in their respective palaces. They were charmingly interspersed on the walls with enlarged family photographs—a Renoir, the sultan and his children, a Monet, the queen and the sultan.

This unexpected final call made my last two days in Brunei even more hectic than usual. After my meeting, I returned to the embassy, opened it up (there was no staff there on Saturdays), entered our secure vault, and prepared a cable reporting on my meeting. It was important that the message be transmitted while I was still in the country so it would be transmitted under my name. I called my communicator, explained the situation, and gave him the option of coming into the embassy any time of his choosing over the weekend or coming in early enough on Monday so that the message would be sent while I was still in country. I believe he opted to come in early Monday morning, and my final cable was an auspicious one—not a routine report about, for example, Brunei's position regarding a UN issue of interest to the United States, but a report of a meeting delivering, and discussing, a letter from my president to the head of state of my host country.

Recuperating in Singapore

Departure time arrived. I flew out of Brunei one last time, thoroughly exhausted from the hectic pace of the preceding weeks—

démarches, farewell calls, and farewell social events hosted by a wide array of Bruneian officials, members of the diplomatic corps, and friends. I sorely needed decompression. It was April 30, 1996, and I had retired from the State Department after thirty-three years of service. A new phase of my life was beginning.

First I had to recover from the exhaustion of those final weeks. To the rescue came my dear Singapore-based friend, Joyce Rasmussen, the director of the Singapore office of the U.S.–ASEAN Business Council. We had become fast friends during the course of my tour in Brunei. When I visited Singapore on business, I always alerted Joyce to my travel plans, and she arranged fun things for us to do there. When my departure loomed, she insisted that she be allowed to make my hotel arrangements in Singapore. She seemed to know every American (and major Singaporean) businessman in Singapore. She arranged for me to have a suite on the fiftieth (or so) floor of a major hotel overlooking the harbor. It was beautifully appointed, offering fruit, candy, hot and cold hors d'oeuvres on tap at the free cocktail lounge (also boasting an incredible view) just down the hall, and other luxuries. A special treat was the beautiful bathtub, situated so the bather could enjoy an unobstructed view of the bustling Singapore harbor—or, tiring of that, watch the television installed just above the tub. Exhausted from my departure labors, I soaked in the tub at great length, luxuriating in the gorgeous harbor view, at that height safe from prying eyes.

I managed to loaf thoroughly for the rest of the day and most of the next. The following evening, I was feted at the residence of Joyce's boss with a party that drew together many of the American businessmen whom I had gotten to know, and work with a little, while in Brunei. Several of my colleagues from the embassy in Singapore also attended, including my excellent defense attaché, Colonel Richard Welker, and his lovely wife, Melinda. It was a delightful evening, a gesture that I much appreciated.

The next morning I left Singapore as a private citizen. I reflected, as I began my homeward journey, on the incredible thirty-three-year adventure that had, in more than one way, taken me a long, long way from home. I was, and I remain, grateful for the opportunity to have served my country in the Foreign Service.

CPSIA information can be obtained at www.ICGtesting.com
Printed in the USA
BVOW032101050612

291838BV00001B/5/P